AN ECONOMIST AMONG MANDARINS

A biography of Robert Hall (1901–1988)

KIT JONES

Robert Hall was the highly respected and influential Economic Adviser to the government between 1947 and 1961. He came to England from Australia as a Rhodes scholar, became an Oxford don and a wartime civil servant. Within two years of returning to Oxford after the war, he was recalled to Whitehall. His appointment as Director of the Economic Section, first in the Cabinet Office and then in the Treasury, came at a crucial time in the development of the modern economic state, when governments were just taking on responsibility for managing the general course of the economy. As the senior members of the Treasury were rooted in a pre-Keynesian age, Hall's influence grew rapidly and was at times dominant with ministers. He was involved in all aspects of economic policy. This book puts a new slant on the events of these years as well as assessing Hall's role in them.

THE NATIONAL INSTITUTE OF
ECONOMIC AND SOCIAL RESEARCH

AN ECONOMIST AMONG MANDARINS

Published by the Press Syndicate of the University of Cambridge
The Pitt Building, Trumpington Street, Cambridge CB2 1RP
40 West 20th Street, New York, NY 1011-4211, USA
10 Stamford Road, Oakleigh, Victoria 3166, Australia

© The National Institute of Economic and Social Research 1994

First published 1994

Printed in Great Britain by Redwood Books, Trowbridge, Wiltshire

A catalogue record for this book is available from the British Library

Library of Congress cataloguing in publication data applied for

ISBN 0 521 47155 9 hardback

Contents

Illustrations

(Between pages 116 and 117)

Preface

This book is the result of a suggestion made to me by Sir Alec Cairncross and Lady Roberthall when I retired from the National Institute of Economic and Social Research in 1990. I had known Robert Hall since 1947, as I myself worked in the Economic Section for most of the time that he was the Director. Subsequently I saw a fair amount of him when I became the Secretary of the National Institute of Economic and Social Research while he was the Chairman of the Council of Management.

I have discovered that Robert Hall made many friends in his lifetime and won the respect and affection of a great many people. Everyone to whom I turned for help – his family, friends and colleagues – has been most willing to talk or write to me about him and I am most grateful to them all. Among them I should like to acknowledge the following: Sir Fred Atkinson, Arthur Brown, David Butt, Kathleen Campbell Brown, Lord Franks, Richard Fry, Lincoln Gordon, K. H. Huggins, Lord Jay, Bill Kerr, Michael Maclagan, Sir Kit McMahon, Richard Malpas, Sir Lees Maynall, James Meade, Robert Neild, Paul Nitze, Sir Henry Phelps Brown, Lord Plowden, Sir Austin Robinson, Lord Roll, Paul Samuelson, Lord Sherfield, Felicity Skidmore, Neil Tanner, Lord Thorneycroft, Nancy Trenarman, Bruce Wemham and Anthea Wilkinson. I owe a special debt to the following who also read the whole book in draft: Sir Alec Cairncross, Liliana Archibald, Christopher Dow, John Grieve-Smith, Chris Huhne, Joan Kelley, Lady MacDougall, Dick Ross and David Worswick. They made many helpful suggestions. Any weaknesses or errors that remain are my responsibility alone.

I am also especially grateful to Rosemary Venton, Hall's niece, for the help she gave me from Brisbane about Robert Hall's life before he left Australia, and for her hospitality when I visited Queensland; also to the Honorary Archivist at Ipswich Grammar School, Queensland; Margaret O'Hagan of the Fryer Library, University of Queensland; Susie Penfold for sorting out the letters Robert Hall had written to his sister between 1920 and 1980; and Rob and Sharyn Hall for producing their family photographs and guiding me through them.

The official files at the Public Record Office have been a major source of material for this book, and I am grateful to the Controller of Her Majesty's Stationary Office for permission to reproduce a number of memoranda from Crown Copyright material. I have made free use of published work on the period, especially that by Christopher Dow and Sir Alec Cairncross; and *The Roberthall Diaries* have also been an invaluable guide.

I should also like to thank the Leverhulme Trust for the award of a research grant for the project; Fran Robinson of the National Institute of Economic and Social Research for helping to prepare the text for publication; and Joan Kelley for preparing the index.

KJ

CHAPTER ONE

Introduction

Robert Hall's claim to fame is that he was the Economic Adviser to the British government for fourteen years. In that position he played the role of economic statesman of the highest rank and his directness, calmness and common sense, and his endearing traits of character won the trust and affection of all who knew him. His achievement was all the greater because his period in power came at a crucial time in the development of modern economic policy. He played a role as impressive as the most outstanding of other confidential government advisers of the twentieth century. But, like them, he gave his advice to ministers, and his activities were not in the public eye – his name did not appear in the daily press and he was interviewed on the radio only a few times. He himself published rather little, a couple of short books and perhaps two dozen articles, but there were two circles where he was a distinguished and admired figure. The first was in Oxford, where he was a popular don and later head of a college; and the second was Whitehall, where he was the highly respected and influential Economic Adviser to eight Chancellors of the Exchequer between 1947 and 1961. During these years his hidden impact on the lives of his fellow citizens was prodigious, through his contribution to economic policy and the maintenance of full employment. His character and achievements are not widely known. This memoir is designed to tell more people about him.

This is the story of Robert Hall's career, built up through his own testimony and the recollections of colleagues, family and friends. It is not an intimate personal biography, but it does begin with his childhood and early life, in order to trace the development of those qualities which made his career so successful and self-fulfilling. His early life in Australia taught him self-dependence and a capacity to face problems squarely; to establish the limits of what could be done; and then to apply a logical mind to sorting out the best way to tackle them. It was also the basis of his complete blindness to class distinctions and his good-humoured modesty and eclecticism.

He was born in 1901 in Australia, the son of a mining engineer, and from the age of two lived on a remote station in Queensland where life was simple and somewhat primitive, and their upbringing taught boys to be independent. After graduation in engineering at Queensland University, he came to Oxford as a Rhodes scholar and, like many ambitious Australians who saw the England where their parents or grandparents were born, he never went back.

The choice of PPE at Oxford broadened his outlook after reading engineering at Queensland. His mathematics course in the latter undoubtedly helped him quickly to acquire an understanding of the way in which complex political and economic systems work, which later seemed to some of his colleagues to be almost intuitive. His mathematical training also provided the basis of rather severe judgments of the role mathematics could play in economic analysis and forecasts.

Hall described the three turning points in his life as winning the Rhodes scholarship to Oxford in 1922, gaining a lectureship at Trinity College in 1926 with a fellowship the following year, and his appointment as Director of the Economic Section of the Cabinet Office in 1947, a role later formally redefined as the Economic Adviser to the government. Each event was unexpected and he seized the opportunities presented by each whole-heartedly; in retrospect it seems as if the first two were leading to the third and the peak of his career as the government's Economic Adviser.

The Rhodes scholarship determined the direction of Hall's interests. It was because he chose to read PPE at Oxford that he developed his curiosity and concern with political economy and the affairs of the state, although the economics course he took was very sketchy and he learnt more as he taught his own students than as a student himself. His Fellowship at Trinity which lasted for over twenty years, including the war years, enabled him to further his knowledge of the workings of the economy, at a time when Keynes's ideas began to circulate in Oxford; and the research he pursued there gave him a close insight into the business decisions which have an important impact on the economy as a whole. It was as a don too that he acquired the arts of persuasion and the negotiating skills that he was to use so successfully as a wartime civil servant. In the Ministry of Supply he also learnt the art of being effective in a large organisation. These skills were reinforced during the war at the British Raw Materials Mission in Washington. There he also made many friendships with Americans, which were later to prove helpful when he was at the Treasury.

After the war, like many wartime civil servants, he returned to his university. But, within two years of returning to Oxford, he was offered the post of head of the Economic Section, from which James Meade had been forced to retire prematurely in 1947 because of ill health. His appointment came at a crucial point in the development of the modern economic state. It is only in the second half of the twentieth century that governments have taken on responsibility for managing the general course of the economy. Earlier in the century, people hardly thought in these terms. Chancellors of the Exchequer knew that their job was to manage their government's own finances and to raise taxes to pay for the government's expenditure, but not to do much more. The Bank of England was then a private corporation and, though it accepted public responsibilities, it guided money matters according to inherited rules, rather than with an eye to achieving this or that effect on the economy as a whole. This was the situation up to 1939.

During the war the economy was run by means of a vast apparatus of direct controls. Even before this apparatus was dismantled after the war, the climate of opinion about how the economy should be run had changed radically: Conservatives and Labourites alike had begun to have more ambitious ideas for the role of the State in economic matters; and a wider function for the Treasury as the main economic department was beginning to emerge. This was the age when Keynesian economics was being built into the routines of the constitution. A quarter of a century or more later there was to be a monetarist reaction from the ambitions of the postwar governments and the high priority that they gave to the stabilisation of employment. But the reversal of policy has been only partial and governments still attempt – not very successfully – to steer the economy, even though the priorities have changed.

It was only in 1953 that the Economic Section was moved from the Cabinet Office to the Treasury. However, from the start, Robert Hall operated as part of the Treasury. Though only knighted himself in 1953, he was always in effect one of the Treasury knights. They, however, were all of an earlier generation than Hall and their careers were rooted in a pre-Keynesian age. Intelligent, competent and industrious though some of them were, they tended to be ill at ease in advising about the level of the exchange rate or the consequences of letting it float, and still less confident about the desirable level of the budget surplus.

This was one reason for Robert Hall's great, growing and at times dominant influence with ministers and civil servants. It also accounts to some extent for the influence of the small group of economists under him, young though most of them were. In the early days after the war the Economic Section consisted mainly of academic economists, most of whom returned to their universities as soon as they could, and were replaced by economists newly graduated or those just back from HM forces. When he took over, Robert Hall thus found a young inexperienced group, and for many years it was one of his chief cares to keep their numbers up. Partly by choice, partly by necessity, he recruited a series of short-term appointees from university departments, but the total number in the Economic Section (excluding those on secondment elsewhere) was never more than twelve to fourteen at any one time – a very different world from the vastly enlarged, largely permanent, staff of the present day government Economic Service.[1]

To his young assistants, and to many others, Robert Hall must have seemed a contrast to his two predecessors. He did not possess the commanding manner of Lionel Robbins who had been head of the Economic Section in the war years 1942–5, nor the academic reputation of his immediate predecessor, James Meade, but he soon proved himself at least equally effective. He arrived at the time of transition, when power was slipping back to the Treasury from other departments. The Chancellor – Hugh Dalton – regarded himself as his own economic adviser.

Robert Hall was fortunate that Cripps succeeded Dalton as Chancellor of the Exchequer soon after his own appointment. He thus became the first Director of the Economic Section who had the chance to see full employment policies put into effect. Cripps accepted and welcomed such policies. It was only with later Chancellors that Hall had battles about the need to maintain a large budget surplus when the economy showed signs of over-stress, and about the acceptability of running a budget deficit to ward off a recession.

He soon gained a reputation for exceptionally acute economic judgment and an ability to get to the heart of the matter. On paper he was lucid and brief. He was able to distil what he needed from a vast number of often long and complicated papers written by his staff, and would quickly absorb the ideas in a mass of documents circulating in Whitehall among departments. When he arrived in Whitehall in 1947, the British economy was at a low ebb, still facing many, apparently almost insuperable, problems, some of which were a legacy of the war. Hall was virtually unflappable in the face of these. He described himself as 'fairly steady' and he never overlooked the exigencies of party politics.

For all his courtesy and tolerance, Hall felt very strongly about some of the events in which he took part. Although he did not show it, he was a very emotional man; he was especially distressed by a notorious episode in 1952, when the Bank of England and some senior Treasury officials concocted a plan for the convertibility of sterling, which he regarded as premature and ill thought out. He was extremely angry at the impropriety of the attempt to push ministers into accepting the plan without adequate consideration at the official level.

In retrospect the 1950s appear as a golden age in terms of employment, inflation and growth. Unemployment did not rise above 2.5 per cent; inflation, though a worry to Hall, averaged only 3 per cent; while output (GDP) grew at a fairly steady 3 per cent.[2] Spotting the moment when an economy is on the turn, either up or down, is, as most economists who have engaged in the business of economic forecasting will agree, one of the most difficult tricks in the trade. There can be many false dawns. In the 1950s there were fewer statistics and as many or more revisions to them than there are now, and information was not available as early. Indeed the statistics we have today and the speed with which they are produced, fallible though they still are, owe much to Hall's pressure for improvements; he had such a feel for what was going on that he never failed to spot the turning points. Where action was not taken in time, or was insufficient, it was invariably because of the interference of some political manoeuvres, which made the Chancellor reluctant to follow Hall's advice. The most notorious example in his time was the April 1955 budget, which cut income tax prior to an election when all the signs were for an upturn in the economy and balance of payments difficulties.

No attempt is made here to give a detailed historical account of the years 1947–61. There are a number of these already.[3] Rather this book skims the surface of these events, summarising the part played by Hall and describing his relationships with others involved in the affairs of that time, with a little background to make sense of his role. The regard in which he was held by the ministers he served and the officials with whom he worked is evidence of his skill in dealing with people.

Hall's career within the Treasury lasted fourteen years, a very long time for undertaking responsibilities of this kind – and for long unmatched. He retired from the Treasury on reaching the normal retiring age of sixty but his interest in the economic problems of the state continued and was frequently expressed in the House of Lords. He also advised two business companies (Unilever and Tube Investments) sat on a number of committees and for a short time was head of an Oxford college. All this was a far cry from the Australian outback where Robert Hall's story begins.

CHAPTER TWO

An Idyllic Australian Childhood[1]

When Robert Lowe Hall was born on 6 March 1901, in Tenterfield, New South Wales, Australia, his father was away in Brisbane and, on receiving the news of the birth, he knelt down and gave thanks, not only for the safe delivery, but also for the end of several years with no pregnancies. He and Robert's mother had been very disappointed when, having had two children, no more had appeared. They had hoped for a large family, both of them having come from a family of ten. Robert's father was English and his mother was a first-generation Australian with a Scottish father. Hall did not leave Australia until he was twenty-two, but the English and Scottish background was very strong. There are varying views about whether Hall had an Australian accent, most saying that he had, although not a pronounced one; this was perhaps because his parents limited his contacts with other children during his early years. But in Queensland, where he spent his childhood, the accent would not in any case have been as pronounced, at that time, as the Sydney accent. The Queensland background was also very strong. Hall had the ethos of the outback; he was cheerful and confident and prepared to tackle anything. On horseback he rode with a long leather – with his legs straight – and a jaded horse did not suit him. As a true Australian he would always light a fire when on holiday – on a beach or wherever he stopped – and he needed only one match; he always carried a knife to strip the wet exterior from driftwood. These habits remained with him all his life. But, at the age of twenty-two, he left Australia without regrets. He fell in love with England and never wished to return, although throughout his life he had bouts of nostalgia for Silverspur, where he grew up.

6

Hall's father, Edgar Hall, was born in 1861. He came from Queensborough in Kent, where his grandfather had been Mayor. Edgar Hall read chemistry at Owen's College, later to be the University of Manchester, following which he joined a family business in the chemical trade in England. Partly because he had weak lungs Edgar's own father went with his wife and several daughters to Sydney. Here he was later joined by the rest of his eight daughters, and finally, in the 1880s, by Robert's father, Edgar, the only son. After a period of lecturing at Sydney University, Edgar was tempted by mining and in turn became the manager of a number of mining companies, and was based for a while in Brisbane.

Robert Hall's mother, Rose Helen, was born in 1863, the daughter of Archibald Cullen, the son of the minister of Balmaclellan in Kirkcudbrightshire, Scotland. Archie had two brothers, one of whom became an army doctor who saw service in the Crimea and in China. The other, together with Archie himself, went to Australia in the 1850s, where he became the head of the Queensland civil service while Archie took up land near Tenterfield, holding several 'stations'. These were large pastoral properties of which the first was Boonoo Boonoo near Tenterfield. Archie Cullen had already met his wife-to-be Margaret Merton who, accompanying her father, had ridden with pack horses from Brisbane in 1857; a lively account of her recollections of Brisbane and the ride appeared in the Warwick (Queensland) daily paper when she was about eighty. Robert's mother was therefore a squatter's daughter, 'squatter' in Australia being a landed proprietor who had substantial capital but who had negotiated a Crown lease only when compelled to do so. Rose's own mother was the grand-daughter of a sister of Robert Lowe, a somewhat eccentric politician who, after a stormy career in politics in New South Wales, went to England and became Chancellor of the Exchequer in Gladstone's ministry.[2] As Robert Hall was called after this ancestor, he made inquiries about him when he went to work in the Treasury some eighty years later. He found that Chancellors had come and gone so quickly that they left no memories behind them. However a small black and white photograph of him was found in the basement, which must have been brought in from the old Treasury building.

Rose and two of her sisters went with their own mother to Scotland in 1873 when Rose was ten and they lived in Kirkcudbright with an aunt who had stayed at home. They went to school there and returned to Australia after about seven years in Scotland. Robert's mother and two of her sisters lived to be over 100.

Robert's parents met in Tenterfield. His father's mining activities brought him to the district and he became a frequent visitor at the Cullen station, then Undercliffe. Edgar was thirty-one and Rose twenty-nine when they married in 1892. They said they knew at once that they had been waiting for one another and there was never any doubt in the minds of their children that it was a very happy marriage – something that Robert thought was probably the greatest environmental blessing that could be conferred on children. The marriage remained entirely happy throughout their lives, in spite of the financial misfortunes which pressed so heavily on Robert's father for the last thirty years of his life.

Edgar Hall remained a mining man and, besides managing, he became a consultant and travelled widely. In about 1896 when their two children, Garry and Helen, were old enough to be left behind, Edgar and Rose went on a visit to the mining areas of the west of the United States, which by then had far overtaken Britain as a mining country. There had never been much hard rock mining in Britain, the exception being the Cornish tin mines, and they were running down in the 1880s, with Cornish mining engineers and miners emigrating all over the world. The most striking result of the visit from Robert's point of view was that the home then became full of mementoes of the visit, as well as copies of the monthly magazines sent by friends they had made in Oregon. Thus the family grew up surrounded by American as well as English journals and books of all kinds, and the house was full of illustrations and photographs, mainly of the mining areas of the Rocky mountains.

At about the time of Robert's birth, Edgar was asked to inspect and report on a find of silver-bearing ore just over the Queensland border, near Texas. This had been found by local workmen who had endeavoured to work it themselves but were not doing very well. When Edgar began to write his report he found that the site had not been given a name, and he began by describing it as a silver-bearing deposit in the spur of a low range of hills. He suggested that it be called Silverspur, which it was and has so remained. He undertook to supervise the operation and soon after bought out the owners and formed his own company. He built a house and moved his family there in 1902 – Robert's elder brother and sister and Robert himself. As Robert was then less than two years old, all his childhood memories began at Silverspur, where two more children were born, David in 1903 and Margaret in 1906 when Rose was forty-six.

The house that his father had built was on the beginning of the spur which ended just after the mine shaft and had a magnificent view. Seventy years on and after seeing a good deal of the world, Robert still thought that this view would stand comparison in its own way with any other in the world. He wrote:

The house stood on the ridge of the little spur which ran North a few hundred yards to the site of the mine, and immediately behind it the spur took an upward slant and in a mile or so reached the skyline, with two tall hills called the King and Queen. From these the skyline ran away to the East in a series of ridges, with a mountain called Tooliambi rising in a pyramid over the ridges. Thence the ridges swept around getting further and further away, so that in the South-East we saw the tumbled mountain ranges of New England in New South Wales. To the North and West the mountains were further away than those in the East and ended due West where there were ridges of smaller pine-covered hills about six or eight miles away. The skyline returned to the Queen by means of a large round bare hill, called in typical Australian nomenclature the Bald Hill, about two miles off.

The only really flat country was around the numerous creeks which flowed, except in dry times, to the Dumorosy, always called THE RIVER, and the flat ground each side of the river itself. Except here there was nowhere that one could walk more than a mile on the flat. Hilly country and small mountains were therefore Robert's familiar surroundings and all his life he felt more comfortable on slopes; his spirits flagged on plains and soared on hills.

Unfortunately the site of the house was stony with hardly any topsoil and no hope of a well, so that all the water had to be collected in tanks from the roof. For Robert's mother, who was a keen gardener, there could hardly have been a worse site, and when her sons were old enough they were often enlisted to bring a little soil from less stony spots, to collect the pats of dung from the cows which fed in the paddock or on the common which surrounded the village, and to carry water when it could be spared. Robert and his younger sister inherited their mother's passion for gardening, but their youthful memories were of forced labour.

The village itself straggled about the mine buildings, themselves a sort of wonderland for a small boy who was kindly received by most of the workmen. The mine was the *raison d'être* of the village of Silverspur and its sole support.[3] Its whistle and the school bell regulated the routine of life and the noise of the rock-breaker was a constant background to existence, so that when the mine was working three shifts and stopped for any reason in the night everyone woke up.

The mine buildings were built on the last part of the spur, beginning with the carpenter's shop which Robert found the most entrancing. Here the carpenter always addressed him as an equal and told him innumerable stories about his earlier days. He explained the various processes of carpentry to Robert, including how a coffin was made and how to make picture frames, and he taught him:

Wise men nor fools
Can't work without tools.

According to his sister-in-law Alice, Edgar created a model mining village. There were two general stores, a barber's shop and one or two miscellaneous shops, a baker and a butcher. The village school, Silverspur state school, was at first manned only by one schoolmistress. Later she was joined by her daughter and later still she was replaced by a schoolmaster. Beside the school grounds lived the doctor. There was also a saddler, a dressmaker and a mounted policeman. There was a library and a village hall. The village was thus reasonably well provided with the essential facilities for those living there. It was a predominantly self-contained small community, a thriving and, as far as the children were concerned, a happy place.

The children were taught to look after themselves as soon as possible. They were all given some instruction about riding (though this was minimal), swimming and the use of firearms, and were told that if they got lost and could do no better, they were to follow the fall of the ground which would lead them to a house in at most five miles. The great safeguard was the universal opinion that it was shameful to be lost or to have an accident, so that although their mother would bind a wound and console the wounded as tenderly as a child could desire, the children would come with apologies rather than appeals.

To Robert there were three smells which had the special quality of bringing back a particular moment of the past exactly as it was experienced, so that it was re-lived rather than remembered. The first and most vivid was the smell of the mine shaft which, whenever he revisited Silverspur in later life, would make his heart turn over. The second was the sulphur-dioxide from the kilns which blew in clouds over the village. There must be few people who actually enjoy the smell of burning sulphur, but the tears it brought to Robert's eyes were those of nostalgia and a reminder of the children in line on the school verandah and the coughs, deliberately exaggerated by the children and stifled by the headmistress. The third was the smell of the sawdust – especially from the cypress pine logs which grew among the eucalyptus in the forests and provided the softwood for all the buildings.

In spite of these smells, the air of Silverspur was remembered as very clear and pure, probably because the wood burned practically clean and the sulphur fumes were quickly dissipated in the great bowl of the hills. Similarly Robert would remember the delicious quality of the drinking water, especially when, for most of his later life, he was faced with Oxford or London mains water.

From a very early age the children were often taken to Stanthorpe, forty-five miles away from Silverspur, to visit their grandmother and two aunts who lived together in a house built and owned by Edgar Hall. This was the way to the outer world. Further on, at Warwick, lived Robert's maternal grandmother and visits were also made there. The journey to Stanthorpe was one of mingled excitement – because of the many changes in the appearance of the countryside – and weariness, since it took a day and a half to make the journey with a horse and sulky, which was the usual form of transport. An observant boy, the landmarks remained so fixed in his mind that Robert could still describe the journey in detail seventy years later, noting especially the climbing of a series of ridges, Little Billy, Big Billy and Cocoa, running in three steps up to the tableland, at least a thousand feet above Silverspur; the gates through the wire fences which divided the various stations; the public houses where they stayed overnight; the creeks; and the great variety of wild flowers and eucalypts, including the famous string bark:

Stringy bark will light your fire
Green hide will never fail yer
Stringy bark and green hide
Are the mainstay of Australia.

Also remembered were the changes in the soil, especially near Stanthorpe, once the centre of a prosperous alluvial tin mining area where the earth was mostly a dazzling white quartz sand.

One of the main attractions of his grandmother's house was that a railway ran through the grounds only a stone's throw away from the front verandah. It carried four trains a day and was worth the journey all by itself. Clearly an adventurous boy, he delighted in standing on the bridge which carried the railway forty feet above a creek, ready to take refuge on a tiny platform with no side rails if caught unawares by a train. Heights and edges never bothered him.

Around the creek below, the endless variety of the water and the granite provided a magnet that never lost its power. It was an entrancing playground for a child not afraid of water and whose own home was perched on a stony hill, where the nearest running water, and not much of it anyway, was a mile away. Robert found Quart Pot Creek a paradise.

It was at Stanthorpe when he was six that he was given a pony named Ruby. His one or two lessons consisted of being put up and led round the field and then left to his own devices: this was the custom in a country where all men were expected to ride well, and it was thought pretentious to regard it as an accomplishment. One of Robert's uncles later gave him a lesson or two and taught him the jingle:

Your head and your heart keep up
Your hands and your heels keep down
Your knees keep in to your horse's sides
And your elbows into your own.

A quick learner, Robert was able to ride the pony back to Silverspur at the end of the holiday.

Apart from Stanthorpe and Warwick, there was one memorable visit to Brisbane where a new pattern of untold splendour was observed in a fashionable café full of mirrors and elaborate furniture. From Brisbane they went to Southport where they bathed on a beach of pure white sand plentifully strewn with shells and as deserted as the scrub. The waves rose well above the children's heads in transparent blues and greens before they curled and hung and fell in foaming white. This beach is now the Gold Coast, covered with hotels and apartments, and one of the most expensive strips of land in Australia.

By the time he was five Robert was longing to go to school. The Silverspur state school was a two-roomed wooden building with a corrugated-iron roof and a small verandah where the mistress stood as her pupils assembled. For the first four years he was taught by the schoolmistress and her daughter. Together they kept six classes occupied and disciplined. Primary schooling was provided free by the state government and the curriculum was laid down in detail so that the Education Minister could say exactly what each class would be doing at any particular time. Robert learned with great speed, in particular reading at which he was so good that, after a few weeks, he was made to read something in front of the whole school. He had made enough progress in conventional behaviour by then to be acutely embarrassed by this and to feel that the mockery he suffered in the next break was no more than he deserved. On the other hand his handwriting and drawing left much to be desired, because he appears to have lacked the ability to see on a blank page just where the pencil should go. Up to the time he left Queensland he could divide his teachers into two groups: those who regarded this inability as a grave moral defect to be cured by severity; and those who agreed with his own passionate conviction that legibility was all that was required of an education and penmanship should be left to the penman. As subsequent secretaries could confirm, in later life his writing was always legible.

Everything that did not require manual dexterity came easily to him, so that he enjoyed his school days. Many things he could remember after reading them only once. But the great charm of those days came from his now having friends among his school fellows which he had scarcely had until then. His father was obviously on good terms with his employees and his mother was the principal organiser of collective social activities, but his parents seem to have believed that there ought to be strict limits in their children's contacts with other children, perhaps because they hoped they would speak with more of a family accent than with a township one. The children were simply kept at home on some chore or other and later Robert was taught French by his mother before school when he might have been playing with other boys.

However during Saturdays and school holidays he managed to escape and soon began to roam the countryside with other small boys. Until he went to boarding school he and the other children all went bare-footed most of the year. The soles of their feet grew so hard that they did not feel the stony ground or even the sharpness of the bricks and slag heaps.

Early roamings were either in the wooded hills above the township or to one of the creeks. The country had so recently been opened up and was so lightly populated that there was plenty of animal and bird life and small fish in the creeks. The children killed everything they could with sticks and stones, but that was not very much – mainly snakes, kangaroo rats (small hopping marsupials), and goannas (large lizards) which ran up trees and could be stoned. They fished with lines on bamboo rods, making a fire to cook and eat the fish straight away, and they collected birds' eggs. Robert sometimes played tricks on his father. On one occasion he put a dead snake on the path attached to a piece of string which he wiggled from his hiding place when his father came along. To Robert's delight his father was taken in and jumped repeatedly on to it to kill it. Another time he moved the garden thermometer in to the sun for a little while and hugged himself with glee when his father came indoors exclaiming at how high the temperature was.

Robert was a strong boy and always wary of using his physical strength in fights with his brother and other boys. Consequently he never hit anyone as hard as he could have done. He could seize and floor any boy of about his own size who attacked him, but he did not then know what to do with his attacker. Years later he compared this problem with that which he had in the world of argument, where he also felt handicapped. In those circumstances it was because his objective was always to get at the truth, whereas he sometimes could not be sure that his opponent was not just making debating points.

Religion does not seem to have had a strong influence in the home and did not leave him with any particular religious belief. In later years he described himself as an agnostic. Edgar and Rose regarded

themselves as having a public duty to support the protestant religion and, as the various protestant ministers who came in turn to
the parish stayed with the Halls, Robert came to know a number of
different services and hymns on an equal footing.

Christmas was an especially exciting time. There was much interest and pleasure leading up to it and then, Robert said later:

on the day itself, the presents were distributed at breakfast; in
my early years these were substantial. Beside the pony already
mentioned, I had a bicycle when I was nine. We almost always
got as a collective present bound volumes of *Chums* and the
Boys Own Paper – never much in the way of toys except when
we were in Stanthorpe and there were aunts to be tapped. Soon
after breakfast all was bustle and stir as we got ready for the
picnic. The Australian determination to eat meals exactly like
those in lower middle class Victorian England was modified by
having a cold turkey and ham, prepared in advance, and eating
the whole meal by the river about six miles away, or if at
Stanthorpe by Quart Pot Creek. At Silverspur, we gradually
collected over the years a number of the neighbouring
overseers or managers of the large estates. Everyone drove to
these gatherings· and the children spent most of the day in the
water.

The men made a fire to heat the plum pudding and to
make the tea essential to any outdoor meal, and the women did
all the rest. After the meal everyone talked or slept or bathed
or fished at will, until four o'clock, when there was more tea
and Christmas cake. Then the horses were caught and we went
our ways. It was an ideal way to spend the day on which everyone eats too much and tends to be tired and short-tempered.

So passed the first four or five of his school years. He must have
been one of the brightest pupils, but there were several boys of
about the same standard. At this stage he was only a mediocre ath-
lete, having no eye for a ball, but this does not seem to have been a
great social handicap. He was fortunate to be born into a society
where difficulties were always shared and a helping hand offered
unobtrusively. His parents were usually scrupulously honest – although he never quite recovered from the shock of the one inconsistency that he observed to her high standards when his mother
attempted to pass him off as six on a train journey, when he was in

fact seven. Robert himself intervened with, 'But I am seven' – to the embarrassment of the guard rather than of his mother. Robert thought his mother indomitable, although when his wife eventually met her in 1936 she found her arrogant and bossy; and her grandchildren thought her formidable. Edgar's good qualities did not include understanding children, so that Robert's relationship with his father was less satisfactory than with his mother. But in spite of that he felt later that his early years had been a golden age.

My parents were happily married, were kind and tolerant, as were my teachers and school-mates. I had a robust constitution and a happy disposition, and endless entertainment on the mine and roaming freely about the country. Life was so interesting and the world so full of enchantment, that it was not surprising that the magic which illuminates the childhood of almost everyone not born to hunger or cruelty, lit my world very brightly.

CHAPTER THREE

Growing Up

Robert's early childhood appeared to him in retrospect as almost completely happy. His life until he was about twelve remained in a very special category. But then a cloud darkened the family skies. Until then the Hall family had been relatively well off: meals were regular and abundant, Christmas presents had been lavish, holidays were good, there was a maid in the house. But in 1912 the mine failed. As they had gone deeper the contaminates had increased, so that the proportion of silver was reduced. The amount of copper, essentjal to the final smelting process, as it carried the silver to the bottom of the furnace where it could be tapped for the smelter, also fell.

Edgar decided that a different process would be more efficient. A new furnace was purchased which required air to be blown through the charge. The process turned out to be a failure. The mine never paid again. Edgar continued to search for ways of rescuing it. But his hopes for its survival faded when wood became scarce and coal could not be transported economically. The railway line had been extended only as far as Texas, ten miles away from Silverspur, and there was no prospect of any further extension. Edgar never again drew a salary even when he made great efforts, all unsuccessful, to start up the mine again.

The consequences of this misfortune were far-reaching for the whole family. The eldest son, Garry, who had left school and begun an engineering course at the fledgling University of Queensland left it after the first year and went to work in China to earn enough to continue the course. The elder daughter, Helen, returned home from school. Plans for Robert were changed so that he took

17

the examination for a state scholarship which would pay the bulk of his fees at a secondary boarding school. However David, the youngest son, whose education had been set back for a year as a result of contracting polio, was kept at a paying school because he failed in his first attempt at the state scholarship examination. His parents assumed he would never be up to it and continued to send him, entirely at their own expense, for a further two years to a private school. Robert thought, even then, that David would have passed the examination the following year and would have been able to go on to university like himself. As it was, in due course David became an engineer for the Main Roads Board with a reputation for the toughest job. Margaret, the youngest, went to school only spasmodically, though at fifteen she went for two years to the famous girls' grammar school at Toowoomba, but she was not allowed to attempt the examination which might have enabled her to go university.

Paying towards the education of the two youngest children naturally accentuated the effects of the financial stringency imposed by Edgar's loss of salary, and put the whole family to shifts which might have been alleviated if they had not under-rated the real ability of their youngest son. From then on Rose and Edgar's sole income became Rose's inheritance from her father – some £250–300 a year – and for the rest of their lives they got along on this.

Robert always felt that his parents made it harder for the children, because at no time was it explained to them that their father had lost all his income. The younger children at least were left to discover and accept the extreme shortage of money from direct experience without any explanation.

One feature of my father's character was his almost unconscious way of looking at his children as an extension of himself. He was quite unable to explain to any of us what had gone wrong, or that he was reduced from comparative affluence to comparative poverty. But at the same time he felt that it was a matter that concerned us all equally; and that he should be the last person to reap any benefit from his anxious struggles to protect the other shareholders.

Rose did her best to mitigate the impact on the children within the resources that she had and the constraint imposed by the targets she had set herself. She was too proud and loyal to say anything

which might reflect on Edgar. So began stress and worry for Robert
and a resentment which he never really overcame.

All this left some scars, at least for my sister and me. As I
grew older, I had a longing to conform to conventions which
were   almost non-existent for a child in the atmosphere of
Silverspur. I gradually encountered the conventions dictated by
the incomes of my group; and this was a set of conventions to
which my extreme poverty almost ruled out   my conforming.
The combined effect of being brought up to think we were not
poor, and of never having the new situation explained to us –
coming down in the world and not admitting it – was traumatic
to a child anxious not only to conform himself, but that all his
family should also.

He was grateful to his school friends who did their best to prevent
him feeling any shame, but did not wholly succeed. One result of this
was a compulsion throughout his life to economise on things which
were   bought for him or which he had to buy in the years from the
ages of twelve to twenty-two, such as cheap food and clothing. But
this did not spill over into the more expensive things he was to buy
in later life. He   always took much more trouble to find cheap
groceries and shirts or to walk rather than take a bus, than to look
for a bargain when buying a new car. Most of his life he worried
about money, even when he was earning a relatively good salary
from the 1930s onwards. Only in 1936, when   Robert went to Australia after his father died, did he realise that he had never properly
understood just how poor his parents had become.

At Silverspur I went through his papers which had been put
aside for me to look at. It was a most painful experience to find
out in this way   how he had struggled to make a little money,
with practically no success, and what a miserable thing at least
this aspect of his life had been. But although I understood and
was deeply moved, I could not and for the   rest of my life have
not been able to overcome the resentment I felt.

In 1914, having passed the state scholarship examination easily,
Robert entered Ipswich Grammar School as a boarder. This was a
two-day journey driving his own sulky and staying one night on the
way. Ipswich Grammar, then a fair-sized school by Queensland standards, was the oldest grammar school in the state, with a fine
reputation. R. A. Kerr who became headmaster in 1915 has been
described as one of the 'greats' in the history of secondary educa-

tion in Queensland.[1] The school was rather different from what Robert had imagined from reading the sort of school stories that appeared in *Chums* and the *Boys' Own* papers. It was a humane school where bullying was strongly discouraged, where punishment was generally by detention rather than caning,[2] and where the food was rather better than he had been having at home since the failure of the mine. Except for Latin, lessons were no problem and the school records for his first three years show that he was always top of his class.[3] The school appears to have let him down in only two ways. His teachers did not inspire him to overcome his laziness about learning the complexities of Latin nouns and verbs by heart; and while he could read French fluently from an early age, he was hardly ever made to converse in it or even read it aloud so that his accent remained very poor.

There were about thirty boarders and fifty day boys. Of the new boys six were boarders and it was with them that he went through the school. One of these, Herbert Burton, struggled to pass him into top place; he was also his closest friend and remained so until his death seventy years later. With some eight day boys the class was usually fourteen, but with them there were nothing remotely like the close ties formed with the small group of boarding contemporaries. There was hardly any talk about families and there were no girl friends until their final year; conversations about sex were frequent and impersonal. All the relations between the boys were strictly platonic.

Games were compulsory – rugby union in the two winter terms and cricket in the summer. Robert enjoyed the football and became captain of the second fifteen in 1916. But he detested cricket where he could neither catch the ball nor score any runs, possibly because he was myopic. His main sport was running and he ran in all the school sports.

In such a school it was a social handicap to be a bad cricket player but Robert managed to maintain some standing because he was so good at other things. In particular his intense curiosity about sex and the freedom his parents gave him to read had made him much better informed than his school-mates, so that he was a kind of court pornographer and walking dictionary. This offset to some extent his inability to catch or hit balls.

Attendance at Sunday morning church service was compulsory.

On the way back from the Anglican church the boys passed the windows of the local newspaper and one Sunday in 1914 there was a typed statement saying that Britain had declared war against Germany. Like nearly all Australians at that time the boys took it to mean that Australia was also at war. Every Australian state had been given independence when they had asked for it, there was no feeling of oppression and, although new arrivals from England were slightly looked down on and called Chummies they were absorbed very quickly. Many people still spoke of England as home.

The war seemed to have only one effect on school life: all the boys had to join the school cadet corps and Robert became a quartermaster sergeant. All the senior boys had to join up when they left at eighteen. Robert's elder brother, Garry, who by this time was working up in Queensland, joined up early in 1915 and was killed in France. Rose was too proud to show her distress, but his father was overcome and wept openly at intervals during the next few days, saying to Robert at one point, 'I suppose I'll have to make do with you now.' Although very saddened for his parents, Robert himself was less affected as his brother was eight years older than him and had been at home very little. But he had expected to receive Garry's counsel as he got older. He knew already that his school friends would be more likely to look to him for advice than to be able to advise him. He felt that it was unfair of fate to have left him thus alone.

Garry was remembered as a good brother who had, amongst other things, introduced Robert to guns at an early age and taught him how to shoot. There were possoms and wallabies and, after 1910, rabbits and foxes; but no koala bears which had already been wiped out of this part of Australia. The many birds included wild duck and pigeons. Garry had taught him the jingle:
Never let your gun
Pointed be at anyone
Whether it unloaded be
Matters not to you or me
All the pheasants ever bred
Won't make up for one man dead.
In spite of this there were a couple of accidents which Robert described:

Out shooting rabbits with two friends and one gun among us, one of them, who was holding the gun which was cocked, when it should not have been, slipped and the gun went off. The flame which followed the charge burnt his shirt and blackened his shoulder. The one thought of all three of us was how he could conceal or explain away the ruined shirt in order to avoid a thrashing. The worst thing I ever did was on a different occasion, when I pulled the left-hand trigger while lowering the right-hand hammer of a shot-gun. I felt very silly, although the gun was pointing where it should have been, into the ground in front of me.

But Robert never considered himself a good shot – the same lack of coordination of eye and hands that held him back at cricket – and by the time Garry was killed he was already losing interest in the sport. Many years later however, he showed himself to be much better than most Englishmen when the staff of the Economic Section visited the Battersea funfair during the Festival of Britain in 1951. Most of the men in the Section had made a poor showing at the rifle range and blamed the system where it was thought that the stall-holder altered the aim of the guns. Hall picked up a gun and from left to right floored all the dolls.[4]

Meanwhile the passage of time had brought him to the lower sixth and he was expected to get a university scholarship. At the end of 1916 all his class took the junior public examination. There was a gold medal for the best pass in the state and Robert won it with eight merits (distinctions) and two passes. This was the Byrnes Medal and he was especially pleased to win it because his father had won a medal when he was at King Edward's School at Kings Lynn. In his father's case the medal was one given annually by the Prince of Wales to the head boy, and Robert's father had gone to Sandringham to receive it.

In 1918, in his final year at school, Robert became head boy. He passed the senior examination with equally good results and was elected to a scholarship at St John's College, a residential college at the University of Queensland.[5] These results – merits in three subjects and passes in another five – were relatively rare. The scholarship winners were placed in order of merit and Robert was placed seventh. In spite of the excellent school reports and high examination marks, he did not regard himself as particularly outstanding, but this may have been partly because his form included a number of boys who were especially successful in later life. In addition to

Burton who became professor of history at Sydney University, there was also R. Stanley who became a judge and Bill Kerr who was one of the leading research men in the sugar industry in Australia.

St John's College was across the river from the university on the cliff top of River Terrace, Kangaroo Point. It consisted of three rambling wide verandahed Queensland houses in which about thirty students resided under the protection of a warden, a burly former English rugby international. The college routine was not unlike that of his boarding school, but much less regimented and groups of students would gather in the common room to talk and argue late into the night.

At the university Robert enrolled for and completed the first year components of an applied science degree. He then transferred to the second year of the engineering course and in due time became a Bachelor of Engineering. During his first year he was the representative on the Students' Association. In his second year he was appointed secretary of the University Union and he also took part in the activities of the Dramatic Society, including reading Finch M'Comas in Shaw's *You Never Can Tell*. He took part in several debates, speaking against the election of the university Senate by students, the nationalisation of the medical profession and the control of industry by the workers. He also spoke for the motion that university training is no benefit in later life. In 1921, the question of the amalgamation of the University Union and the Students' Association was discussed and Robert was one of three undergraduates who drew up the constitution of the new body. He then became the first secretary of the reconstituted Union.[6]

At university his closest friends were Herbert Burton, his former school friend, P. R. Stephensen (Inky), and Edmund Dimmock, all of whom were at St John's College. These four became lifelong friends who all later found their way to Oxford. They did a lot of things together. They were all very short of money and trying to work moderately hard, but they also enjoyed student fooling and practical jokes. The university was a very sociable place so there was ample to do, apart from work. There were plenty of dances and university functions.[7] A lot of students went to church on Sunday – perhaps twice if they were keen on any of the women students, because they could then walk home with them. Although shy and with a hesitant manner, Hall was popular with women students; he was of average height, with dark wavy hair and blue eyes and he was very good-looking. In his letters to his sister he occasionally expressed concern that he was neglecting his work because he was having such a good time, and would have to 'knuckle down' if he was to pass his finals.[8]

In the college, Hall was particularly interested in the library and he was the business manager of the college magazine. He devoted a fair amount of time to running and ran for the college both in 1919 and in 1921 when he won the mile championship at the university sports. He represented Queensland at the inter-varsity sports in 1921 and was awarded a half-blue. The following year, his final one, he won the mile and the half-mile championships and represented Queensland in Adelaide that year. He was again awarded a half-blue, but this was the last time he ran competitively in Australia as he was beginning to find it too exhausting. Football also featured in his activities, both in university and college teams, and he took up rowing. His sporting successes gave him great satisfaction and went a long way to compensating for his poor performance at cricket.

Until he was twenty-two, Hall's life was probably not very different from that of many other middle-class Australian boys, although he had experienced one unusual occurrence – the loss of the family income. Clearly exceptionally clever, he had chosen to follow in his father's footsteps and study engineering. On the surface there were few signs of his subsequent career but there were already signs that he would be successful in whatever he decided to do. He had shown himself to be a good 'all-rounder', competent at everything he chose to do. In spite of neglecting to work, he had no difficulty in obtaining his degree. He was a doer and already knew that he would be able to advise others better than others could advise him. But his future was not to be in Australia like that of most of his contemporaries. The following year his life was to change dramatically. He departed for England, settled there and returned to Australia for short visits only seven times in the next sixty-five years. The man responsible for this turning point in his life was Cecil Rhodes, who had created the Rhodes scholarships for clever young men from the white colonies to study in Oxford and then return to their countries of birth to ensure that white supremacy continued.[9]

CHAPTER FOUR

The Young Australian in Oxford and London

In 1922, the course of Robert Hall's life took an unforeseen turn which made a complete break in the direction he was expecting his life might take. When he was almost at the end of his course in civil engineering at Queensland University, Inky Stephensen appeared one afternoon and said that, as the competition for that year's Rhodes scholarship was very weak, he had decided to become a candidate; and he suggested that Hall might as well apply also. In those days the Rhodes scholarship was thought of as the crown of an under-graduate's career and Robert had never considered himself to be in that sort of class. But he was persuaded to try for it knowing that his parents were keen. Although the entries closed the next day, he managed to complete the forms with the help of the Registrar, who was a friend of his aunt. To his astonishment he was chosen.

He was sitting his final year engineering examination in October when the Registrar gave him the glad news. After a short inter-view with the selection committee, he ran like a deer to Parliament House, where there was a post office, to send a telegram to his parents. On his return he was congratulated by his fellow students, including Stephensen who, it seems, bore no resentment that Hall, not he, had won the scholarship.

Hall gave an interview to the local newspaper, the *Courier* – pre-sumably his first ever press interview – before returning to his ex-amination. He said his selection came as a surprise as he did not think he had much of a chance, but he was particularly pleased because his parents were very keen on him gaining the distinction. He acknowledged his debt to his two headmasters at Ipswich Grammar School. He had quickly made up his mind what he wished to study at Oxford – political theory and economics – with a view to entering public life in Australia. The excitement at home was intense, but as usual his father handed out little praise. His father's reaction was to send him a telegram saying only that he hoped Robert would try to justify the choice of the selection committee. Nevertheless Robert knew he was pleased. In a letter to his sister he played down his achievement: 'As for the Rhodes, of course I am very pleased – mostly because father and mother seem so glad. But don't feel too impressed will you – I don't feel proud at all.'[1]

A job with an engineering firm at Dalby, north-east of Brisbane, filled in six months of the year before Oxford. He earned some useful money, but thought it would be much pleasanter to be in some sense one's own boss. He spent a few weeks with his family at Silverspur and visiting his relatives in Stanthorpe and Warwick, before returning to Brisbane for a few days. He then departed for Sydney, where in August 1923 he embarked on the SS Suevie for England and Oxford, arriving in late September.

It must have been a shock docking at Tilbury and travelling up to London through the slums of the East End. It would have been smoky and smelly, something he was unlikely to have experienced in Australia where even Brisbane was then just a small town. In Oxford his first impressions were of the cold, but he noted that the climate made the country very beautiful. It did not take him long to become accustomed to England and the English way of life. One home in Oxford where he was immediately welcome was that of the Cannans, Edwin and Rita. Edwin Cannan was a professor of economics at the London School of Economics, but lived in Oxford. Rita was a cousin of Robert Hall's mother. He thought her a wonderful person, who welcomed everyone into her home. She was especially kind to Robert and remained a friend to him and his family all her life. Edwin was both a socialist and an orthodox economist. Robert found him a difficult character, who had no respect for anyone's opinion but his own.

When Hall arrived in Oxford in October 1923, the school of philosophy, politics and economics – Modern Greats as it was called – was only two years old, having opened its doors to students in 1921. Prior to that, economics was not considered a separate academic subject. It was just something an educated person should be able to talk about. There was usually only one question in a general paper in Greats. Consequently there was no tradition of an Oxford school of thought as there was in Cambridge. The members of the Political Economy Club were mainly philosophers and historians. Though the Drummond Chair of political economy was an old one and there had been some distinguished occupants, there had been no serious students for them to teach and few teaching colleagues.[2]

In 1921 D. H. Macgregor succeeded Edgeworth as the Drummond Professor. He was a shy man and, when he came up against a hostile environment of College independence, he easily retreated into his own shell. He had been a student of Marshall at Cambridge and liked testing economic theories against real life and his lectures had a definite Marshallian flavour. Among the other lecturers and tutors there were very few who were also interested in either applied economics or economic theory. These included Roy Harrod who had just been appointed as a lecturer at Christ Church after reading Greats and modern history; he had however spent a term in Cambridge where he was supervised by Keynes.

When Hall arrived, the dominant influences in the PPE course were still those of the economic historians and philosophers. In the study of political economy the emphasis was placed on the history of economic thought and on the writings of Adam Smith, Ricardo, Stanley Jevons, Marx and so on. The whole time Hall was a student – three years – the scheduled lectures continued to lean towards this historical approach. But things were beginning to change; the number of dons in favour of this way of teaching economics had begun to decline and a gulf between economics and economic history began to emerge. Many of the historians and philosophers who had been active in developing the PPE course had retired or died or become heads of colleges. They were replaced by younger dons who believed that Marshall and Pigou ought to be read at Oxford in addition to or perhaps even in place of Smith, Ricardo and Jevons which were the recommended books in the early PPE examinations. But this was all happening too slowly for Hall to benefit much from the change. He always felt that he was not given a good grounding in economic theory when he was a student and had to learn it later while he was teaching his own students.

Hall's tutor at Magdalen was T. D. (Harry) Weldon, who was in fact the first PPE tutor there. He had read Greats, obtaining a First in 1921, only two years before Hall arrived. At this time Magdalen was an intellectual backwater. There was no economics tutor; Weldon taught all three subjects for PPE. His speciality was Kant but his real interest was politics. Hall was one of his very early pupils, only about four years younger than he was. Weldon had a powerful effect on his students. He particularly liked Australians, Americans and Canadians. 'My tutor is such a nice man', Hall wrote to his sister. But the fact that there was no specialist economics tutor meant that Hall's tuition in economics was inadequate.

The scholars all sat together at a separate table. A large proportion of the students had been at public schools and not all of them welcomed the 'colonials'; on his first day Hall received a rebuff from the student next to him which rankled for a time. In a further letter to his sister, Hall wrote that Magdalen was 'the swankiest college of the swankiest university in the world. It is full of Etonians who are young in years, but come into the world with a very self-possessed manner and come to Magdalen to hunt foxes with neighbouring packs. But they are quite approachable after the first fortnight.'[3] The Rhodes scholars all joined the Colonial Club which met once a fortnight: someone would read a funny paper, or songs were sung. The club met at a café and included Americans as well as colonials. In his early letters home he described the life as cloistered and secluded. But within a short time, he was meeting girls, playing rugger constantly and a lot of bridge. In Paris for his first Christmas in Europe, he spent his time in cafés with American friends and was fascinated to see Chinese, Negroes and Indians, with the French, English and Americans. His stalwart white Australian feelings were rather outraged at first, but in time he became accustomed to it. He found Paris warmer and more cheerful than England with everyone casual and a free and easy atmosphere. But he also saw in France the hatred of Germany and, in Italy at Easter, the fascists asserting their dominance. He hated such intolerance. He met some charming Americans but was troubled by their aloofness from the less fortunate world of Europe.

After a term of economics, he told his father that it was the most troublesome subject because it was still in such an uncertain stage, with all the authorities contradicting one another. He felt more at home in his other subjects and had ideas of his own already. He noted that the tutorial system did make them all think for themselves. He attended the annual Rhodes dinner given by the Trustees to all the Rhodes scholars in England; there he listened to speeches by Lord Milner, Lord Grey and Rudyard Kipling, whom he thought spoke exactly as in his books. 'If I return an imperialist, I will not have come here in vain', he wrote, 'for that is what Cecil Rhodes wanted to happen to us.' He concluded one letter: 'I don't think I'll stay in England ... I have been too much soaked in Australia to be really happy anywhere else.'[4]

Hall was unable to find a job in the long vacation so he visited Devon and stayed with the Bishop of Salisbury, who was a friend of his father. He found the sea a joke – half the beaches were all stones and the rest only half sand; the temperature did not appeal to him and there was no surf. He was homesick: 'all the country is lovely, but I should like to see some bare lands and straggly gums'. He still felt lonely in spite of knowing a lot of people, but this feeling was not to last much longer.

Hall's time as a student coincided with a number of his Queensland friends. Herbert Burton had come to Oxford the previous year as a Rhodes scholar and then Stephensen, the friend he had beaten in 1923, won the scholarship for 1924, so that by an extraordinary set of chances, Burton, Stephensen and Hall were all Rhodes scholars at Oxford in the academic year 1924–5. Burton then returned to Australia, but Stephensen remained in England for some years and Hall saw a great deal of him, at least until about 1928 or 1929.[5]

The arrival of Stephensen in 1924 was greeted joyfully by all the Queenslanders already there. Herbert Burton and Robert Hall met him at Tilbury and took him to a boarding house in Bloomsbury and then to a cheap French restaurant near Piccadilly Circus, and his arrival was celebrated for several days. He and Hall remained close, but with life in Oxford centred on the colleges and Stephensen at Queen's, they both had many interests and acquaintances they did not share. However, though they saw little of one another in term time, they usually spent some part of each vacation together either in London or Paris.

In the early 1920s, many Rhodes scholars spent at least part of their vacations in Paris because it was one of the very cheap places where one could live pleasantly. They stayed in modest lodgings and ate in cheap restaurants, and they spent much of the day in cafés, reading, writing, talking to friends and playing chess or cards. They wandered around the Latin Quarter, visiting bars and drinking aperitifs. Hall discoursed on the world economic situation in which he was already greatly interested. He wrote home: 'I am becoming quite an authority on the French for food and appreciating the best things on the menu.'

After Stephensen's arrival, there were many visits to Paris. At Christmas 1924 and again the following summer, they were there together with Herbert Burton and Jack Horsley, all former students together at St John's College in Brisbane. Hall found Stephensen intensely attractive and a great deal of the colour in his early life was associated with this unconventional friend. Hall himself was very conventional so that it was an attraction of opposites. Hall worried about the future, while this was of minimal concern to Stephensen whose interests were inclined towards the literary and artistic. He provided a sense of excitement and romance to a much greater extent than any of Hall's other friends.

Hall found his second year at Magdalen very different from his first because the students all knew one another so much better. 'No more do I sit through a meal in dignified silence, surrounded by Etonians and Harrovians preserving their own dignities by means of a similar course. No longer do we rack our brains for civilities and platitudes. Nor am I asked if I am an American. Tea parties and bridge parties are in full swing. The mornings are devoted to staying away from lectures or attending tutorials, and the afternoons to Rugger or running.'[6] He decided to make one last effort in the senior sports and then give up running and play rugger all the time. He was a wing three-quarter and wished his sister could see him with the ball under his arm, tearing down the line.

Later in the academic year he was taking work more seriously. He reported that he wrote two essays a week, one on pure reason and the other on a political topic. There was less reference to economics in his letters home. He noted that he had the measure of both his tutors: 'poor deluded Fellows, they think that I work hard and burn the midnight current. They would throw sevens if they knew the low way in which I construct my essays.'[7]

During his final year Hall worked harder to make up for lost time. For the 1925 Christmas vacation three of them took a flat in Chelsea, Hall himself working hard for his finals the following summer. Jack Horsley had been in the Sudan where he had an engineering job and was on leave in London and rather inactive; Stephensen worked, read and went out. The three of them decided to cook the Christmas dinner collectively, which somewhat tried the patience of all of them. Each one of them confided separately to Stephensen's girlfriend, Winifred, that it would all have been done much better and more quickly if the other two had not been there.

By Easter 1926 another Queensland friend had arrived in England. This was Jack Lindsay whose father, Norman, was a well-known Australian artist. It was Lindsay's intention to start a press and his main asset was a large number of drawings by his father. Jack himself was the other asset. He was a brilliant classical scholar, a poet, capable of immense hard work where anything to do with literature was concerned, and with a strong critical sense founded in a creative rather than a critical talent. Stephensen became involved with Jack Lindsay in the setting up of the Fanfrolico Press;[8] and spent most of his vacations in London with Winifred whom he later married. Hall liked Winifred very much, describing her as one of the nicest women he had ever known, valuing her for being good-humoured, sensible, honest and straightforward, and for her sense of humour and common sense.

Hall took his finals in 1926. He was awarded a formal First on all round high marks, the lowest being in the logic paper which was his special subject. He wrote to his sister that he was at a loose end and hoping for a job in Oxford. By this time he knew a great many people in Oxford. He had learnt to drive a car. His brother David came over from Australia for six months and most of the summer was spent with him. They toured England and then paid a visit to Paris. David was then in Oxford with him until the following Easter.

For the first few years after he graduated his friendships with Stephensen, Horsley and other Australians in Oxford and London continued. He still spent holidays abroad with them and he acquired a small house in London at 10 Pond Place. He continued to take a great interest in the activities at the Fanfrolico Press, where the aim was to publish finely printed and illustrated books. But the Press failed and Hall came to Stephensen's aid, lending him and Winifred his tiny house in Pond Place, paying their bills with the milkman and grocer and giving Winifred ten shillings a week. Hall described this as a not very generous provision, but it enabled them to live. Winifred was able to manage, and preferred it to a larger sum which would have made no difference to their basic position. They stayed several months until Norman Lindsay came to the rescue, organised a job for Stephensen in Australia with an advance to pay his and Winifred's fares, as well as that of their son Jack. In the end they departed in good shape and Hall paid their debts.

This was the end of what had been a very close relationship between Hall and Stephensen for about twelve years. Neither were good correspondents. Stephensen became involved in the First Movement in Australia. This was a political pressure group with fascist undertones and he was interned during the Second World War. Hall saw him for the last time in 1936 when he was in Sydney. But until 1927 or 1928 they hardly kept anything from each other and always resumed their friendship just where they had left off.

As a student at Oxford, Hall had not shown much sign of his subsequent successful career. He was just another clever young Australian, not needing to work too hard to obtain his First, and enjoying his life to the full. He was a good sportsman and enjoyed the outdoor life. He had made a large number of friends and was in great demand at parties, dances and as a house party guest. He had adjusted to a certain level of society in England. But he was still expecting to return to Australia, without much idea of what he was going to do in the future, when a second unforeseen event occurred in his life.

CHAPTER FIVE

Oxford Don[1]

The second unexpected event in Hall's life was his selection by Trinity College to succeed Frederick Ogilvie in October 1926, first as their lecturer in economics and then, in the following year, as the economics Fellow. He was to remain at Oxford for thirteen years, until the war took him away, and then to return for another two after the war, so that fifteen years of his life were spent teaching. Aware that his training in economics had been inadequate he took the view that he had been appointed because he had got a First, rather than for his knowledge of economics, which he then set about improving.

The economics course Hall had taken was indeed very sketchy, but the engineering course in Queensland had given him a good mathematical foundation, and he found the elements of theory – at that time supply and demand, the quantity theory of money and the principle of comparative cost – were easy enough for him. But he found teaching the subject much more difficult. He had to teach himself in order to teach his students. The new PPE school rapidly became so popular that most colleges were compelled to appoint economists, nearly all young and mostly keen and conscientious. In the next twelve years until the start of the war they all grew up together. They included – in addition to Harrod who has already been mentioned – Maurice Allen, Philip Andrews, Russell Bretherton, Eric Hargreaves, Charles Hitch, James Meade, Henry Phelps Brown and Redvers Opie. Hall later described the organisation of economics at Oxford in the late 1920s as a mixture of vacuum and chaos. The dons had to find their own way to organise their teaching.[2]

Along with the other economics dons, Hall directed his students through the historical survey of economic doctrine enshrined in the books recommended for the course, so that it led up to Marshall's principles of economics. But the emphasis was already shifting away from the historical survey towards a greater emphasis on economic theory. Hall's lectures on wages, for example, in 1927 would have been much more theoretical than his predecessor Ogilvie's lectures on questions in applied economics in 1923; and from about 1930 onwards Keynes's work became the core of his teaching.[3]

Hall, as a tutor, combined theory and practice and most of his students found it a stimulating discipline to have to go over essays with him in tutorials either singly or with one or two contemporaries. The essays typically consisted of explaining and criticising the ideas of Adam Smith, Ricardo, Marshall and Keynes and covered the standard economic theories of these economists. He was particularly skilful at sizing up what his students could take in and in simplifying obscure and difficult points to help them to grasp them. Those who benefited most liked his plain Australian no-nonsense approach. Others thought him unimpressive though kind and polite; and some were later astonished when he reached such eminence in Whitehall. He was perhaps less good as a lecturer in the early days as a don, because he lacked assertiveness, a weakness he overcame later on, although he was always tongue-tied when speaking to a group. His mathematical background and his clarity were very evident, but he never wasted words and his manner of speech sometimes made him seem uncertain when he was no such thing. He was a very popular don, not least with the women students of Somerville College, who at the end of the 1920s included Clarissa Goldschmidt (later Kaldor) and Peggy Joseph (later Hemming).

Hall did not find the work of being a don too onerous and he continued to have a very active social life. He contrived to have a good time partly at other people's expense as he was still short of money to begin with, having debts to pay off. 'My finances are always in a miraculous condition of unstable equilibrium', he wrote to his sister.[4] He continued to spend many weekends in London and later in Kent. In later life he realised how much free time he had in his first few years as a don. He had a strong desire to travel, to avoid stagnating and grooves at all costs and Oxford and term time seemed to be less interesting than the rest of the world and the vacations. He wanted a car badly after driving the college President to Devon in 1927 and then he complained that his afternoons were taken up with teaching Cannan to drive – and his progress was slow. His lack of money did not prevent him from planning trips to Europe every vacation. Various affairs with girls went wrong and he was restless. Then he became engaged – to Jean Millar – but she had frequent bouts of illness and died of tuberculosis in 1931. He was greatly distressed, although he had become aware that it was bound to happen and it was unlikely they would ever marry.

A visit to Australia in 1929 unsettled him. On his return to England, he wrote to his sister:

> You were all just as I remembered you so that it seemed uncanny, and I now have an absurd feeling that the past six years did not exist ... I do feel it would have been more satisfactory to have stayed, because I was much happier there than here. This life is adequate in its way, the chief advantages being long holidays and material comforts and after a while one begins to take them for granted. I have been pleased enough with this term and have not been longing for it to end, but it is a dead sort of existence and I was alive at home.[5]

In spite of this gloomy letter, he was soon writing more enthusiastically about the life he was leading and, during the 1930s, he was to marry, settle down and become more integrated into the life of an Oxford don. Marrying into an English family he gradually ceased to have any regrets about leaving Australia except for the nostalgia for Silverspur itself.

Hall was most influenced in his own development by three books. The first was Cassel's *Theory of Social Economy*, in the last part of which he introduces his readers to the general equilibrium analysis developed by Walras and Pareto, of whom at that time Hall had never heard. With enough mathematics to understand and enough economics to appreciate the equations he found that all the problems of supply and demand became clear to him in a flash.

The second book was Pigou's *Economics of Welfare*, covering the place of the state in the economic system. Pigou showed that the resource allocation which would result from the free operation of market forces would not necessarily be optimum from a welfare point of view. Government intervention by way of taxes and subsidies could improve it.

The third book and perhaps the most important was Keynes's

Treatise on Money which was published in 1931. The ideas of Keynes had a similar impact on Hall to the one made by Cassel's *Theory of Social Economy* earlier – problems fell into place and he was never the same again. The *Treatise* is a difficult book because Keynes's concept of what determined the level of economic activity and unemployment evolved and developed as the book went through successive drafts. Hall took the difficulties in his stride and understood Keynes's message – that the automatic working of economic forces did not necessarily, of itself, lead to full employment. But, strangely enough, he did not have the same attitude of respect for and enlightenment from Keynes's *General Theory*, which for most of his generation was the revelatory book.

We have, from his own account of the books that influenced him most, a picture of the sort of intellectual approach he brought to economic problems throughout his professional career: first, the importance of relative prices in allocating resources; second, the limitations of market prices in producing an optimum allocation of resources and the possible need for government intervention to achieve it; third, and most important, the recognition that the overall level of economic activity was not self-adjusting, but needed to be managed by deliberately designed fiscal and monetary policies.

Hall found that it was to political economy rather than to economic theory that his commitment would develop. Like many of his contemporaries he had to watch the humiliations caused by the mass unemployment of the 1930s and the then current doctrine that this was either an act of God or because wages were too high. Thus employment policy, and the damaging effects of unemployment, became a dominant concern throughout his career. To a practical man like Hall, the Keynesian revolution was essentially the acceptance of monetary and budgetary policy as instruments for correcting excess and deficiencies of effective demand. Keynes had also drawn attention to the need to frame monetary policy so as to prevent unacceptable inflation and had condemned the use of monetary stringency to bring down wages because it worked through depression and unemployment.

When Keynes's *General Theory* was published in 1936, it made less of an impact on Hall probably because the effect of the *Treatise on Money* had been so great five years earlier. He recognised that there were many theoretical improvements in the *General Theory* compared with the *Treatise*, but thought that the practical consequences of the theories would have been clear from the *Treatise* even if there had been no *General Theory*.[6]

During the late 1920s, Edwin Cannan was doing his best to stimulate the development of economics at Oxford and he organised regular meetings of the Oxford economists, calling his group 'Some Oxford Economists'. No philosophers were allowed to become members. Its meetings were usually held in the Cannans' house and the members discussed both topics in economics and issues relating to the development of the teaching of economics. This created a sense of community among the Oxford economists and strengthened their hands in proposing reforms of the syllabus and arguing the need for more resources for research. As a result of their pressure, and their complaints about the running of the school, there were revisions to the curriculum. A further factor in strengthening the influence of the economists was the growth in student numbers. When Hall arrived in Oxford in 1923 there were only 85 students reading PPE. By 1927 when he had been teaching for a year there were 141, and by 1933 there were over 275. The number of economics dons had risen from six in 1927 to fifteen in 1932.[7]

In 1931 the Hebdomadal Council decided to conduct a review of the financial needs of the university for the next few years. At this time, in spite of the growth of the PPE school, there was no faculty composed of or including economists as such, so that the economists had no representative on the General Board of Faculties. This was a big drawback to any developments in the method of teaching economics. Hall was one of the economists who launched a drive to have their board of studies raised to the status of a sub-faculty. They succeeded in 1932 when the Faculty of Social Studies was established and one of its first decisions was to set up the sub-faculty of economics. Until then there had been little exchange among the economics dons about economic theory or applied economics as distinct from the teaching structure. None of them knew what the others really felt about the subject. But from 1932 the sub-faculty provided the economists with a base from which they could pursue their objectives and Hall was active in helping to develop the economics curriculum along more professional lines. It also provided more encouragement to the dons to engage in research in economic theory, applied economics and economic policy, rather than in economic history.

From then until the war began in 1939, the economics sub-faculty was a stimulating place to be. Trade cycle theory had a high place in undergraduate teaching. Economists were looking for explanations of the depression. The primary importance of Keynes's *General Theory* lay in its claim to provide a theory of the general level of activity in which under-employment of resources occurs. This contrasted with earlier theory of an equilibrium where the factors of production were fully used, apart from those trapped by friction in places or industries other than those in which there was a demand for them. It was the unemployment mystery which began to hold the Oxford economists together.[8] Hall himself was always more fascinated by the policy implications of Keynes's *General Theory* than the basic structure of the system. In fact Hall was not a theorist. He was more interested in using theories to help in finding solutions to practical problems.

A second interest of Hall's that developed in Oxford arose from the work on monopolistic and imperfect competition in the books of Edward Chamberlain and Joan Robinson. Hubert Henderson went to Oxford in 1934. He felt strongly the lack of contact between theoretical analysis and realistic investigations, and he thought one of the most useful things the Oxford economists could do would be to meet regularly as a group, to discuss where information was most needed to test the theories. First those questions where information was likely to be available should be identified and their significance thoroughly discussed. The economics Fellows responded enthusiastically, details were worked out and the Oxford Economists Research Group was set up. Hall was one of the nine original members.[9] The same year, 1935, saw the start of the Institute of Statistics under the direction of Jacob Marshak, which housed a wide range of empirical studies. Hall was associated with that body also.

The group started work at the beginning of the Hilary term. A successful application to the Rockefeller Foundation raised enough funds to employ a research assistant. The general objectives were to investigate the influences determining the trend of economic activity since 1924 and to find out what factors affected the decisions of businessmen in manufacturing industry. The two more specific topics which particularly interested them were the effect of interest rate changes on the level of capital investment and stocks, and the policy that businessmen adopted in fixing the prices and output of their products. The first of these reflected the desire to know whether government action taken to control the cycle would trigger off the right responses; while the second was inspired by a disagreement about whether a reduction in money wages would reduce costs and prices or whether it would lead to increased profits, prices remaining unchanged.

The methods of investigation were to interview top businessmen in Oxford and to follow these up with interviews at the firms during the vacations. Henderson, the chairman of the group, had a great number of contacts and would invite company chairmen or chief executives to dinner at All Souls. Members of the group would join them after dinner for an informal discussion at which it was hoped the businessmen would talk openly about their policy. Most meetings were in fact lively and open. The field interviews were much more structured. A questionnaire would be submitted and discussed at each interview, written up and circulated for comment.

With regard to interest rates, the businessmen detailed the methods used by their firms when determining capital expenditure projects and these appeared to ignore altogether changes in interest rates, from which it was concluded, perhaps incautiously, that variations in interest rates had no direct influence on investment decisions. The results of this investigation by Meade and Andrews were published, with an introduction by Henderson, in the first issue of *Oxford Economic Papers* in 1938.[10]

Hall and Harrod gave some results of the second study on pricing policy in papers they read to the British Association, Section F, in 1937. Although neither of these papers was published in the proceedings, they aroused great interest so Hall, together with C. J. Hitch, wrote a paper for publication in *Oxford Economic Papers* in May 1939.[11] This included the evidence on which the British Association papers had been based and what had been collected since. It also extended and modified the theoretical structure which had been emerging. Hall and Hitch emphasised that the data had been collected by various members of the group, but only they were responsible for the presentation and the speculative part of the paper. The most striking feature of the answers was the number of firms which claimed that they did not aim to maximise profits by the equalising of marginal revenue and marginal cost. The firms worked on a 'full price' formula, that is, average direct costs plus overhead

costs divided by expected output, plus a profit margin, often 10 per
cent. Businessmen did not see prices as market-clearing as economists did. They felt that the full price was the right one, the one that
ought to be charged. Sometimes they accepted a traditional price
which had proved acceptable to consumers and adjusted the quality. A few firms admitted they might vary the price up or down in
exceptional periods thus modifying or increasing profits.

These results were thought to cast some doubt on the
general applicability of the conventional analysis of price and output
policy in terms of marginal revenue and marginal cost. The typical
case was found to be neither pure competition nor pure mo-
nopoly, but one of oligopolistic competition where only a few
firms were in direct competition with one another. A firm might
fear that while the other firms would follow its lead if it lowered its
price, they would not do so if it raised its price. Diagrammatically,
the firm would see a demand curve with the elasticity of the lower
branch less than that of the upper – that is, a demand curve with a
kink in it. The implication of the Hall–Hitch picture was that
prices were not determined only by profit maximisation, a doctrine of most economists at that time, but partly by the particular
history of the industry. A further implication was that prices would
tend to be stable in the face of moderate changes in demand or
costs. This was Hall's idea, but it was Hitch who saw its importance
so they wrote it up together. Hall and Hitch thus became known as
the inventors of the 'kinked' demand curve theory of oligopoly
and their article on 'Price theory and business behaviour', first
published in 1939, became the centrepiece of *Oxford Studies in the
Price Mechanism* when it was eventually published in 1951.[12]

A third interest of Hall's arose from the philosophical side of
the degree course. He believed that the only indication of purpose
in the physical universe, as we know it, is the apparent drive towards more and more complex organisms, and that human values,
including the increasing stress on the value of the individual in
democratic societies, will lead only to destruction, unless we use our
minds to ensure that these values do not conflict with our survival.
He was much affected by a phrase of Winston Churchill's, who
spoke of each generation being only the life tenants of the national
heritage, having a duty to hand it on to descendants in at least
as good shape as they received it. Though there is room for argu-

ment about the definition of good shape, this, Hall felt, was a good practical maxim for those who wanted their society to survive. He published a little book on *Earning and Spending*, expanding some of these ideas.[13]

In 1937, he published a book on *The Economic System in a Socialist State* based on a series of his lectures.[14] Hall's interest here was in the economic problems of a socialist state from a theoretical rather than a practical point of view. He rejected the view that some simple form of direction would be adequate and that a rough method of choice would give a rude plenty, which is all that is really wanted by the average man. Even if a socialist state established a mechanism through which it could ascertain its relative errors of overproduction of some goods at the expense of underproduction of others, it might still be unable to enforce productive methods which would give it sufficient quantities of all goods, unless it made some use of a price system.

He argued that at that time few socialists had grasped the complexity of the modern economic structure which functions so unobtrusively that it is easy to take for granted the interrelations of its parts. He felt it was the duty of all who advocated a change in the economic order to acquaint themselves with the probable implications of such a change. He concluded that a socialist state which seeks to equalise incomes as far as possible, and to do this by owning all property itself, must use a price system to some extent.

Hall was thus busy with both his teaching and research and had fitted easily into academic life. He described himself as a socialist but he was not a particularly active member of the Oxford Constituency Labour Party or the New Fabian Research Bureau founded by G. D. H. Cole. Like James Meade, then Fellow of Hertford, he was in favour of both Keynesianism and the removal of inequality, but he was less concerned with fundamental alterations in the structure of society of the kind envisaged by some socialists. He did however help to draw up proposals for the Labour Party's finance and trade committee together with Roy Harrod and Redvers Opie.[15] When the Master of Balliol stood as an independent candidate in the parliamentary by-election for Oxford City in 1938, he wrote a speech for him.

Hall lived in college until the end of 1932 when he married Margaret Linfoot. Margaret was a student at Somerville, where the

Principal, Lucy Sutherland, sent her PPE students to Hall for tutoring in economics. Margaret studied with him for two years and one term. She gained her First and they were married in December 1932. Margaret's mother had died when she was thirteen, but other members of her family came down to Oxford from Leeds for the wedding, which was held in Trinity College chapel. Margaret's father was one witness and the other was Ronald Syme, one of Hall's Australian colleagues. None of Hall's family were able to come from Australia. Their honeymoon was spent at Gara Rock in Devon, where Hall had been in earlier years with Dr Blakestone, President of Trinity College.

They went to live in Banbury Road. In a letter to his mother, Hall described with some excitement the setting up of their first home.[16] His life ceased to be that of a self-indulgent bachelor and there was no more talk in his letters of dashing up to London at the weekends. Instead, the house was often full of visitors, the garden needed attention and cooking skills were practised. Margaret kept the accounts and was clearly better at it than he was. There was no more talk of being in debt and the following year they bought a car. A daughter was born in 1936. There was a Trinity tale that, when Hall informed Dr Blakestone of Felicity's birth and told him what they were calling her, 'Blinks', as he was called, said 'Felicity Hall: it sounds like an institution.' The Halls were an extremely popular young couple. It was easy to be friendly with them and they were very hospitable. Visitors were almost certain to meet some of the up-and-coming young dons, especially economists, and also some of the livelier members of the womens' colleges. Although Hall was fairly preoccupied with his college, he found time to cycle, to play golf and to ride. He acquired an allotment and wrote to his mother that he thought he had an instinct for gardening. He also relaxed after teaching by playing darts and poker. There were evening card sessions in Trinity. During the vacations there were more holidays at Gara Rock and one with the Phelps Browns at St Bride's Bay in Pembrokeshire. There were also reading parties with students.[17]

Hall's closest colleagues among the dons at Trinity were Henry Price, Cyril Hinshelwood and Ronald Syme. As well as an outstanding philosopher and a very popular lecturer, Henry Price was a man with wide and somewhat unusual interests, which included gliding, collecting carvings of owls, and matters supernatural. These were all perhaps outcomes of his First World War experience when he was a member of the Royal Flying Corps. He was a keen walker, with a long stride and a disconcerting habit to some of lengthening it when going uphill. Price was more serious than Hall's other colleagues; Hinshelwood and Syme were more fun.[18]

Hall made friends easily. His slight Australian accent made him seem classless. Although he was not as colourful a figure as some of the Oxford dons, he was an original in his own way and thought deeply about problems which were things to be solved rather than grumbled about. He was free of arrogance and laziness in spite of appearing nonchalant and *dégagé*. As a number of students and younger dons found, he was a good person to turn to if they were in difficulties and he was both wise and kind. On one occasion he lent his car to a young don to transport his gear from Oxford to Salisbury. He was kind and welcoming to Kaldor when he was a newly arrived *emigré*. He was also very discreet, so that his advice was often sought on personal problems and the advice he gave was always practical. His pupils saw a fair amount of him and regarded him as a friend. During the 1930s, Hall, Henry Price and Christopher Cox became tenants of Seatoller House in Borrowdale from the Egremont estate.[19] They took reading parties of students there. Mornings were devoted to study and afternoons to walking the fells. Hall was a keen and energetic walker, so that with Henry Price he was able to 'raise his spirits' on the hills of the Lake District.

In 1933, at the age of thirty-two, Hall was made Dean of Trinity having been Junior Dean since 1927. The function of the Dean is to have charge of the discipline of the undergraduate members of the college. He may impose or recommend a variety of penalties for the breach of college regulations, the usual penalty being a fine which is donated to the library fund or used for repairing damage. He may also withdraw permission for various activities or privileges. The Dean may also recommend that the offender be sent down, rusticated, no longer be allowed to live in college, or be deprived of his scholarship. A disciplinary committee sits as a final court of appeal. The Dean's permission has to be sought for a number of activities, such as holding parties or meetings and forming societies.[20]

In his first term as Dean, Hall had to address the students on the subject of behaviour. 'I hope I avoided being too moral' he wrote to his mother. In the same letter he commented on the President: 'He directs business as he pleases and, though we do take decisions against him sometimes, we are worn out and he thrives.' Hall appears to have been an understanding Dean. On one occasion he was especially tolerant. The Trinity Torpid boat scored six bumps in the annual race. The college gave a bump supper in honour of this and it was the usual uproarious and rather drunken affair. After dinner a bonfire was started in the garden quad and one undergraduate decided to remove a passage door from its hinges to add to the flames. He was caught in the act by Hall, who remonstrated with him. The undergraduate defended his action as an excellent idea, on the grounds that the door was not only ugly but served no useful purpose. Hall allowed him to continue, the door was not replaced and no fine was ever imposed.[21]

Hall's good sense and lack of pomposity had a good deal to do with the virtual absence of any 'them and us' feeling often prevalent between undergraduates and dons. He could skilfully lead off into harmless pursuits none-too-sober young men who were becoming dangerously wild in their ritual abuse of next-door Balliol, but he very much disliked drunkenness and took to leaving parties early when he had had enough to drink himself. Many years later at the Economic Section Christmas parties, he always contrived to dilute the alcoholic fruit cup.

Hall was remembered by many as one of the outstanding personalities of the Trinity Senior Common Room in the 1930s. Trinity in those days had a curious institution called the Tutors, a sort of inner cabinet of three senior Fellows. It was Hall, in a lighter moment, who summed up the younger Fellows' opinion of them in a parody of the Athanasian Creed: 'Palters incompetent, Reggie incompetent and the lovely Thebe incompetent. Yet are these not three incompetents, but one incompetent?'[22] Nor was he beyond practical joking himself when he was a young don. He and Cyril Hinshelwood, the chemistry don, found one of the senior dons much too pompous. One afternoon they emptied half the contents from a decanter of port, substituting sugar and water in quantities which would achieve the correct density. They were delighted when that evening, the senior Fellow smacked his lips as usual, commenting 'Delicious.'[23]

In 1938, Hall was made bursar of the college. His predecessor had not adopted a very professional approach towards the management of the college estates. Although his term of office proved to be short, Hall proceeded to update the tenancies of the agricultural land owned by Trinity and to negotiate with Sidney Sussex College, Cambridge for a similar revision on land owned jointly with them. He also began a scheme for the college to buy North Oxford houses and lease them to Fellows, whose stipends were then reduced by the amount of the rent. This was a way of easing the housing problems of the younger dons. It also put the college into less unprofitable investments than some others they held.[24]

The 1930s passed pleasantly for Hall. Another daughter, Anthea, was born in 1939. The one sadness was his father's death in 1935. From 1938 he became increasingly concerned about the European political situation. He wrote to his sister that he had no sympathy for the British government, which had not lifted a finger to stop the aggression by Germany, Italy and Japan, but had allowed themselves to be blackmailed at every turn. The government was a disaster with no policy at all and – worst of all – no rearmament.[25]

As far as economics was concerned, he had developed as an applied economist rather than as a theorist. His interest was not so much in theories as in the uses to which they could be put. By 1939 he had a few publications to his credit and a reputation as a sound, but not brilliant, economist. He had shown little sign of the kind of intellectual inspiration which would have placed him in the same class as some of his Oxford contemporaries, like Harrod and Meade. The story of these years gives little hint of his future eminence; he seemed in some way to be marking time. But there was plenty of evidence that he had a natural gift for dealing with people, which was to be one of his strengths in his subsequent career. At Trinity, he had learnt the practical skills of negotiator and operator, which were to be put to good use in the Ministry of Supply and the British Raw Materials Mission in Washington during the war, and then in his years in the Treasury after the war.

CHAPTER SIX

Wartime Civil Servant in London and Washington[1]

As for so many people, the war made a complete break in Hall's life. From a job he found congenial, but not particularly exacting, and from which he could enjoy his family life, friendships, hobbies and holidays, he was catapulted into a hectic job in Whitehall. He had no time for anything but work, usually in the office until 11.30 p.m., and even then there was not enough time to do everything properly.

During 1938, when it looked as if war was likely, a number of university people had been approached and their names placed on a register as being available for whatever they were wanted to do. Hall by this time was thirty-seven, so that he was not wanted for military service. Instead, about three weeks after war broke out, he received a telegram asking him to attend the Ministry of Supply for an interview. When he went he found they were recruiting rapidly and he was offered a job straight away. He started work the following week in the Raw Materials Department of the new Ministry of Supply.

On the eve of the war the British Empire and the United States exercised a dominant control of world raw materials resources. Reserves were plentiful. There were some restriction schemes on output in existence as a result of excess production during the world depression in the 1930s, for example in rubber, but the allies could feel reasonably secure and would only face shortages as a result of major defeats in theatres producing supplies or as a result of heavy losses at sea. Neither of these possibilities had been seriously considered until war was declared, so that no large stocks had been acquired and no alternative sources had been developed. Indeed the production of substitutes at home would have been unthinkable in peacetime, when commodity producers were suffering from the decline in world production and trade.

By the time war was declared in September there was some control machinery in existence and some programmes of requirements had been worked out, but these were of a rather skeletal kind. When it set up the Ministry of Supply in July, the government had announced the resumption of some powers it had discarded twenty years earlier, transferring to it the Board of Trade functions in respect of the Essential Reserves Act (1938). The ministry was made responsible for the whole range of defence supplies, including the acquisition and maintenance of reserves of essential metals and other raw materials required in connection with defence and agriculture.

On 1 August 1939, when the new ministry began work, personnel were transferred from the Board of Trade as the nucleus for a raw materials department to be organised under a minister or parliamentary secretary, with a senior civil servant as its head, two assistant secretaries, six principals and supporting staff. Fennelly, the head, was quickly pressing the Treasury for more staff, and by October the net effect of his proposals was an extra twelve principals, six of whom were found by promotion and six by temporary appointments from outside the civil service, one of whom was Robert Hall.

As the agitation with the Treasury to increase the size of the department indicates, the staff were all very pressed to start with, because of a ministerial decision to institute controls for nearly all the important commodities immediately. The plan was to use the existing trade associations and personnel as controllers, who would acquire and generally direct materials in the most efficient manner in the interests of the war. The Board of Trade had been negotiating with trading interests on various matters for many years, so that the contacts were already there for the building of the machinery by which the Ministry of Supply would control the design, inspection and supply of all army requirements and of common user articles for the army, air force, navy and civil defence.

The work that Hall immediately became involved in was organised in the following way. Munitions demands were worked out

by the military strategists. These had to be broken down into estimates of raw materials. These estimates were passed to the raw material divisions which had to find out how far the materials were
available and subsequently ensure that the right amounts were
available at the right place at the right time. At any of these stages
the margin of error might be great. Moreover, if strategy changed,
munitions estimates changed and this radically affected the raw
material estimates.

Hall began as the civil servant in direct contact with the hides
and leather control set up at the start of the war. The main function
of this control at that time was to arrange the supply of raw material
needed to obtain leather for the services, raw hide being 60 per cent
of the value of finished leather. Hides and skins were imported from
a large number of countries, with domestic supply making up the
total available. Cattle were the most important source, so a large
proportion of supplies was a by-product of meat production. An
increase in demand for leather does not therefore lead to an increased
supply, but rather to rising prices. Consequently a most important
function of the leather control was to keep prices down. Hall was
thus involved in the arrangements which were made for all tanners
to purchase hides through a pool. This meant that in effect there
was only one buyer in the United Kingdom. The pool did not actually buy hides. All the usual channels of trade were maintained but
no purchase could be made without the approval of the pool. Before
long the pool determined what was to be bought and arranged the
purchase.[2]

The distribution of leather from producers to users was for the
most part regulated under rationing systems using existing trade
channels, but licences were required for the quantities they could
purchase. There was also a complicated machinery for regulating
prices, because of the extreme variety of leather and the absence of
homogeneity.

These arrangements involved Hall in much correspondence and
consideration of the trade. His duties included supervising and coordinating plans for imports and the distribution of supplies,
advising on progress of previously laid plans, or deciding (with the
controllers) the extent of any departure from these plans; the making of voluntary agreements which needed constant supervision;
frequent revision of control schemes; additional statutory orders;

and the development of the centralised buying arrangements. There were also the demands from the Export Licensing Department, the Ministry of Economic Warfare and others for information, while other matters which concerned him related to the diversion of supplies, shipping programmes and priorities, and an ever increasing flow of policy questions and enquiries of all kinds. Hall reported directly on all these matters to the head of the department because the assistant secretary, to whom he was technically responsible, was too busy on the wool control.

Until the collapse of France in 1940, Hall lived in London during the week, in a small flat in the Gray's Inn Road, either eating in restaurants in the evening or cooking his own dinner. This was the period of the phoney war and Hall marvelled that there had been no air raids. 'What a fool Hitler has been', he wrote to his sister, 'we would have been in a shambles if he had bombed us all at the beginning.' He escaped to Oxford on Saturdays: 'I can hardly bear to be away from my allotment and you can imagine with what anxiety I rush up at the weekends.'[3]

He went to Paris early in May 1940 to a conference on leather and found Paris still moderately gay. Belgium and Holland were invaded while he was there. Back in Oxford he and Margaret decided that she and the girls should go to Australia where his sister had offered them a home for the duration of the war. It was a hard decision, but Hall, along with many others felt that England was going to be invaded. Margaret was desolated, but the children were too young to go alone. Felicity was only four and Anthea was not yet a year old. The plan was for Margaret to stay with them in Queensland until they were settled and then return to England to do some war work.

After their departure the Halls' home in Oxford was commandeered and used by the university to house staff from London University who were evacuated to Oxford. Hall still managed to go to Oxford most weekends, staying with the Cannans, but he gave up the allotment. He was finding the work fascinating. He had been taken off the hides and skins control and moved to the general branch of the Raw Materials Department, which he liked much better. He had been promoted to Assistant Secretary and 'there was never a dull moment'.[4]

In addition to becoming an expert on one group of commodities, he had learnt how the government machine operated and also demonstrated that he had mastered the problems involved in the commodities control system. He had also learnt to deal with the people with whom he had contacts in that post. He had learnt all this in a relatively short time, as indeed all the most successful temporary civil servants did.

The general branch handled the coordination and contacts with other government departments on the broad questions affecting raw materials as a whole, including shipping. It was also the liaison for all the policy-making decisions that might be made by a minister or ministerial committee. The branch was headed by Charles Morris, also an Oxford don.

It was part of Hall's job to represent the Raw Materials Department on the various Whitehall committees and to discuss with the operative branches how the decisions affected them and to pass back their reactions. Shipping space had become more and more limited so that the raw material controls had to be tightened, and much time was spent on the problems this created. Another committee was looking at the export surpluses in various countries, and the coordination of changes in purchasing programmes involving surplus commodities was added to Hall's responsibilities. In a letter to his sister he described his job as very interesting, but very strenuous: 'I am badly overworked for the first time in my life. It isn't only that I am at it from the moment I get up until I am too tired to do anything at 11 p.m., but that there is no time to do anything properly.' He missed Margaret and the children badly. During the air raids in 1940–1 he slept in the office, which was much safer than his flat.

Although there were surpluses of some commodities, a succession of military disasters in Europe bore heavily on supplies of others and, at the same time as supplies were falling, the pressure of demand for them intensified as America began to rearm. Then in June 1941 Germany attacked Russia. From the time of Dunkirk until lend-lease became effective in October 1941, the main worry was paying for the materials rather than their availability. Every device was used to gain dollars for essential purposes and to restrict the use of dollars to essential needs. By the beginning of 1941 nearly all Britain's available dollars had been committed. It was a race against time. The Lend-Lease Act in March 1941 marked a turning point. There was less need to earn dollars by exporting, and export markets were sacrificed as the dollar problem ceased to exist.

In June 1941, when the German invasion of Russia brought Russia into the war, Hall was put in charge of a small section called Allied Supplies which helped primarily with getting supplies to Russia. Lord Beaverbrook had been appointed Minister of Supply and most inquiries on supplies to Russia went to him rather than to the junior minister in charge of the Raw Materials Department. The Allied Supplies section was therefore more directly involved with the minister himself.[5] Hall was baffled by Beaverbrook, who was either unaware that he frequently reversed decisions, or was unconcerned about doing so, but he thought that Beaverbrook probably did more to stimulate aircraft production by going on as he did than anyone who was concerned about consistency.

The work that took up Hall's time and energy in the six or so months during which he headed this section brought him into closer contact with the American official also engaged in these matters, as the attack on Russia brought closer collaboration between the British and American governments and resulted in combined handling of supplies. The American representative in London was Averell Harriman. He sat on British committees and went to Moscow with Lord Beaverbrook, who negotiated and signed in Moscow on 1 October the First Russian Protocol which was designed to regulate British and American supplies to Russia. It listed the specific supplies to be delivered and although it did not bind the suppliers to provide the shipping, in fact Britain and America did so.

The extensive demands from Russia faced Britain and America with a deficiency in materials and shipping, so that there was much to-ing and fro-ing on these matters in the Allied Supplies section and in Whitehall more generally. Supplies to Russia had to be met out of what was becoming a British–American pool. For example, a large part of the British reserve stock of aluminium was released to meet urgent Russian requirements, in the hope that the stock would be made good by America. By the end of October 1941 it looked as if raw material resources would be a limiting factor on meeting the requirements of the three countries and would force cuts in those requirements. While Russian resistance to the German attack, and the consequent start of the second front, had brought a significant easing of Britain's strategic burden, it had added to her economic burden. But the situation was soon to change again.

Up to December 1941, Britain had borne the main strategic and economic burdens of the war. After the Japanese bombing of Pearl Harbour, however, the war became global and Britain's burdens were eased somewhat when the United States became fully involved. This led to another change in post for Hall as it introduced alterations in the Anglo-American supply arrangements. At first it was feared by Britain that the United States government might freeze supplies of raw materials, but this fear turned out to be groundless. Instead, following a visit by the Prime Minister, new arrangements for the allocation of raw materials were agreed in Washington which included the setting up of the Combined Raw Materials Board. Until that time, in addition to the Embassy which covered foreign relations and was also closely associated with the Ministry of Economic Warfare and the military service representatives, there were a number of separate missions. They communicated with their home departments in London by cable and on the economic side were loosely coordinated by the British Supply Council.[6]

The British Supply Council had included a Raw Materials Mission at an early stage when direct procurement from the United States began. At its core were commodity sections under directors from the relevant trades who received their instructions directly from the controls at home. After the agreement between Churchill and Roosevelt on coordinated procurement, the Raw Materials Mission became independent and, apart from its procurement function, provided the British staff for the Combined Raw Materials Board. It was to the Raw Materials Mission in Washington that Hall was sent early in January 1942. There he was reunited with his wife.

Margaret Hall had arrived in Washington about six months earlier. Finding it impossible to obtain a passage from Australia to England, she had managed to procure one to the United States. She made tremendous efforts to find a way of travelling to England and, when she failed, found herself a job with the Office of Price Administration. Eventually her plans materialised in December 1941 with the offer of a post in the Ministry of Food in London, which qualified her for a priority flight home. She had no sooner done this than she received a telegram from Hall telling her to delay her decision. He had been posted to Washington. It was not easy to find anywhere to live. Washington was overcrowded and they considered themselves fortunate to find a small flat about five minutes walk from Hall's office. They were both working very hard, but they were not disposed to grumble and they both found their work very absorbing. They managed to escape from Washington about one weekend in three, to stay with friends about thirty miles away.[7]

Technically the Combined Board consisted of two men: Sir Clive Baillieu, the head of the British Raw Materials Mission, and Mr William Batt, the representative of the American War Production. George Archer went from London to be the official head and Hall went out as his deputy and head of the General Division.[8] As George Archer was away in London from time to time Hall became acting head of the Mission on these occasions and he developed a very good understanding with Baillieu. Britain and America had begun to dominate the raw material markets of the world, even before the Combined Raw Materials Board was set up. The new machinery completed the process.[9]

The General Division dealt with questions affecting several commodities, such as shipping, coordinated buying and relations with third countries. When Hall arrived the allies were facing a series of acute scarcities caused by the cutting off of supplies by Japan and the sudden vast increase in the demands of American industries for strategic materials. Allocations were sometimes made on the basis of relative populations and industry, sometimes on an historical basis and sometimes using a more complicated formula. In the case of rubber, where Japan cut off 80–90 per cent of world supplies, the main answer was provided by establishing the capacity for new synthetic production. In the case of tin, Japan had not only reduced supplies but had also eliminated smelters, so that the United States had to re-enter the smelting business; there was a drastic curtailment of tin consumption and an increased use of substitutes.

The task of the Combined Raw Materials Board was to assemble the facts on matters which were of urgent common concern, so that they could make recommendations to the national authorities as a common strategic interest. Their power to recommend was strong as most of the problems could not be handled by either government individually. However, interdepartmental struggles were rife in Washington in 1942 and the Combined Boards did not in themselves make the partnership effective. They were helped by the very close relationships built up between the two national ad-

ministrations at many levels, some of which led to personal friendships. It was a unique partnership. Hall thought the Americans very
easy to get on with for those with the right temperament and found
them anxious to help and to cooperate.

The British and American administrations became geared together
at every level so that, when a problem finally reached a meeting of
the Combined Board, it had behind it agreement on the essential
points right back down the line. The machinery for maintaining contact between the two countries was an advisory operating committee, which prepared in advance measures which in due course
emerged as recommendations of the Combined Board. The committee then followed these up to ensure that they were carried out.
Hall thus learnt from experience that negotiations begun low down
the line and carried up to the board by the American officials were
more likely to endure.

Business was conducted by cable, rather than the usual civil
service method which was by file, and this speeded up operations
because it meant that everyone who had to be consulted in London knew more or less simultaneously what had to be done and
what decision was needed. In addition to the more formal channels of communication between the British and Americans, there were
the wholly informal relations of daily meetings and hourly telephone
talks. The delegations' offices were on opposite sides of the same
corridor in the Willard Hotel and they shared the same luncheon
room – the Bradford Lunch Room. It was here that some of Hall's
friendships with Americans began.

The official history of the war concludes that the Combined Raw
Materials Board was the most successful of the combined boards
and attributed the success to a number of factors. One of these
was that the common emergency brought together some of the
ablest, most devoted and energetic officials from both countries who,
although they continued to be national officials, performed functions beyond the national interests.[10]

This contact of an international kind certainly appealed to Hall,
who got on with his American colleagues in a very similar way to
that with his own colleagues in the Raw Materials Mission and in
the other related missions such as the Food Mission in Washington. His philosophy of international relations was illustrated when
someone in a moment of frustration referred to 'those bloody

Americans'. Hall reproved him, commenting, 'You can say "that bloody American" but not "those bloody Americans".'[11]

In spite of his burly appearance (Hall put on a stone in Washington) and abundance of physical energy Hall was always calm and equable. His staff never saw him excited or angry. His relations with other members of the mission were always friendly without being in any way intimate. He demonstrated that he did not believe in making enemies, and he made use of every casual meeting to get thoughts and information from the other without giving anything away himself. These were characteristics which were observed by his staff in the Economic Section some ten years later. He wrote regularly to colleagues in London reporting on events in Washington. In one letter he commented, 'I have my finger in most pies here.'[12] A reply from Charles Morris expressed his appreciation of Hall's reports. In a letter home in August 1942, he wrote that he was involved in completing forward programmes, as the mission was expecting a request from the Americans. He reported that the statistical section was gradually improving and that a new Lend-Lease appropriation statement had been prepared by working through all the requisitions of the past year. These had been supplemented by information in cables on future intentions. All the estimates had then been discussed with the supply officers.

He also reported that he had established some sort of working relationship on specific enquiries then going on into copper, but that steel was in the utmost chaos because there were so many bodies involved on both sides of the Atlantic. He doubted whether anyone knew the whole picture and wrote that it was almost impossible to find anyone on the American side capable of giving a decision that would be adhered to.

In September of the same year he wrote to Charles Morris that things were getting much tighter and they were bound to have difficulties in the next few months. The main problem was local confusion about jurisdiction: 'even the service departments are sick of the present system as they have to spend all their time standing over their contractors with an axe, to make sure no-one jumps new priorities over them'.

By this time Hall had become the regular liaison with the Combined Production Research Board and he kept a general eye on policy points. He was recalled to London for three months early in

1943, in order to report on the situation in Washington and to be put in touch with recent developments in London. It was a beautiful spring and he enjoyed seeing all his government friends and going to Oxford where he found that the peaceful features of college life were unchanged. It had been an exciting time to be in Washington, but he felt out of the war too much and the sacrifices that everyone in Britain was forced to make made the American way of life seem too opulent.[13]

On his return to Washington, he was made the British representative on the Combined Conservation Committee in addition to his other work. By this time the North American Supply Missions had grown into a large organisation resembling an overseas Whitehall. Things were working more smoothly; as far as raw materials were concerned the worst was over, and this was reflected in the amount of work he had. While in England, he had found many people taking a great interest in postwar problems and his own interest had been thoroughly aroused. From then on, he devoted more and more time to the ideas developing about the shape of the postwar world and the institutions needed to achieve the aims of a new international order.

CHAPTER SEVEN

Postwar Plans for a New Economic Order[1]

From the summer of 1943, when he returned to Washington, until the end of the war, Hall spent less and less time on Combined Raw Materials Board work and more and more on postwar economic problems. He had became involved in the discussions between the United States and Britain on economic matters connected with the shape of the postwar world, particularly in such matters as commodity policy and cartels. But his interest extended more widely than this into the ambitious economic plans that were being formulated among the English-speaking nations. These plans were based on the assumption that the peoples of the world would expect to live in peace and prosperity and would be willing to accept something like a common code about international relations. In the new world, labour and capital were to be free to pursue their own interests in response to market forces, but governments were pledged to a commitment, new to the majority of them, to intervene to moderate and iron out the cyclical swings in economic activity of which the 1930s depression had been so traumatic an example. An integral part of the pledge was to refrain from action in the international field, for example by restricting imports or exports, which sought short-term advantages at the expense of other nations.

Discussions on these matters with the Americans had their origin in the Mutual Aid Agreement in February 1942, when negotiations over the terms of Article VII on lend-lease made it clear that the Americans wanted to see the confusion and national individualism which had marked the world economy in the 1930s replaced by forms of international cooperation. American officials were very conscious of their country's wealth and their creditor position and had begun to feel that they had the power to mould the postwar world in the way they wished it to be. They were also aware that their aid would be needed to rehabilitate Europe and that this put them in a strong negotiating position. They leaned towards freer trade and wished to see the end of trade discrimination, with a gradual reduction in tariffs.

While the British agreed with these objectives, it was the Americans who pressed for new international organisations to regulate the world economy and they felt that a useful start could be made in the currency field, which would provide a basis for further action on trade, investment and employment. Consequently, currency planning began soon after the signing of the Mutual Aid Agreement and two plans took as a starting point the ideas on monetary cooperation which had been circulating before the war. One of the plans was by the American, Harry White, who was in the United States Treasury, and the other by Keynes who was an adviser to the British Treasury during the war. Both plans provided for the control of exchange rates by an international agency; and both made a provision for supplementing international liquidity and a mechanism for multilateral clearing.[2]

The Keynes proposal was much the more ambitious of the two. An International Clearing Union was to be established, requiring no initial members' deposits, but giving each country an 'overdraft' or 'quota' to supplement its own reserves if necessary to meet deficits on its balance of payments. This was to give debtors time to make the necessary changes to their economies to reduce or eliminate their deficits more gradually than by deflating and increasing unemployment. Under his scheme, as much of the strain of adjustment was to be on the creditor countries as on the debtor countries.

The White Plan on the other hand required initial deposits from members. There was to be no automatic supply of currencies to deficit countries; in all cases the fund was to have the right to oblige members to carry out measures to correct the disequilibrium in their balance of payments. The scheme that eventually emerged in the Bretton Woods Agreement in 1944 was more like the White Plan than Keynes's Clearing Union.

Keynes was also proposing an international investment board and an internationally supervised scheme for the stabilisation of primary commodity prices by the operation of internationally held buffer stocks. This scheme was known as 'Commod'. The need for a policy towards primary products was already apparent in 1943, because the economic blockade had led to the accumulation of surplus stocks of some commodities in some of the colonies. But there were also the longer-term problems of the instability of primary product prices and the resulting fluctuations in the incomes of those countries producing primary products. These had been particularly acute in the 1930s. The basis of Keynes's proposal was that there should be an international system for purchasing stocks at times of abundance, and for selling them at times of scarcity and rising prices, that is a 'buffer stock system'.

The Economic Section of the Cabinet Office, which Hall was later to direct, and in particular Professor Lionel Robbins and James Meade, were also thinking about postwar economic policies and there had been a lot of discussion in Whitehall with the Treasury taking the lead. There were various different approaches; Meade himself was especially concerned with commercial policy, working on proposals for an international trade organisation and there was much apprehension about the future. It was not clear how far America understood the problems that Britain would face; some officials thought that if there could be international arrangements, then British problems might be easier to solve.[3] Hall had joined in some of the informal discussions in Whitehall.

The first conference to discuss postwar economic policies was held at Hot Springs, Virginia in May–June 1943, shortly after Hall's return from London. It had been called suddenly by President Roosevelt in March. In a letter to the Prime Minister he wrote that the United States government believed the time had come for the United Nations, and other countries associated with them in the war, to begin joint consideration of certain fundamental questions confronting them and the world, after the attainment of complete military victory. All the allied nations were invited. As a first step, the conference was to explore postwar plans for production and trade in foodstuffs and agricultural raw materials and the possibility of improvements in levels of consumption. Secondly, it was to consider the possibility of international arrangements, institutions

designed to promote efficient production and adequate supplies
and equitable prices for both producers and consumers. Thirdly, it
was to explore trade, financial and other arrangements to obtain
adequate supplies and markets. Finally, it was to explore the possibility of policies for improving nutrition. The conference thus
provided an opportunity for discussing a wide range of policy options.[4]

Hall attended this conference because of the specialist knowledge
he had acquired while working at the British Raw Materials Mission. Earlier in the year, he had taken part in the pre-conference
discussions in Whitehall. These had a rather panicky flavour, as the
British felt they had not been given enough warning about the
talks. Hall returned to Washington with a collection of briefs on
agricultural raw materials, the briefs on foodstuffs being the responsibility of the Ministry of Food. He was thus implicated right from
the start of the series of discussions with the Americans and others
on the shape of the postwar economic world. He felt that he had
been very privileged to attend the first conference.

It was this conference that agreed to establish an interim commission to draft a constitution for a permanent Food and Agriculture
Organisation. This makes it sound as if it was easy to reach agreement. But in fact the conference opened in an atmosphere of 'abso-
lute bewilderment, compounded of resentment, suspicion and
ridicule', according to Richard Law, Minister of State at the Foreign Office, who was leading the delegation. It had no direction
posts to guide it. In the event the British delegation took over
and led the delegates through the maze.[5]

Hall's role was that of an expert adviser to the delegation. Although the Ministry of Supply felt that a Food and Agriculture
Organisation might have too much opportunity to extend its activities into the field of commodity policies, Hall was not so concerned
about this, because he thought that the problems of the better
distribution of food were closely linked with the broader international problems of trade and payments and that if the new organisation could improve distribution this would be very helpful.

By this time Hall knew personally many of the Americans taking
part in the conference and must have been very useful to the
delegation from London. He had also acquired a pretty good knowledge of the way things worked in the United States. Professor

Robbins, who was a senior member of the British delegation and kept a diary, described Hall as 'one of the most knowledgeable and agreeable members of the British community'. From Hall, Robbins learnt much of the stresses and strains of the British set-up in Washington, as well as those of the United States machine.[6] Although the British were admired for their resistance to Hitler, the Americans were critical of their colonial policies and sceptical of Britain's ability to become again a world power. Something else that the British needed to take on board, which Hall had learnt at the mission, was that the Administration in the United States was subject to the annulling power of Congress. Everything always had to be acceptable to Congress, and foreign negotiators needed to be aware that promises made to them or concessions negotiated might evaporate in practice. Nor did the American officials hesitate to make use of this if they thought it would help their cause.[7]

The next round of discussions took place in Washington in September and October of the same year. These were informal non-committal talks confined to the United Kingdom and the United States. The British delegation was again led by Richard Law and it became known as the Law Mission. Hall was again in evidence at delegation meetings and he was a member of the sub-committees on commodity policy and cartels. He took part in all the informal discussions between the British and American groups.[8]

He argued against an American proposal to adopt the principle of maintaining price ratios between agricultural and industrial commodities in the course of the trade cycle. He also wrote a note on a differential price system, opposing a system where the home consumer would pay a higher price than foreigners and in a discussion on prices he reminded the meeting that primary producers had no mechanisms for adapting themselves to economic depressions. As Hall and other economists saw it, commodity agreements were needed to avoid the sort of situations which had arisen before the war, when the productive capacity for many primary commodities greatly exceeded effective demand. In most cases this had given rise to agreements among the producing countries to restrict production, in order to maintain or improve prices and so protect the primary producers. Consuming countries were not consulted and felt their interests were ignored. It was thought that remedial action should be on an international scale. Commodity policy had a particularly close link with commercial policy so the groups worked closely together. The commodity policy group considered that there could be little hope for an agreement that did more than bring out where the two sides agreed or disagreed.

Highly complicated and technical issues were involved. The conference was attempting to frame arrangements which would ensure the free flow of primary products into consumption, together with any measures that might be necessary to protect the producers of those products. This latter requirement was essential for the British delegation which was also representing the colonies who were large producers of primary products. In addition to special measures on commodities, however, an orderly world economy and currency and trade policies were needed to achieve such protection.

On cartels, Hall thought that their regulation, rather than their prohibition, might be more appropriate because in Britain, where firms were often small, mergers could be useful. It would be difficult in some cases to prove the existence of price agreements, for example where one large firm became a price leader. There was a danger that a prohibition, drafted in such wide terms as some of the group were contemplating, would catch the innocent as well as the guilty. Hall was displaying the practical approach to economic problems that was the basis of his success in Whitehall after the war. He was also drawing on his experience of visiting firms associated with the research he had done in Oxford on how firms fixed their prices.

The Americans feared that in the absence of special measures of international regulation, cartels would be likely to take action which was inconsistent with a liberal commercial policy and with Article VII of the Mutual Aid Agreement. The beneficial effects of any reduction of barriers to trade that were imposed by governments would thus tend to be thwarted. Restrictions on production, productive capacity and technological advance might follow.

Employment policies were also on the agenda and Hall was on the sub-committee to exchange ideas on this subject. This concluded that it was desirable to have an organisation with wide terms of reference. Its function should be to promote international action to maintain high levels of employment and the coordination of economic policies by some sort of supreme council.

The conference reached agreement on the objectives of commodity policy, but advised that individual committees should deal with the detailed matters relating to each commodity, and that importers and exporters should be evenly balanced on these committees. Hall was to become the British representative on a number of these committees or 'Study Groups' as some of them were called. The main difference of view with the United States arose on the value of buffer stocks in offsetting cyclical fluctuations in prices where the Americans were more sceptical, and the final report concluded that further study was necessary. The final agreement stated that international commodity arrangements should be in harmony with general expansionist policy, and the primary objectives should be that they should mitigate violent short-term swings in prices, help to counter business cycles, ensure that price adjustments would follow changes in basic conditions of demand and supply and provide action on an international basis – a tall order indeed. An international commodity organisation was to be established and the policy methods for achieving these goals were to be buffer stock and quantitative regulation arrangements.

These discussions therefore did not carry much further the general principles on commodity policy agreed at Hot Springs. It also proved impossible to reach agreement on the International Clearing Union at this meeting, but four months later a joint statement was issued after a conference at Bretton Woods on the establishment of the International Monetary Fund, though without committing either government. The most successful negotiations in September–October 1943 appeared to be those on commercial policy, but in fact the proposals met with considerable ministerial opposition in Britain from the protectionists in the Cabinet such as Beaverbrook, R. H. Hudson and Leo Amery, while Ernest Bevin was unhappy about the idea of fixed exchange rates. There were also efforts by the Bank of England to persuade the Cabinet to reject the International Monetary Fund. The war ended before the final decisions on commercial policy were reached.

Early in 1944, Hall was expecting to be recalled to London. He and his wife had become increasingly restless and anxious to have the children back with them, and they had agonising discussions on how to get them home. Hall was very concerned that his wife should not return to England without them, as he thought it would be much more difficult for her to go to Australia from England than from the United States. She therefore set about finding a way to fetch them but she was not to succeed until the following year.

In the meantime Hall was back in London with a new job, which was exactly what he wanted to do, that is working on postwar commodity policy and more specifically on stabilisation proposals for individual commodities, in line with the Law Mission's tentative conclusions. At a meeting of the Interdepartmental Group which had been set up in Whitehall, he favoured a new international body, rather than one based on the combined boards for food and raw materials which already existed in Washington. But this would take time so the boards would have to deal with problems that would not wait. He pointed to the danger of *ad hoc* bodies pursuing separate policies out of line with the general objectives.[9]

On specific commodities, there were departmental discussions on wool and copper in which Hall was involved. In January 1945 he was again in Washington at a meeting of the Rubber Study Group which he had helped to promote. Consideration was also being given to study groups for wheat, cotton, wool, tin and sugar, and discussions on their likely trends were taking place. Hall's brief was to secure the best possible agreements both as a major importing country and also (at the time) as representing important producers of some primary commodities in the colonies. This called for considerable skill on Hall's part, balancing what might have been opposing considerations. As a negotiator, his reputation was established.

In 1944–5, it was vital that the cost of imports did not rise too much, so that Hall and his colleagues were working to reach agreements which aimed at a plentiful supply at reasonable prices, which would prevent extreme fluctuations. But they were also concerned that the agreements should allow for increased efficiency as well as higher consumption. Hall recognised that it was most important that Britain should not join any agreement which would result in artificial scarcity, high prices and inefficiency. There is no doubt that in postwar circumstances these agreements provided some stabilising elements when they were needed. Hall was one of a very small number of Whitehall officials responsible for negotiating these.

The Hall family were together again in Oxford at the end of 1945 and able to resume a normal social life. Margaret Hall had departed for Australia at the end of 1944 having at last found a way of getting there. She obtained a short-term appointment with the United Relief and Rehabilitation Administration (UNRRA), to work in Sydney for three months, covering meetings of the committee of the Council of the Far East; and then, after leave to travel home, to work for another three months in London setting up links between UNRRA in Washington, Sydney and London. She arrived in London with the children in July. Felicity the elder daughter was just four when she left England and remembered little about her father. But he was immediately recognisable, standing on the wharf at Liverpool to meet them, because he looked exactly like the photograph they had with them in Toowoomba. Anthea, the younger, was only a year old when she went away and had no memories of him, but soon thought him wonderful. Hall was very much moved at seeing the girls again. For a few months while their mother was working with UNRRA in London, they all stayed with Margaret's sister. It was a difficult time until Margaret was released from her UNRRA contract after a three-week visit to Washington for another meeting of the Far Eastern committee.

In the meantime in Oxford, Hall reorganised the house in Banbury Road, taking the girls there in time to start school in September. They were all back together there in October. Margaret was one of the first women to be appointed to a lectureship at an Oxford men's college – Lincoln in 1946 – and the following year she became a lecturer and then Fellow and tutor at Somerville College. Until Hall moved to a full-time post in London in September 1947, he spent a lot of time with the girls, cycling or walking with them to school, sharing with their mother the hearing of their prayers and reciting poetry to them in a sonorous voice to lull them to sleep. He cooked the meals at the weekends which his younger daughter, accustomed to Australian food rather than the meagre British rations, found dull and distasteful. The years 1946 and 1947 were not exactly comfortable in Britain with the fuel crisis in February 1947 and the swingeing cuts in imports leading to even stricter rationing than during the war. To the two girls returning from Australia it must have seemed much worse than to those who had not been out of Britain. Moreover, living in Queensland they had never experienced cold. To Felicity, the elder, all this was out-weighed by the warmth and love of her parents, but the younger, Anthea, looked back on those early years in England with a shudder.

Although Hall returned to Oxford in October 1945, he was able to organise his teaching into three days a week and when the Raw Materials Department of the Ministry of Supply was transferred to the Board of Trade at the end of the war, he was appointed there on a part-time basis and so continued for almost two years. He spent two days a week in London during term time and more in the vacations on Board of Trade matters. He was appointed to a sub-committee set up to review the whole question of buffer stocks and began to press for changes in the departmental responsibil-ity for commodity policy. He felt increasingly that work on com-modity policy should be centralised in one place.

The Treasury had been made the central coordinating body for commodity policy with a committee chaired by Sir Wilfred Eady, but it had not met for a long time. There had been little systematic coordination and only a rushed series of *ad hoc* meet-ings in connection with the setting up of the Food and Agricul-ture Organisation (FAO) and the preparatory conference for the International Trade Organisation. Hall sensed that the Treas-ury's preoccupations with balance of payments problems meant they were unlikely to take any lead. He thought the Board of Trade was the most suitable department to do so, since com-modity policy was so closely connected with matters of interna-tional commercial relationships which were the Board of Trade's responsibility. He also felt that it was important that a single body of people with specialised knowledge should deal with all commodities, since one of Britain's problems was to ensure that the Americans did not get away with the adoption of one set of principles where it suited them and then try to impose a different set on the world when it did not. With these arguments he convinced Sir James Helmore that his department – the Com-mercial Relations and Treaties Department – of the Board of Trade should take over responsibility for commodity policy.[10]

During 1946, Hall was abroad several times attending meetings of study groups and an FAO conference in Copenhagen. By late that year he knew that commodity policy had moved away from an overall solution, with an authority which had power to operate for a predetermined number of commodities and had become one which dealt with specific problems of each commodity. He found it was relatively easy to reach a series of individual agreements – they had made good progress on rubber, tin, cotton and wool – but almost out of the question to form an international authority with power to act without reference to individual cases. He became convinced that the United States would never be a member of an international commodity agreement and so felt that there ought to be an attempt to create machinery for officials to negotiate buffer stock schemes where they suited British interests.

The same year – 1946 – Hall was also at the preparatory commission for the international trade conference. This included representatives of some European and Latin American countries, as well as the British Commonwealth and the United States. It prepared the outline of what was to be the charter for an International Trade Organisation. It covered a much broader field than that of barriers to trade, and included questions of internal policy connected with target levels of employment. But this body was never set up. Although a charter was agreed at Havana in 1947/8, it was ratified by only one country. In its place a much more modest agreement was the sole survivor, though this was still very important. This was the General Agreement on Tariffs and Trade (GATT) which contained only the draft clauses of the charter on tariffs and import restrictions.

Hall then attended the meeting of the United Nations Economic and Employment Commission in New York in January 1947. This body had been set up by the Economic and Social Council the previous year to implement the employment pledges in the United Nations Charter, to monitor performance and make recommendations. It was a particularly ineffectual body. At the first meeting Hall wrote back to Whitehall that he was finding it very painful as so few of those in attendance knew anything about the subject on which they were supposed to be representing their governments. 'If we go on as we have begun', he wrote, 'we shall be here till Christmas, but no doubt the party in favour of going home will gradually gain a majority over all other points of view.'[11]

Hall was the British delegate to all the meetings of this body which was finally wound up in 1949. He himself helped to abolish it. He felt quite clear that the commission was much too ignorant to allocate the responsibilities requested of it. The first meeting had adopted a resolution to initiate regular reports on world conditions and trends, giving particular attention to any factors preventing full employment and reporting on the most appropriate action to achieve full employment. However this did not take very far the British wish for the adoption of a resolution which would actually commit countries to a full employment target. Hall lost patience. He thought it unfortunate and ironic that it was impossible to whip up as much enthusiasm as he would have liked for studies of full employment, because everyone was preoccupied instead with what he regarded as useless researches on economic development.[12]

During the first half of 1947, Hall was also sending memoranda to Sir James Helmore, head of his department, on a variety of practical points, attending meetings of the new committee set up to handle commodity matters, and writing papers for the Buffer Stocks Working Party of which he was also a member. He managed to achieve a great deal in his two days a week. The Board of Trade certainly had their money's worth out of him.

In addition to being a part-time adviser at the Board of Trade from 1945 to 1947, and teaching three days a week, Hall began again the research that he had abandoned at the outbreak of war. He became preoccupied with the subject of imperfect competition, developing the ideas arising from the kinked demand curve that he and Charles Hitch had written about in 1939 and its relationship with the size of firms.

Hall's experience in Whitehall and Washington during the war convinced him that he liked operating in the world of current affairs, reading up a subject thoroughly and then working hard at a particular problem. He also enjoyed a period in which he could turn things over in his mind without much conscious interference, so that he could work out the best line to take. But in Whitehall he had also learnt to work against deadlines when it was necessary. He had worked very hard – five times harder than ever before in his life, he told his mother – but, unlike some wartime civil servants, he was not longing to escape from Whitehall back to teaching. Rather he found that he liked the mixture of Oxford and Whitehall and was very pleased to carry on as a part-time adviser. The war had established his reputation, especially with the Board of Trade, Treasury and Economic Section.

It was therefore perhaps not surprising that his name should be the first to come up as a possible Director of the Economic Section when James Meade retired because of ill health in 1947.

CHAPTER EIGHT

A New Job

The year 1947 saw a third wholly unexpected event cause another break in the course of Hall's life. Early in that year the Permanent Secretary of the Board of Trade (Sir John Henry Woods) made it clear to Hall that he did not approve of arrangements which involved academics working part-time in Whitehall; Hall was therefore expecting their early demise and the end of his own appointment. At this point, he received a message that Sir Edward Bridges, the Permanent Secretary to the Treasury, wished to see him. This was followed by a summons from Sir John Henry who, far from dismissing him, gave him a drink and urged him to accept the proposal that Bridges was about to make. This turned out to be that he should become the Director of the Economic Section to follow his friend and former colleague in Oxford, James Meade, who had been forced to resign because of ill health, after less than two years in the post.

The Economic Section was the first group of professional economists to operate full-time as government economic advisers. They began early in the war as the staff of the Stamp Survey, to review the economic and financial war contingency plans. When the Stamp Survey was wound up at the end of 1940, the staff was split into the Central Statistical Office and the Economic Section, both located in the Cabinet Office. The Economic Section remained there until 1953 when it was transferred to the Treasury. During the war, it was staffed by academics recruited as temporary civil servants. For twenty years after the war the number of staff averaged about twelve.[1] They were a mixture of economists recruited on five-year contracts, short secondments of young economics graduates from other departments and – an innovation by Robert Hall to deal with a continual shortage of experienced staff – secondments from the universities for two years. The Section was an advisory body and it had no direct responsibility for economic policy; the policy adopted by the government might or might not reflect their advice.

Although Meade had several times suggested that he might join his staff, it had never crossed Hall's mind that he might become the Director. He thought that there were a number of economists, even at that time, who were better qualified than he was for the post. He considered that, although he had been a moderately successful civil servant, he was far from the heights which had been scaled by some of his ex-Oxford colleagues. On the other hand, most of them wanted only to return to academic life; and he himself had always felt capable of further progress than he had in fact made in the Ministry of Supply. Moreover it was clear in his mind that if Bridges saw fit to choose him, he must have consulted some person or persons in whom he had a good deal of confidence. In fact Bridges had consulted both Robbins and Meade and both of them had advised Hall's appointment.

Hall went back to Oxford and spent a troubled weekend discussing the proposal with his wife and in the end they decided that he should accept the offer for a three-year period, but that they would not move house to London. Hall wrote to his sister, 'It will be a very interesting job as long as I am not hung on a lamp-post by the angry population at the end of my term.'[2] Trinity College, which had treated him with great generosity both during and after the war, added to his debt by agreeing to release him for three years. He had until September to sort out the teaching arrangements. In the event Tony Crosland, then one of Hall's best students and about to be awarded a First in PPE, was given a temporary appointment to take over Hall's teaching commitments.

For the next fourteen years up to 1961 Hall was to be in effect the Chancellor's Economic Adviser serving three Labour Chancellors, Dalton (only briefly) Cripps and Gaitskell and then five Conservative ones, Butler, Macmillan, Thorneycroft, Heathcoat Amory and Selwyn Lloyd. He was also given the title Economic Adviser to the government in 1953, when the Economic Section was moved to the Treasury, in recognition that Hall advised other ministers as well as the Chancellor. Plainly he had found his role.

Years later he wrote, 'It is hard to think of a more congenial post to one whose overriding interest is in the economic functions of the State, and especially in the use of its powers to put an end to the unemployment which made such a nightmare of the interwar years.'[3]

When Hall started work as Director of the Economic Section, Britain still faced many difficulties despite the fact that the war had been over for two years. The first Labour government with an overall majority, which had come to power in 1945 with Attlee as Prime Minister, had ambitious plans for the social services and was committed to a full employment policy to be realised by a somewhat vague economic policy. The most critical problem of the transition from war to peace was the balance of payments. Most of Britain's overseas investments had been used to pay for the war and this, together with an adverse shift in the terms of trade, meant that exports would need to be much higher than before the war. But it would clearly take time to achieve this, since the whole economy had been mobilised for war. When the United States brought lend-lease to an abrupt end in 1945, there seemed to be no alternative to a loan and this was negotiated by Keynes. On strictly commercial terms this looked generous, with a low rate of interest and a provision for cancelling interest in any year that export earnings were insufficient to pay for the prewar volume of imports. But there was a very stiff condition attached, which was only accepted by the government under duress. This was that the convertibility of sterling must be restored within one year. The American loan, together with a credit from Canada, were expected to cover deficits for three years. In fact they were used up in half that time, as much as two-fifths as a result of capital movements.

Hall was transferred to the Economic Section from the Board of Trade on a part-time basis on 1 June 1947, mainly to work on the draft Economic Survey for 1948–51. But as the balance of payments position worsened, he had to spend more and more time on that, including a good part of August when he was meant to be on leave. Convertibility had been substantially introduced before 15 July, the date agreed under the loan agreement, and the drain of gold and dollar reserves was disastrous.

The Chancellor wrote a paper for the Cabinet and asked for Hall's views on the situation. Hall advised that part of the drain must have been of a capital nature and of drawings on the sterling reserves held in London by other countries. He thought that the Egyptian settlement had been too generous and reminded the Chancellor that the Indian one was still to come. His recommendations included calling on the first year's instalment of 'drawing rights' from the International Monetary Fund, cuts in food consumption and action to reach export targets. He warned the Chancellor that he might be driven into a situation in which Britain would be unable to carry out the loan agreement obligations (that is convertibility and non-discrimination) because world recovery had not taken place at the rate envisaged when the loan was negotiated in 1945. The United States should be warned of this with a full explanation of the reasons. Until this time there had been no reference back to the Americans for a change in the conditions or to request further help, even though it had become clear to many that the move to convertibility was inappropriate.

In Hall's view, the foundation of Britain's case should be that both the United States and Britain had been proved by events to have taken too optimistic a view of the speed of world recovery during the years when the plans were made, largely under the influence of President Roosevelt, for the postwar economic structure. The difficulties were mainly beyond Britain's control; they included the deterioration in international political relations, with its consequent burdens, and the delay in the recovery of world food and raw material production which had resulted in a rise in world prices. He was very anxious that there should be consultations with the Americans:

> My own belief is that the only hope for either country to secure in the long run the kind of world which was envisaged by such organisations as the IMF, Bank and ITO is that there should be not only a strong USA, but also a strong Britain. And relations between the two countries should be as friendly as possible and should certainly not be marred by either relationships of donor and recipient, nor by an atmosphere of mutual recrimination about broken pledges.[4]

Following Hall's minute to the Chancellor, Hall-Patch, a Deputy Under Secretary at the Foreign Office, visited Washington and reached agreement on a suspension of convertibility. This was done on 20 August, after a week when $237 million had been paid out of the reserves, as much as the total deficit for 1946. At home, measures were taken to reduce rations, already low, following a reduction in food imports, and there was an agreement with the sterling area countries to limit their dollar imports. These measures reduced the dollar drain to more manageable proportions, although it was clear the reserves were no longer adequate. Fortunately, the concept of the Marshall Plan had been sown in June in a speech by General Marshall, the United States Secretary of State, at Harvard; this appeared to imply an offer of financial aid to Europe provided the countries themselves could agree on their requirements and work out a programme to put Europe on its feet. This was seized on by Ernest Bevin, who called the European nations to a conference designed to follow up this American speech by organising a plan for the recovery of Europe. Thus, although the British economy was at a very low ebb when Hall was appointed the Director of the Economic Section, there was a possibility of further United States aid on the horizon.[5]

In September Hall was able to take up his new position full-time and give his whole attention to the job. He began with some big advantages. He had a good knowledge of how the civil service worked as a result of his wartime experience, and he was also familiar with the Anglo-American machinery as a result of his two years in Washington. Moreover he was well versed in the current situation and the problems the government were facing.

Hall's job was not an ordinary civil service post. However all his dealings were to be with senior civil servants or ministers, and he needed to work out his role within the civil service machine. He knew already from his civil service experience that there was practically no pretence that an outgoing tenant of any post should have a period in which to indoctrinate his successor. This was the result of two articles of faith: first that everything material to the conduct of government business should be on files and secondly that the ability and training of the administrative (or top) class of civil servants should make any member of the higher civil service capable at once of grasping the essentials of any situation with which he or she would have to deal. There was an elaborate system of keeping other departments aware of anything one department might be contemplating in which another might have an interest. In addition, every civil servant was expected to know when he could take a decision and when he needed to refer it to a superior. The most certain way to get a black mark was to get one's superiors into a row with their colleagues because they had not been informed or, alternatively, to take a decision which turned out to be a mistake, without having proper authority to take that decision.

True to civil service custom, Hall was left to his own devices when he entered upon his new job. In other ways, however, the job was completely different from the usual civil service position. The Economic Section in fact had no responsibility for taking or carrying out any decisions. Its advice was available to any department which asked for it and to any committee on which it was represented. It had been very active during the war in working on postwar economic problems as well as the operation of the war economy itself. Lionel Robbins, the second Director, and James Meade, the third, had played an active role in the international negotiations referred to in chapter 7, which had led to the establishment of the International Monetary Fund and the International Bank for Reconstruction and Development, and in the attempt to set up an international trade agreement, which was later watered down to the General Agreement on Tariffs and Trade. They were also involved in the drafting of the commitment to a high and stable level of employment which was adopted by all members of the United Nations.[6] As we have seen, Hall himself was on the fringe of all these discussions and he firmly believed in the need for such institutions and the sort of powers they had been given.

The concern of British governments with the management of the economy dates from the formal acceptance in 1944 of responsibility for maintaining a high and stable level of employment, which was set out in a White Paper on employment policy. This led to a concern for much more than that, including the course of prices and the balance of payments, and also to some extent the rate of economic growth. As a result governments became generally responsible for the management of the economy for the first time other than in a war. In the postwar world it was intended that the Economic Section would be the body that would advise ministers on the conduct of this wholly new employment policy (later to become known as demand management and later still as macroeconomic policy) which was to be carried out in a way consistent with maintaining a fairly stable exchange rate and an open trading system. Meade had given a good deal of thought to these matters, and he foresaw that budget, exchange rate and monetary policies would become the decisive elements in economic policy once the direct controls used during the war were eliminated. But when Hall arrived none of the senior Treasury officials had thought through what would be involved in carrying out such a policy. The senior Treasury officials with whom Hall was to work during the first few years were Bridges, the Permanent Secretary and the three Second Secretaries, Wilfred Eady, Bernard Gilbert and Henry Wilson-Smith. But the man with whom he was to work most closely was a temporary official, like himself. This was Edwin Plowden, who was appointed by Stafford Cripps to the new post of Chief Planning Officer early in 1947. They both found the Second Secretaries frustrating and sometimes obstructive. Eady had worked in the Ministry of Labour for twenty-one years before joining the Treasury in 1942. He had a reputation for energy and resourcefulness and for his creative skill in negotiation, but the war years had told on his health and he was sometimes slow to grasp all the arguments. He was determined not to be diverted from ensuring that arrangements would be workable. Hall found him 'rather mad'. Gilbert was more of a thorn in Hall's side. He had been in the Treasury since 1914 and Hall frequently disagreed with him and thought him lazy and and uncaring; he was to conclude later that Gilbert had consistently thrown all his weight in the direction of doing nothing. Wilson-Smith he spoke of more highly; he was younger and much more energetic, but he left the Treasury at the end of 1950 to go to Guest, Keen and Nettlefold, a most unusual step at that time. Among the third secretaries, the next in seniority, was Herbert Brittain. Hall found him 'on the whole a force for good though not a very strong one. He really understands the Treasury, he carries out policy loyally and resolutely...His main weakness in my time has been that he has never initiated anything or even been conscious of the changes of problem until these were pointed out to him...But how much better in all respects than Eady or Gilbert.'[7]

When Hall took over the Section, it was attached to the Cabinet Office as it had been throughout the war and this served to emphasise its independence from any specific department. It gave advice at its discretion and also had the opportunity to comment on any economic matter. But by 1947, it was clear that the Chancellor of the Exchequer would be the key figure in an economic policy which looked to changes in public revenue and expenditure and monetary policy as the principal instrument for avoiding recessions. The Chancellor did not consult his Cabinet colleagues about what was to be in the budget and informed them only at the last stage when it was too late for them to make any changes. In fact everything about the budget was then, and for many years later, 'top secret'; even the existence of the Budget Committee itself was secret. Although there were still wartime controls in existence which in some ways made planning the economy easier, the object of policy was to get rid of them as soon as possible, that is as soon as supplies were sufficient to allow market forces to take over the allocation of resources without a large increase in prices.

Although the Chancellor had asked Hall for his views on the economic situation soon after he arrived in the Cabinet Office, Bridges had warned him, rather apologetically, that Dalton regarded himself as an economist able to cope himself with any problems that might arise and that this would limit any scope Hall might have had to affect Treasury policy. He was not too surprised therefore when he was not consulted about the supplementary budget which Dalton had to introduce in November 1947. It was this budget which in some ways set the pattern for the disinflationary budgets of the next three years with which Hall was closely associated. After some tax reductions in earlier budgets, Dalton felt constrained to raise taxes, as a means of deflating demand, although Hall thought he did not go far enough. The three Cripps budgets firmly resisted any relaxation in taxation.[8]

Not wanted by Dalton, Hall quickly involved himself in a great many other economic matters which were dealt with in interdepartmental committees, both official and ministerial. Some of these were called working parties in deference to Churchill's complaint during the war that there were too many committees. The Economic Section could be and usually was represented on the official committees which dealt with matters on which the Treasury often took the lead. The Section also received papers of ministerial committees dealing with economic matters including those of the Cabinet itself. Hall therefore discovered that it was very well informed with the chance to intervene and express its views at the official level and to write briefs, if it thought fit, for the Prime

Minister or for the Lord President of the Council or for both – but not for the Chancellor of the Exchequer.

The main weakness which soon became apparent was that the Section knew very little about matters dealt with by the Treasury alone, including the side of the Treasury which dealt with revenue and expenditure, and matters connected with the funding of public debt and the management of the money supply. Indeed the latter, as Hall gradually discovered, was largely in the hands of the Bank of England.

Hall believed that an economic adviser could only be useful if he took as his starting point the policy objectives of the government and the extent to which parliament and the community could be persuaded to move towards them. If he did this, his briefs would then be more likely to be effective. To start with he wrote briefs for the Prime Minister and the Lord President, but he could not feel they were sufficiently interested to take much notice of them. Moreover looking through past Economic Section briefs, he discovered that by his standards most of them were too long. He also found their tone somewhat unhelpful in that they tended to assume that a competitive economic system gave the best results. He thought this was not tactful to ministers who were impressed by what they thought were the achievements of a planned economy during the war.

During the first few months, while he was still part-time, he was essentially learning the ropes and finding his way around. He had time to read his way into the job, to become more familiar with the current economic situation and outlook, both in Britain and to some extent in the free world, and to get to know his staff and the officials in the departments concerned with the broad economic policy interests. At this stage Hall was not very impressed with the staff he inherited. A number of senior economists had departed at the time that Meade left and among the ten or so remaining many were young and inexperienced. Later he came to recognise and be grateful for the ability of some of them, and to be frustrated when he met with 'establishment' opposition to their promotion. He then had to argue for an increase in the permitted seniority in the Section (which had been reduced after the war). Nor was he very successful when he pressed for an increase in his staff and this was a worry at intervals throughout his time as director.

A few months before Hall's own appointment, Sir Stafford Cripps had been appointed to a new post of Minister of Economic Affairs, owing to the dissatisfaction felt in the Cabinet on the way economic affairs were being handled. Cripps was initially located in the Cabinet Office and had been given a small planning staff with Sir Edwin Plowden as its chief executive. Plowden was given very extensive powers, although they were operationally ill defined. At the time of his appointment Cripps was told that he could look to the Economic Section for advice on economic matters. This looked to Hall a better way forward than ineffective briefs to the Lord President. Soon after he began work full-time, Hall rang Plowden to suggest a meeting. Plowden was at home recovering from jaundice, but invited him to lunch at his home near Dunmow, offering the official car, already at Plowden's disposal, to transport him to Dunmow and back. Hall found Plowden looking rather odd, with his face marked by jaundice and an incipient beard.[9] In these circumstances formality went by the board. They quickly became friends as well as colleagues and formed a close working association which lasted until Plowden left Whitehall in 1953. Plowden had been a wartime civil servant in the Ministry of Aircraft Production and Cripps had selected him for his outstanding qualities to be his Chief Planning Officer.

Both Hall and Plowden attended Cripps's weekly meetings for senior staff. They were supposed to be drawing up schemes for a 'planned economy' which was the declared aim of the government. As the Minister of Economic Affairs had been given no powers over the Treasury, which controlled the budget and to a predominant extent the import programme, he had little scope to plan. After the suspension of convertibility Hall was asked to write a paper on the economic outlook, mainly to stress the difficulties stemming from the exhaustion of the American loan and the need to concentrate on the balance of payments problem which was rapidly becoming a dollar problem. Britain's exports were increasing satisfactorily, but they were going mainly to areas which could pay in sterling from the balances they had accumulated during the war, and which had never been blocked in spite of earlier intentions that they should be. Consequently British exports were not earning the dollars to pay for goods only available from the United States.

A new committee on the balance of payments was set up in September 1947 under the chairmanship of Leslie Rowan, who had been at No. 10 as one of Churchill's staff, and had been appointed a Third Secretary. He was an extrovert, a captain of a team, always energetic and efficient and good at getting things done; but he tended to get into intellectual difficulties when dealing with central problems of economics, which required a grasp of the interaction of a wide range of forces. Hall found him to be temperamental and, when opposed on a matter of policy, inclined to treat it as a moral issue. In spite of such reservations, Hall felt that it was a great step forward to have balance of payments problems in the hands of an interdepartmental committee, chaired by the Treasury, on which the Planning Staff and the Economic Section were represented, instead of being managed by the Treasury alone.

Within three months of Hall's arrival in the Section, the economic apparatus was transformed by one of those wholly unforeseen chances which seem to the chief participants at the time to be a historic turning point, although they are later often discounted by historians. This was the resignation of Dalton as Chancellor in November 1947, for having revealed the tax changes in his supplementary budget to a lobby journalist, on his way into the House of Commons to announce them. This was technically the disclosure of a budget secret, though no one could have benefited from it.

Cripps became Chancellor, retaining the position of Minister of Economic Affairs. He took Plowden with him into the Treasury and, although the Economic Section remained in the Cabinet Office until 1953, Hall was treated as though he was a member of the Treasury and his staff were in a position to have much closer relations with Treasury staff than they had had before. His staff included David Bensusan Butt, who had been closely associated with Keynes and his followers in the 1930s during the preparation of the *General Theory* and who was interested in the work on national income statistics begun before James Meade became Director. There were two or three others who also understood the problems involved in trying to carry out what became known as Keynesian policies, including Christopher Dow, who had studied under Gaitskell at University College before the war. On external policy, Marcus Fleming, the Deputy Director, took the lead, with Nita Watts also playing an important role. Unfortunately Hall found it difficult to get on the right wavelength with Fleming, despite his good sense and intellectual distinction; in Hall's view, Fleming included too many qualifying clauses and subtleties in any papers he wrote or any proposals he made. In the next year or two Hall was able to recruit a few more staff, who were also interested in helping to put into practice Keynesian ideas.

Hall expected his staff to get on with their work while he got on with his. He interfered very little with them after agreeing their area of responsibility and committee membership. His standards were high, which often made him critical, and if he once decided that someone was muddled, or did not produce work on time, he quickly lost faith in him. He hoped his staff would find their own channels to be effective, but most of them were too junior to do this. Hall did not have time to help them to do it, hence there was always some sense of strain in the Section. Some of his staff often felt he did not really need them because he rarely asked their advice and, even when he did, he never indicated whether he was going to take it or not. He really was remarkably self-sufficient. Those who came closest to him were those who worked with him on the national income forecasts and the budget judgment.

Aside from keeping up with a regular flood of papers that had to be read somehow, Hall attended an almost continuous round of official meetings. Among many meetings of less importance, he became a member of the Budget Committee and also of the Second Secretaries' meeting which Bridges held every week for the three Second Secretaries, Plowden and Hall and the Permanent Secretary of the Board of Trade. At these weekly meetings there was a general discussion of what each member was doing and thinking. The Chairmen of the Boards of Inland Revenue and Customs and Excise were sometimes invited and this larger group formed the Budget Committee.

Hall soon discovered that the Treasury was ill equipped to deal with the problems facing the country. Bridges himself he could not have respected more; he was clearly a very able man with great authority, not only by his actual position, but also that which he brought with him as a former Secretary of the Cabinet. He understood in a general way the intentions and methods set out in the Employment Policy White Paper, but at that time, and almost all the time he was there, Hall felt the Treasury was painfully weak at the top levels. He described the Second Secretaries as almost extinct examples of the volcanoes they had no doubt once been; and the Third Secretaries as almost as weak. The outstanding man was R. W. B. Clarke (Otto) – in Hall's view a man of great ability and able to take a forward view. He was lively, full of ideas and very self-confident; and much more influential than his rank indicated – he was not promoted to Third Secretary until 1955 – but he was also somewhat unstable and his judgment was not reliable. Hall had many struggles with him. Clarke believed that the Treasury must not only formulate the general directives of economic policy in its totality, but also act as the coordinator of the policies of individual departments towards the achievement of these objectives. He was a man of great ideas. Hall was not, and distrusted them. He always felt that Clarke was more concerned with being the moving force behind great enterprises and elaborate plans than with the effects they would have when they were carried out – an Alexander or Napoleon who wanted battles to win rather than faiths to establish.[10]

The general weakness of the Treasury, however, left the way clear for Hall and Plowden. They were trusted by Bridges and, as far as the senior staff were concerned, the only person of any standing to cause Hall some concern was Clarke, whom he thought might propose policies with which he disagreed, or ambitious schemes which he regarded as impracticable.

Another factor that Hall had to take into account, in considering his role as an economic adviser, was the position of the Bank of England. From the economic point of view monetary policy was an essential part of the anti-cyclical policy intended to smooth out the alternation between booms and slumps, required to maintain a high and stable level of employment. Demand management, as it came to be known, had also to see that plans took account of balance of payments considerations. At this time, the balance of payments was supposed to be regulated by variations in the import programme and the use of exchange controls. The latter required full cooperation between the Treasury and the Bank of England.

Although the Bank had been nationalised early in 1946, no steps had been taken to integrate it fully with government operations. The Treasury had two divisions which were in continuous touch with the Bank – Home Finance and Overseas Finance. The Home

Finance division was responsible, *inter alia,* for matching the differences between revenue and expenditure through operations for issuing and repaying long-term debt, and for smoothing differences through the floating of short-term debt. In both these operations the Bank acted as the government's agent and in fact decided the ways in which the government's needs should be met. Both might involve changing either the structure of interest rates or the amount of money. Hall found it impossible to discover what policy considerations actuated the Bank in its decisions on these matters; the Home Finance Division however took the Bank's advice without argument or discussion.

Similarly, the Overseas Finance Division, the other division closely connected with the Bank, could produce little information on releases of sterling balances, on the outflow of capital and on the amount of transfers being allowed under the exchange control system. Hall learnt that, in September 1947, Clarke had complained that the Bank had stonewalled for several months on providing information about the inflow of capital into South Africa from Britain, but his complaints had little effect and the Bank continued to keep the Treasury in the dark about such occurrences.

Soon after Hall took up his post full-time, he became extremely busy. He was burning the midnight oil with members of his staff on the Economic Survey for 1948. He was short of staff to attend the numerous new committees which were being set up and to meet the demands for briefs and reports on a host of subjects. But even if he had had more senior staff, it is likely that he would still have found himself overworked. Much of his work could not be delegated, as the demands on him were from ministers or very senior officials. As it was, members of the Section invariably found themselves at meetings with officials who were a higher rank than themselves.

During the winter of 1947–8 the economic situation gradually improved, the dollar drain eased and shortages became less severe. With Stafford Cripps now master of economic policy and Plowden as his chief of staff, Hall's position grew increasingly powerful, even to an extent that was rather scaring to himself; he was often to feel that neither he nor Plowden knew, or could know, enough to justify the responsibilities being thrust upon them. It was said that, if Bridges, Plowden and Hall agreed on a recommendation, Cripps accepted it as if it were the voice of God.

An important development early in 1948 was the approval by the American Congress of the European Recovery Programme, which brought with it the prospect of receiving Marshall Aid. Hall was appointed a member of the London Committee which was set up to run the operation in Whitehall. This involved many meetings about the programmes that the Americans had requested; and other members of the Section were involved in helping to work out the details. Hall was also working on the 1948 budget. He was astonished at the progress made in the six to seven months he had been in the Economic Section and in his diary he recorded his surprise at how much he had come to be consulted and to get his views accepted. 'To crown all', he commented in his diary in March 1948, 'Edward Bridges sent for me this afternoon to ask what I thought about the policy of the Bank and whether we should give them directions about the control of credit.'[11]

It had taken Hall less than six months to find his role in the Treasury and in Whitehall generally. He had quickly established his working habits. From Monday to Thursday he often slept in the office and he was at his desk early to read the daily inflow of papers before meetings started. He worked hard and fast all day, generally leaving around 7 p.m. for a dinner engagement or to dine at his club. He made it a rule not to allow himself to become overtired but, when inevitably he did from time to time, he was usually resilient and recovered fairly quickly. He recharged his batteries at the weekends, almost always catching the train to Oxford around 6 p.m. on Friday. Margaret was now a lecturer and tutor at Somerville College and was also working hard. The girls were happily settled in school. Much of the weekend was spent on the allotment and there was plenty of entertaining. An early train on Monday morning took him back to London in time for Cripps's Monday morning meetings.

CHAPTER NINE

Working with Cripps

Cripps's first budget in 1948 was also the first on which Hall had an influence. He felt that it was a turning point, because it was the first occasion in peacetime that budgetary policy was related to the overall economic situation and the first budget in which an inflationary gap was quantified by the Chancellor using national income accounting. From 1948 onwards, budgets were formulated on the basis of a judgment about what was needed to keep or bring demand into line with the resources available. Budget speeches emphasised that events might turn out differently, but if so changes would be made. At this time special interim mini-budgets were not ruled out. Hall had arrived in the Section just at the point when this could be done; and it was he who established that in future the budget would be worked out in this way. With the assistance of his staff, he was not only able to develop the economic arguments logically, but he was the only senior official who could do so. Except for Clarke, none of the others had a formal economics training, and Hall provided them, not only with the methods and solutions, but with the conceptual framework as well.

This budget contemplated a very large surplus in 1948/9, but all Hall's fears that it would be regarded as too deflationary were unfounded and it had a good reception. Immediately after the budget, he wrote a minute to Plowden:

it seems to me that there are a number of problems about the place of the budget in the national economy, which could profitably be discussed at more leisure than we have had in recent months. In particular, I have in mind the present levels of total expenditure and the question of whether our tax structure provides an adequate incentive to that part of the national economy which depends on private enterprise. It could be argued that we are trying to put altogether too heavy a load on the economy and that this will produce a continuous tendency towards inflation, which can only be checked by taxation so severe as to dishearten the community.[1]

A further paper by the Economic Section, which Hall submitted on budgetary prospects and policy for the next five years, concluded that a considerable budget surplus would be required by general economic conditions, so that it was important to achieve all possible reductions in government expenditure.[2] In this connection, he argued that food subsidies should be examined, with a view to their reduction or abolition by 1952. On taxation, he concluded that a reduction in the standard rate of tax had a high claim and that attention should be paid to the profits tax and depreciation allowances.

He felt encouraged to propose some new studies: one to examine government action to help or hinder competition, which led to the setting up of a committee on controls and efficiency, and another on the level of government expenditure and the impact of the tax structure on incentives. He was also working on a paper on prices and material controls and their effect on the pattern of industry. In addition to asking his own staff to write papers on these issues, he was also active in encouraging some academic economists to write papers.

Although recovery seemed to be going well in the second half of 1948 and the country was approaching overall balance in its current trade and payments, Hall was worried that the dollar balance was actually worsening. The situation was complicated by the large sterling reserves held by countries overseas. These had accumulated during the war, when Britain ran out of reserves, was unable to pay for the imports she needed and so borrowed and ran up debts. These sterling balances were far in excess of what was considered appropriate as monetary reserves by the countries themselves, and the natural inclination of holders was to use them for purchases from Britain or to convert them into dollars to buy goods from the United States. Bilateral discussions in 1947 resulted in agreements about their use, though these proved far from watertight. There was some temporary blocking for some countries and restraint in use by others. Separate accounts were created at the Bank of England for the blocked balances and the releases. The agreements were renewed frequently and releases were substantial between 1947 and 1949.

The release of the balances was criticised by many, including the Economic Section, partly because it was thought that, since the countries which held them had been defended by Britain, they had no moral right to demand payment and partly because of the burden it placed on the British economy. There were also some moves to make intra-European payments easier and some of the proposals for a system of drawing rights by deficit countries made British officials fearful of losing dollars to Europe.

In Whitehall there was much discussion about unrequited exports and the fact that holders of sterling wanted to spend it on dollar goods, rather than in the sterling area. The Bank of England appeared to be finding the problems of managing inconvertible sterling more difficult than Hall thought they should. To support the British position, the government resorted to controls of various kinds, in an attempt to divert exports to dollar markets and to obtain contracts for supplies from the sterling area.

The United States regarded these measures as contrary to the agreements Britain had made with them to work for a world of convertibility and non-discrimination. Moreover relations between the two countries were not very happy; the direct contacts between the United States and Britain, which had been so close during and immediately after the war, were more or less suspended as the Marshall Plan got under way. The need to coordinate the plans of the European countries and to agree on the division of Marshall Aid resulted in the setting up of the Organisation for European Economic Cooperation (OEEC), based in Paris and in which the Americans, although not members, took a full part from the beginning. They did not wish to have direct contacts with Britain, but to work through the OEEC, and they were pressing for a solution to the sterling problem through the European system.[3]

The Bank of England did not like this idea. They were very anxious to restore the reserve function of sterling in Europe and thought that the problems of integrating the existing sterling system with a European payments system were almost insuperable. For the next two years they engaged in tactics to make every move away from a traditional banking approach more difficult. Hall found these tactics very irritating and was extremely critical of the Governor and his staff.

Towards the end of 1948 Hall became concerned about the growth of bank credit which had led to an increase in the money supply. The Bank viewed a reduction in government spending and a budget surplus as the only ways of controlling inflationary pressures; and it was content to let the money supply respond to demand. The Labour governments of 1945–51 ruled out rises in interest rates, which had been at 2 per cent since 1939, because they did not wish to see an increase in the heavy burden of the national debt and because they wished to encourage borrowing for investment. This was so firm a commitment by the government that Hall did not waste time arguing about it, but looked for other effective instruments of control. He and Douglas Jay, the Economic Secretary, proposed that there should be a ceiling on advances. In a letter to Cripps, this proposal was rejected by the Governor of the Bank in no uncertain terms, as impractical and unwise. Hall continued to press for a more restrictive policy to check inflation but he met with little success, as the Bank took the view that because prices were rising more money was needed. Angry minutes went from Hall and Plowden to Bridges, but they resulted in only a little progress, in that it was agreed that the government must borrow more from the market and less from the banks. By this time Hall sensed that the postwar world was facing inflation and rising prices rather than the deflation and falling prices which had preoccupied Keynes and other economists. It was clear that inflation was not going to cure itself. Average wages and salaries were rising and import prices continued on an upward trend. Although output was rising, it was not enough to prevent a rise in unit costs which, if it continued, would pose a threat to exports. Marshall Aid was providing a breathing space, but time would run out fast.

Hall continued to think that monetary policy had some part to play in combating inflationary pressure and that one way was through a limitation of bank credit. He engaged in a correspondence with officials at the Bank, conceding some points but continuing to argue about the need for more pressure on borrowers and the degree of severity desirable. He was not particularly concerned about the hit and miss effects of credit restrictions, a worry expressed by the Bank. That Hall was felt to be making a nuisance of himself is clear from a letter written by Catto, then the Governor, who was in hospital, to Cobbold, then the Deputy Governor. This included the sentence: 'This pressure from the Economic Section on financial and banking matters must be dealt with forcibly, otherwise you will have no peace in the future.' The Bank were unused to criticism and regarded all matters to do with the financial operation of the markets as solely their concern.[4]

As 1948 drew to a close Hall was still very much overworked, covering, as he had to, so many aspects of policy. His concerns for instance included banking policy, the Budget Committee and the economic outlook, food subsidies, export targets, Marshall Aid and the OEEC, and the Economic Survey for 1949. He was able to cope with such a vast amount of work because he was a very fast reader and he wrote concisely. He rarely changed what to many civil servants would have been a first draft and he often wrote speeches for the Chancellor and other ministers at very short notice. He sometimes said that if you persuade a minister to accept your policy, you should then help him to sell it by writing his speeches for him. The demands on him were great but he managed to keep abreast of the situation.

As time went on he became increasingly concerned about the persistence of the dollar problem. While the possibility of devaluation as a means to balancing Britain's postwar external account had been under discussion during the war, the subject received little attention in the early postwar years. There was some desultory discussion between the Treasury and the Bank during 1948. Towards the end of that year, encouraged by Marcus Fleming, Hall decided there was sufficient evidence to show that the sterling/dollar exchange rate was too high and that the time had come to devalue the pound. He approached Cripps about the possibility but Cripps was always temperamentally opposed to the idea of realignment, and still thought the dollar shortage could be met by directing exports. Hall thought to himself, 'Well I'll give it six months to see whether he can do it by direction.' The Bank of England was also opposed to devaluation. Cobbold, then Deputy Governor, thought the only solution to Britain's difficulties was to reduce government spending; this would reduce government borrowing and credit creation, and rising exports and lower imports would follow. Hall too was interested in reducing government spending, but in his case mainly in order to reduce the high level of taxation. However he did not think it very realistic to expect much reduction, given the government's commitments; nor did he think it would solve the exchange-rate problem. In fact, although exports were doing well, there was no sign of the dollar deficit falling in spite of attempts to direct exports.

Early in 1949, Hall minuted Bridges urging an inquiry and recommending a devaluation of the pound.[5] Bridges was also opposed to devaluation; he gave the policy the code name 'Caliban', after a man of underhand nature. Hall's minute began a heated debate in Whitehall, involving both officials and ministers, which continued until August. Hall first set about trying to convince the senior officials in the Treasury – where Clarke was the only one in favour of it – and the Foreign Office. A lot of work was done in the Section, mainly by Fleming and Jukes, on the effects of devaluation. Papers were written on a number of topics: the pattern of dollar trade; the export earnings of both Britain and the rest of the sterling area; the import content of exports; the cost of living effects; and the international repercussions. Inevitably these were complicated and uncertain calculations because of the long chain of cause and effect and the uncertainty of the links in that chain. But they did provide some estimate of the global effect. Armed with this work, Hall succeeded in convincing Plowden of the need to devalue. Then with Plowden's help he set about convincing others.

In the meantime, an international debate had begun, sparked off by the long-term programmes which had been drawn up by the European countries for the distribution of Marshall Aid, and the *Interim Report on the European Recovery Programme* circulated by the OEEC late in December 1948. These concluded that the closing of the dollar gap without further aid was unlikely; a reduction in European export prices was needed to increase exports to the dollar area and reduce imports from it. This was seized on by the Americans, who used it to argue that the question of exchange-rate realignments should be reopened. At this stage the United Kingdom played it all down, arguing that it was a matter for the International Monetary Fund rather than for bilateral discussion, but the Americans pressed the issue after the United States Congress took the line, in voting Marshall Aid, that less aid would be needed if exchange rates were adjusted.

When he was in the United States in May 1949 for a meeting of the Economic and Employment Commission, Hall talked to Oliver Franks, now the British Ambassador, about Anglo-American relations. They were old friends from their Oxford days. All who knew Franks found him an outstanding figure, a powerful operator and excellent chairman and speaker. He was therefore a very good ally for Hall whose qualities were different. They both felt strongly the need to heal the divergence of outlook which had opened up between the two countries. The time had come, they felt, to discuss with United States officials, in a friendly spirit, not only exchange rates but also the nature of the one-world system for which both countries were striving, and the modifications necessary in the conceptions which had guided the discussions between 1944 and 1947. On immediate issues, Hall thought there should be requests for action on rubber and shipping (where the United States was especially protective), the price of gold and, in the longer term, on reductions in the American tariff and an outflow of American capital.

Partly as a result of Hall's discussion with Franks, the latter suggested to the Americans that the talks between the two countries, suspended at the start of Marshall Aid, should begin again. The Americans agreed on condition that nothing firm should be decided and that there would be no publicity. This was the start of Hall's many trips to America throughout the 1950s, when he engaged in wide-ranging discussions with a large circle of American officials, many of whom were already his friends and others who became so. It also resulted in the secondment of one of Hall's staff to the Washington Embassy from where he kept Hall informed on the United States economic situation.

Hall himself went to Washington again early in June, this time with Wilson-Smith, a Second Secretary in the Treasury, for the first of the new round of talks. There was a good deal of discussion about the unbalanced state of Britain's payments and the US Treasury was disturbed by the lack of progress towards convertibility and non-discrimination. Bill Martin, one of the officials, said in a kind, but firm tone that British policy was very perplexing; the British had agreed in various documents to work jointly with them towards a world with free convertibility and non-discrimination but, as far as they could see, policy was moving in the opposite direction and ought not British officials to come clean about it? Hall thought this was very fair criticism, but it did give him the opportunity to explain Britain's difficulties.

Various possibilities were touched on as part of a general scheme to narrow the gap between prices in the dollar and non-dollar worlds. The assumption by the American officials was that Britain would need to devalue before long and that it certainly ought to do so. Hall spent a lot of his time in individual talks with government economists and economic commentators and had to answer a great many questions put to him. This was no problem for him as the whole situation was at his fingertips; he had done a lot of preparatory work together with Fleming and Jukes, and had been thinking about the possibilities for a long time. The talks were considered a success, in that they established closer relations and confirmed that the objectives of the two countries were the same. The Hall/Wilson-Smith visit was undoubtedly a turning point in Anglo-American relations, even if its effects did not last.[6]

Moreover the talks had a very strong effect on Wilson-Smith. They also converted – or at least half converted – him to the need for devaluation, when he heard at first hand the reasons why the Americans supported it. Wilson-Smith was then a highly influential man in the Treasury, because he was in charge of overseas finance and his views carried weight with Bridges. It was not until early July that the Treasury and Bank officials decided that devaluation would have to be part of a package to check the dollar drain. Then, in the middle of the month, Hall heard that Douglas Jay, with whom he had many talks, was convinced of the need to devalue, and shortly afterwards that Hugh Gaitskell, then Minister of Fuel and Power, and Harold Wilson, then President of the Board of Trade, had also come round to this view. Several people claim to have converted Gaitskell. Hall did not make this claim; he and Plowden did have many discussions with him in the preceding months, but Hall thought it was Jay who had finally convinced Gaitskell. At this time Cripps, having been overtaken by ill health, was away in a Swiss clinic for treatment, so that Gaitskell, Wilson and Jay were jointly in charge of economic policy. They set about persuading the Prime Minister and Hall wrote a note for him, to make it clear that the need for devaluation was now the commonly held view of Treasury officials. The note was signed by Bridges, Hall, Plowden and the Second Secretaries, Eady and Wilson-Smith.[7]

The case was made on the following lines. Although the deterioration in the reserve position had been accentuated by short-term speculative factors, it was clear that, as Marshall Aid declined, there was no prospect of being able to earn sufficient dollars to ensure an adequate supply of food and raw materials, unless an adjustment was made to costs and export prices. Without such an adjustment, there was still less prospect of the restoration of a 'one-world' system which had been Britain's objective since the end of the war, in which sterling could again become convertible and there could be an end to discrimination. The necessary adjustment was too large to be achieved without devaluation. The alternative would be a violent deflation, accompanied by wage cuts, which would result in heavy unemployment and a waste of resources. It also seemed unlikely that confidence would be restored in Britain's competitive power without it. Hall then went on to stress the need for cuts in government expenditure of about 5 per cent, or 1 per cent of national income. He also advised restrictions on bank credit and an appeal to the trade unions and the nationalised industries to keep wages unchanged.

By the end of July the Cabinet were in agreement, but the final decision had to await the return of Cripps from his Swiss sanatorium late in August. As a senior minister with great authority in the Cabinet, such a decision could not be taken in his absence. Before he returned, there was a proposal for some sort of continuous Anglo-American machinery for the discussion of economic matters like that which existed for defence arrangements. The Americans were prepared to set this up, provided little was said about it publicly, because they did not want other countries to get the impression that Britain had a direct line to the United States which might discriminate against themselves. Hall was enthusiastic, illustrating the merits of such an arrangement from his own wartime experience with the Combined Boards in Washington.

Cripps returned to London in August and, following a meeting at Chequers, reluctantly agreed to devaluation at an Economic Policy Committee meeting. Hall was irked that action had been held up for so many weeks, and felt that Cripps's illness had been a serious brake on policy. 'One cannot exaggerate the seriousness which Cripps' illness has been to all our affairs', he wrote in his diary. 'The one man that had them in hand, to go off and actually become the chief obstruction – it ought to be a lesson to us all, that if the leader gets unfit he should step right out until he is better, or resigns.'[8]

Towards the end of August Hall flew off to Washington again for the official talks which were to precede the arrival of Cripps and Bevin.[9] To start with, the atmosphere in the Washington talks was not very good. There was a lot of shadow boxing and little progress. Then President Truman made a speech which improved things and the talks eventually ended with a number of concessions by the Americans, including the promise to lower tariffs, simplify customs procedures and increase investment overseas. Hall took an active part in these discussions, explaining the objectives of domestic policy and pointing out the success of this policy except in relation to the balancing of the dollar accounts. He stressed the lack of any prospect of increased competitiveness resulting from a contraction of demand.

In the British Embassy in Washington there was a private meeting between Hall, Plowden and Wilson-Smith (for the Treasury) and George Bolton (for the Bank of England) to discuss the new rate for sterling. As none of the others would stick their necks out, Hall's proposal was accepted that the rate should be between $2.80 and $3.00; he recommended the lower rate to prevent any thought that it might be lowered again. His proposal was based on work done in the Economic Section by Fleming and Jukes.

Cripps and Bevin agreed and the pound was therefore devalued by 30 per cent against the dollar. As Hall and possibly others expected, once sterling moved, there followed a general realignment. There was some indignation in the Commonwealth and Europe (especially in France) at the manner in which devaluation had been carried out and the lack of consultation, but officials had been very much afraid of a run on sterling if it had been known in advance. In the event, almost the entire sterling area, Scandinavia and the Netherlands devalued by the same 30 per cent as Britain. France and Germany devalued by 20 per cent, the Belgians by 12 per cent and Italy by 8 per cent. The change in exchange rates thus went far beyond sterling, as Hall always thought it would,[10] and amounted to a dollar revaluation which was what the world economy needed. When allowance was made for all the parallel devaluations, Britain's devaluation was about 9 per cent on a trade-weighted basis. It proved difficult to isolate the effect of devaluation on Britain's current balance of payments, because of the outbreak of the war in Korea nine months later. However there was a spectacular improvement in the total external situation. The reserves which had been lost during the summer were all regained by the end of March, six months later, and continued their rise in 1950, with a marked improvement in the dollar balance.[11]

Hall's role in all this was clearly central. He noted in his diary that it was the end of a long struggle begun six months earlier. He regarded the conclusion as brought about by the logic of events rather than by himself. But his patient and careful persistence to convince others of what he believed to be the right policy could well have been the deciding factor. He convinced his colleagues that he had a coherent view of what was happening. Although a number of personal relationships were put under a lot of strain, many emerged greatly strengthened. His friendship and method of working so closely with Plowden was of a kind that was extremely rare in Whitehall. Plowden has described it as tendering advice in tandem:

> much of the time, Robert Hall would most often provide an idea or piece of analysis, we would discuss it, and then I would present it to the relevant committee or to the Chancellor as best I could. As such, he loaded the gun and I fired the bullets or as Rab Butler put it, 'I was the vulgarisateur or publicist for his ideas'.[12]

Hall preferred others to make his points in comments in committee. His shyness prevented him being effective. But his seeming modesty increased the respect with which he was regarded. Amongst other colleagues, he had developed a firm understanding with Bridges who consulted him and kept him informed on many matters. William Armstrong, Principal Private Secretary to the Chancellor and later to become the Permanent Secretary to the Treasury, kept in close touch with Hall and was a valuable ally. In Washington he was most appreciative of Franks's diplomatic skills.

This was an exciting time for Hall, playing such a key role. But it was also an exhausting one, with the actual negotiations with the Americans, the briefings, writing speeches in a hurry and preparing a broadcast for Cripps. Hall's version of the broadcast admitted that devaluation was a change of policy, but Cripps altered it at the last minute because he refused to admit to a change. Hall thought this was unwise. The announcement was held up until the IMF meeting, so as to get the Fund's approval, at this time a necessary part of the procedure of changing an exchange rate.

Hall had no illusions about the difficulties and complications of a sterling devaluation. He was aware that it would set the trading world ablaze. The complexity of the operation was enormous, requiring a secrecy which he knew would be very unpopular when the announcement was made. So it proved, but the operation would have been a failure if secrecy had not been kept. In spite of the gloom that had been around in Washington, Hall did not feel at all depressed. After all, he had had his way. He gave himself a pat on the back in his diary, noting that, in his two years as the Director of the Economic Section, he had helped to make changes in the two great instruments available to manage the economy. First, the budget surplus had been increased to £600–700 million and secondly, there was to be a big change in the exchange rate. The next step, that he knew was necessary, was to cut expenditure at home to make devaluation effective. He regretted that so far bank credit had not been tightened up; he had been defeated on this, as he saw it, by 'the direct cowardice or else disingenuousness of the Governor of the Bank of England'.

Hall had crossed to the States three times in as many months to talk about this subject. This brought the total number of his Atlantic flights to eighteen. Out of these the flights had been on time only twice and on some occasions he had suffered delays of as much as twenty-four hours. This was before the jet age and the journey took about twelve hours anyway. On his return to London with the Chancellor's speech after the devaluation talks, he felt he had real VIP status when the captain of the plane was told to get him on to London at all costs, if his plane was held up. In those days a government economic adviser needed great physical stamina. Fortunately Hall had this in good measure.

Back in London, he devoted a lot of time to emphasising the danger that inflation would undo the benefits of devaluation. There were a number of signs of a booming home market, falling unemployment from an already low level and a worsening trade balance. Hall drafted a note for Bridges to send to the Prime Minister, saying it was essential that there should be accompanying steps to reduce inflationary pressure, including a rise in bank rate to 3 per cent. But Cripps argued that no advantage would be gained from such a rise, and proposed instead that the banks should restrict credit. However nothing was done because of the opposition of Cobbold at the Bank. The Bank did not wish to interfere, because the commercial banks were making good profits on their loans and so objected to the idea of restrictions on credit or a ceiling on advances.

It was also hard work trying to convince ministers that cuts in expenditure were needed. The only step actually announced at the time of devaluation was an increase of one penny in the price of a loaf of bread – and even this measure had been hotly disputed in Cabinet. Cripps was infuriated that, although the Cabinet had agreed in principle to deflationary measures, each individual minister was unwilling to accept cuts in his own departmental programme.

Eventually, after a long battle and threats of resignations by ministers, a number of cuts were agreed. These were less than Hall had advised, but he recognised the political realities and consoled himself with the thought that they might prove sufficient if they were actually carried out.[13]

There was also a need to strengthen incomes policy. Towards the end of 1949, the TUC was persuaded by ministers to recommend a one-year pay freeze and the suspension of cost-of-living agreements, provided that the retail price index did not rise by more than 5 per cent. As part of the agreement with the TUC, profits tax was increased and low-paid workers were exempt. Whether or not as a result, the rise in wages and prices in 1950 was remarkably small despite devaluation.

By the end of 1949 Hall was again expressing concern in his diary about the amount of power and influence he had acquired. It was at least recognised by an increase in his salary and a CB in the 1950 New Year Honours. He went as far as to tell Bridges that it seemed to him very rash for the Budget Committee to commit itself so deeply to the advice of one man, but Bridges merely said that the Committee felt that Hall's advice conformed with what was needed. Recent events confirmed his view that the acceptance of the convertibility of sterling as early as 1947, as a condition of the American Loan Agreement of 1945, had been extremely unfortunate and that discussions should have been reopened with the United

States before 1947 for a modification of that commitment. Hall also came to the conclusion that it was time for a change in the government's policy on cheap money and he again began to campaign in the Treasury and the Bank on the lines that it was inflation and not recession that was the problem.

He spent a good deal of time thinking about the problems of a full employment policy, especially the question of the need for a wages policy. The two problems as he saw them were both connected with inflation: first the need to reduce government expenditure and secondly to hold wages and profits steady. He discussed all this, both within the Economic Section where a number of papers were produced, and also with economists outside the government service.

The Labour government's overall majority was reduced to six in the election in February 1950. Before the budget which followed, Hall wrote a paper on budget policy which was discussed in Cabinet. This was written at the request of the Chancellor on the suggestion of the Prime Minister. The need arose because the new Lord Privy Seal, Lord Addison, felt doubts about the policy of having large budget surpluses. Hall attempted to put the defence of the policy into simple language, concluding that any serious departure from it would cause great harm, both at home and abroad.[14] The Cabinet endorsed the policy and the Chancellor's approach to the next budget. In fact the budget introduced few changes and maintained a large surplus on current account; Cripps's speech included a lecture on the function of the budget surplus.

As the economic situation improved in 1950, and the reserves began to rise, pressure from the Americans began once more, both on convertibility and on increasing defence expenditure following the coming to power of the communists in China. Hall did his best to counter these pressures, first at talks in London with an American delegation, when he gave them an account of the fiscal outlook in an effort to prove that Britain could not spend more on defence, and then in Washington in May–June.

In Washington he found the atmosphere much better. Devaluation had removed a lot of the causes of suspicion and conflict. The European Recovery Programme had produced a forum in which short-run problems were more likely to be settled. For the first time since the war it was beginning to look as if Britain would be able to dispense with overseas aid without endangering full employment. Hall re-established some old friendships in Washington and made some useful new contacts, so that he was able to keep himself well informed about the economic situation in the States and about government thinking there. In this new atmosphere it had been agreed that an Economics Minister should be appointed in Washington as head of a UK Treasury Delegation. He would be nominated alternatively by the Bank of England and the Treasury and all cables were to be sent both to the Bank and the Treasury. The first Economics Minister was Lord Cromer. It was also agreed that a member of the Economic Section should be seconded there for two years. Hall nominated Jukes to be the first two-year secondment; he was followed in turn by Atkinson, Grieve-Smith and McMahon.

Hall returned home in a cheerful frame of mind. On his arrival in the Economic Section in 1947, he still believed in the primary objective of reaching a multilateral and convertible trading system, which he thought would confer great benefits on the world. Like many others, he anticipated that the recovery period would be short and then there would be a return to a world not very different from the prewar one, with the great improvement that governments would be able to prevent economic recessions. However, there had been five years of painful readjustment after the end of the war, and the rosy and idealistic dreams of the postwar planners had faded. Hall came more and more to realise that those plans had to be reconsidered in the light of the general political and strategic circumstances of the time.

In pursuit of a high level of employment and the expansion of the social services, the economy had been constantly overloaded in the hope that production would expand sufficiently to meet demand. Marshall Aid, which had been given on very loose conditions because the Americans wished to help Western Europe to resist any strengthening of communism, enabled Britain (and others) to go on expanding. The economy was still at full stretch, even though all three budgets with which Hall had been associated were resolutely non-expansionary in Keynesian terms, retaining high levels of taxation. However, by the spring of 1950, exports had been rebuilt and there was a surplus on the balance of payments; at last he felt that Britain was 'out of the wood'.

Hall had been back in London less than three weeks when the Korean War began. That opens a new chapter in the story.

CHAPTER TEN

The Korean War and Rearmament

The Korean war, which began on 25 June 1950 with the communist attack on South Korea, brought in rearmament on a massive scale. Hall felt sure the Americans would not allow this attack to overthrow their foreign policy, which was designed to contain the power of the communists. He himself was a strong supporter of this policy and he was very relieved when two days later the United States decided to give full support to South Korea, in their resistance to the Russian-backed attack by North Korean troops. Hall was hopeful that this would stop Russia but, if their support should provoke a third world war, then at least the allies would be relatively stronger at that time than they would be later.

The next year or so was dominated by American pressure on Britain. So far from arguing for any reduction in the load on the economy, they put strong pressure on Britain to increase defence spending, undertaking to help her to bear the extra load. They dropped their agitation for convertibility and non-discrimination and, in a discussion with Paul Nitze, then Director of the Policy Planning Staff at the US State Department, Nitze expressed astonishment that Hall was even thinking about them, when there were so many more important things to worry about. He told Hall that it was more important for the British government to maintain full employment and the level of the social services, if she was to be an active and useful partner in the cold war.

But the United States' undertakings turned out to be heavily qualified. As a result, rearmament in Britain led to acute economic problems. It caused a severe shortage of raw materials with sharply rising prices, resulting in a balance of payments problem which United

States support would have eliminated. The consequences dominated government policy for the second half of 1950 and throughout 1951.

In the late summer of 1950, Gaitskell succeeded Cripps as Chancellor. Gaitskell was a very different character from Cripps. Hall found him good to work for in the sense that he was also a strong upright man. However there was a big practical difference. Gaitskell was an economist and very interested in economic problems, which had some advantages. He was realistic and practical but he insisted on long discussions, whereas Cripps was inclined to have fairly short discussions and then decide what to do. The main direction of Gaitskell's economic objectives was still the same, that is how to make full employment work and how to make it consistent with other objectives of policy. However, Gaitskell tended to become bogged down in detail. He would sometimes behave more like an official than a minister, becoming more concerned with economic theories than political judgments. He redrafted speeches, engaged in academic debate when decisions were what was needed and he had a reputation for being late for appointments. The impact on Hall meant that he spent far more time in what he regarded as time-wasting discussions. But one positive result was that he was able to interest Gaitskell in the problem of inflation and also in employment targets at a time when this issue was still live in the Economic and Social Council.

As it happened, however, Gaitskell had little time to spare for the problems of full employment and inflation after the British government decided to rearm. He himself pushed very strongly for rearmament and then became preoccupied with its consequences – as indeed was Hall also. At this time Hall for once worked at weekends – on the economic effects of the defence programme, writing papers and drafting speeches for ministers. He worried about what he thought were excessive demands by the defence ministers and, above all, he was troubled by the air of confusion in Whitehall at this time, with attempts to set up new organisations to deal with the new situation, and *ad hoc* meetings with much discussion and little action. He felt they were all dealing blindly from day to day with what were major issues. In the autumn of 1950 his main concern became to prevent ministers committing themselves on what Britain would be able to afford until the end of the year, when the outlook would become clearer.

Hall was sure there would be some inflationary consequences of the increase in defence expenditure. But he anticipated the greatest threat coming from a shortage of raw materials, and the most serious headache the rising cost of living and its effect on wage demands. So he took himself off to the Ministry of Supply to talk to several of his wartime colleagues there. He learned from them that stocks were being run down. He thought this was madness and that they should be doing just the opposite and building them up. It seemed to him that only he and Plowden were at all anxious about the raw material outlook. In August, he urged that the Americans would look less critically at our assets if these were not too much concentrated in gold, but were partly in stocks of materials.

Although Hall supported the government's decision to rearm, he did feel it would be rash for them to commit themselves in advance of a definite commitment to financial help by the United States. He had a premonition that this might not be forthcoming on quite such a generous scale as had been indicated, either by United States officials, or to the Prime Minister by Lew Douglas, the American Ambassador in London. He was more aware than most that Congress still had to be satisfied, and that the United States officials would want to be reasonably sure of approval before they finally put their proposals forward.

In October, Hall formed one of the delegation which accompanied the Prime Minister to Washington. On the economic side, he was involved in the talks about raw materials and eventually he agreed behind the scenes on how to handle the problems; a small group would call on commodity committees to deal with the critical commodities, rather than letting NATO or OEEC handle things – an arrangement which Hall felt was very reminiscent of the old Combined Raw Materials Board in 1942–3. He noted in his diary that this trip was by far the most exhausting and unpleasant he had ever made. He had been lodged with a member of the Embassy staff and commented, when staying at the Chateau Laurier in Ottawa on the way home, on what an enormous relief it was to be able to go to bed and get up at breakfast in as morose or as detached a mood as one wished – something one could not do in a private home, however comfortable and however kind one's hosts.

It was a winter devoted to the economic effects of rearmament, preparations for next spring's budget and a reconsideration of the possibilities of revaluing sterling. The budget calculations were particularly complex because import prices were rising and this upset earlier calculations of the balance of payments which proved to be too optimistic. This was especially galling to Hall, having advised stockpiling of raw materials by Britain as early as July before prices rose. A decision to do so had been taken soon after this, but the official concerned had carelessly failed to pass on the instruction and no action was taken until October, when the Treasury at last instructed the supply departments to increase their purchases for stocks.[1] By the time the instruction did go out, it was too late to beat the rising prices. One lesson Hall took to heart as a result of this was that, if he felt strongly about something, he should press it himself with ministers rather than pursuing it more formally with officials, as he had done on this occasion.

It was not surprising that Hall was much exercised by the raw materials outlook. After his direct experience of the volatile prices at the start of the Second World War, he knew better than most of his colleagues what the dangers were. It seemed to him possible that the whole rearmament effort might be threatened by raw material shortages and he determined this must not happen. The defence of the West should not founder just because Britain and America were not able to organise the machinery for allocating materials. At home, a new Department of Materials was at last set up; and the defence programme was agreed.

The Economic Section spent much time and thought on these matters at Hall's request. A memorandum from Hall to Fleming in October set out his concern about the whole raw material situation and in particular the effect on employment of shortages of cotton, wool and timber.[2] A note was drafted for the official Economic Steering Committee emphasising the important role that easier supplies of raw materials in the previous year had played in increasing the output of British industries, so enabling us to right the balance of payments, support a large and increasing volume of capital expenditure and permit small increases in current consumption. Many of these achievements could not have taken place without an easier supply of raw materials. Now there were shortages again and Hall advised the establishment of new machinery to deal with those that had developed by allocations[3] – but matters were slow to improve.

Hall was relieved to have the help of Bretherton and Butt on raw material questions. In particular Bretherton, who had joined the Section in 1950, was an expert on the subject from his wartime work which, like Hall's, was in the Ministry of Supply. He supported Hall's view – that it would be better to alter the existing system of bilateral bargaining to one of international allocations in commodity groups – and he felt that Britain would do better on things like cotton and sulphur, if she had kept some bargaining counters in her own hands, for example, wool. A paper by Bretherton setting out the arguments was marked as admirable by Hall.[4]

In the spring of 1951, raw material prices continued to rise, the United States being no less grasping than in 1950 and still building up stocks to an extent that Hall regarded as excessive. However arrangements for dealing with shortages were being developed internationally. Hall argued that the common objectives should be the moderation of United States demand and additional measures to stimulate production. He wished to press these claims on the Americans and to enlist the support of other industrial countries as well as of the primary producers.

It was not often that Hall complained of exhaustion and nerves, but he did so over the 1951 budget speech. In terms of the balance of the economy, the Economic Section correctly estimated that a large part of the additional defence expenditure was offset by the deflationary impact of the rise in import prices.[5] But the increased pressure of demand on the economy as a result of the Korean War and rearmament indicated a tight budget. In fact the budget was expansionary in total in spite of a rise in taxes. There was an increase in income tax of 6d in the pound and increases in profits, petrol and purchase taxes. But these were more than offset by increased government expenditure as a result of the rise in defence spending, only partly offset by the introduction of charges for dentures and spectacles, which led to the resignations of Bevan and Wilson from the Cabinet.

In addition to all Britain's problems, there was increasing concern that she was not going to receive any American aid in the next financial year. At first British officials felt confident that the United States would underwrite the dollar impact of rearmament on the balance of payments, and ministers first took on a £3.6 billion rearmament programme with what they took to be a definite promise of aid.

There then followed a long discussion about 'burden-sharing' under an exercise called the Nitze exercise which raised some doubts that the United States would fully compensate Britain for the balance of payments effects.[6] When the defence ministers pressed for more than £3.6 billion to achieve their target levels of recruitment and supplies, ministers went on to a £4.7 billion programme on the clear understanding that there would be an equitable sharing of the burden. At a late stage, the Americans introduced an arbitrary rule that payments would not be made if that caused a country's reserves to rise. In the case of the United Kingdom, no allowance would be made for the fact that Britain's reserves also belonged to the rest of the sterling area, and that the share of the latter might be expected to rise as commodity prices had increased. Although Hall had uttered warnings about such a danger, even so he was outraged by the American attitude. But he failed to win any concessions when he went to Washington again at the Ambassador's request.

It is not easy to see who was to blame for this muddle – perhaps both sides, the Americans for playing false and the British for being too trusting – but the consequences for Britain were a fall in her share of sterling reserves, with a lot of worry and vexation for the government and senior officials. From the British standpoint it looked like a big let-down by the Americans, who had convinced Attlee that some acceleration of the defence programme was unavoidable. They had made much of the special relationship between Britain and the United States, but when it came to the point they did not play their part in helping Britain over her difficulties.

At home a working party was set up to work out the economics of the increased programme.[7] It is perhaps questionable how far Hall's optimism about the size of defence programme the British economy could afford was fully justified. It made it more difficult to cope with the 1951–2 inflation and caused an overload on the engineering industries, which meant a loss of potential exports, at a time when Western European recovery was really taking off.[8]

But there appeared to be a real risk of a third world war, unless the Russians were made to believe that the Americans would resist aggression. Neither Hall nor Plowden wanted to see a situation similar to that in 1938, when the Treasury had advised Chamberlain that the economy could not support the rearmament programme then

proposed. The communist threat in the 1950s came both from the
armed forces of the Soviet Union occupying Eastern Europe and
from its support for communism in Western Europe and the rest of
the world. Their military might was very menacing and the outlook
looked much more threatening, as a result of the victory of Mao
Tse-tung in China and the attack on South Korea.

Both Hall and Plowden remained convinced that it was the right
decision in the circumstances of the time. The Truman Administration had made it very clear that they would not be able to persuade
Congress to agree to a major rearmament programme, unless one of
their allies – and this meant Britain – also made a substantial increase in their defence programme. Hall was persuaded of the need
to go along with this – here he was acting as the 'whole man' and not
just the economist – in spite of the fact that it was bound to put a
great strain on the balance of payments. He was convinced by the
American officials that rearmament by Britain was an important
factor in Congress agreeing to adopt the very large United States
rearmament programme. At that time no nation apart from Britain
was in a position to act as a partner in the need to show the communists that they would not be allowed to spread their creed throughout the world. Moreover he and other officials were very conscious
of Britain's debt to the United States for Marshall Aid, which made
them wish to respond to an appeal for their help if they possibly
could.

Hall continued his campaign to keep commodity prices down.
He rejected the idea of revaluing the pound. He persuaded the Chancellor to take the matter up strongly in the OEEC and even to broaden
the case from the need to hold prices down, to a plea for world
economic stability. He himself spent a lot of time pressing his views
in Washington and Paris. He was acutely conscious of how influential he and Plowden had become in all matters to do with the
economic problems of rearmament. What they advised was likely to
be done, if it was at all politically possible.

The Cabinet was much weakened, having lost Cripps and with
Bevin also in poor health. Ministers allowed themselves to be
bounced along by the Americans who then let them down over aid,
but then carried on, thinking all would be all right in the end. The
Prime Minister and the Chancellor were both very upset about what
they regarded as broken promises. Attlee had been given the impres-

sion that the Americans would help by their Ambassador in London, Lew Douglas, and never forgave him. Gaitskell learned by hard experience that the American proposals for burden-sharing meant very little. Hall himself felt let down by the shifts of ground of the Americans.

In the first quarter of 1951, the balance of payments deteriorated as expected. Over the summer, it was worse than expected. Although a reduction in raw material prices was beneficial to the United Kingdom balance of payments, this was offset by the lower sterling area dollar earnings. Britain's deficit with Western Europe rose; and the nationalisation by Iran of the Iranian oilfields in May meant less income from oil sales and more costly dollar imports. Economic policy was under continuous review and there were further attempts to gain American dollar aid. But these were unsuccessful. The Americans were tough bargainers and they always had an ace up their sleeve – they would not be able to get this or that commitment through Congress – but on this occasion they had expected the British to press harder than they did for the United States to provide more finance.[9]

As a result of further meetings in Washington, a new initiative was proposed and a committee of three experts was set up to report to the NATO Council on the whole issue of rearmament and 'spreading the burden' among member countries. The experts became known as the Three Wise Men – Harriman, Monnet and Plowden, each with a deputy. These three set out to reconcile the requirements with the realistic capabilities for the defence of Western Europe. Hall was a member of the Whitehall committee set up to monitor their progress.[10] The Wise Men concluded that there should be no further increase in Britain's defence effort in view of the strain already felt; and that Britain's programme required assistance both with steel and with her dollar and overall balance of payments problems. Other countries were urged to make substantial increases in defence expenditure. But the United States was not to be committed to any further increase even though Hall and others thought she was capable of very much more.[11]

By early autumn it was becoming clear that the balance of payments had swung from a healthy surplus in 1950 to a large deficit in 1951 and gloom had set in. The rise in import prices alone was sufficient to account for this. The last months of the Labour government were completely overshadowed by a developing external crisis. By October the drain on the reserves was very high owing to rumours that there might be a devaluation. Preparations were made to cut imports, which in the event were put in hand by the new government, blaming its predecessors for the necessity. Hall argued that some of the rapid rise in imports must have gone into stock. He was right, as it turned out. When the figures became available they showed a large rise in stocks in 1951; and later figures also showed the balance of payments deficit to be less than was thought at the time. But that did not help the government. There was feverish activity in Whitehall when the situation deteriorated and the prospect of a change of government – there was to be an election on 24 October – led to the usual practice before an election of preparing a whole flock of papers on every conceivable subject. Hall himself was writing on new budgetary methods, and on the actual experience of fiscal and monetary control.

Attlee waited until Gaitskell was in Australia and Morrison was in Canada before the dissolution was announced.[12] Hall thought it was the worst time for the government to call an election. The economy was feeling the heaviest of the strain of the Korean War, because of the increase in food and raw material prices. The electorate was aware that the cost of living was rising and the gold and dollar reserves were seeping away. But in fact the government had been so weakened by the loss of Cripps and Bevin that the strain on other members of the government, with the tiny majority they had, made it inevitable that an election would not be long coming.

Hall felt it was particularly unfortunate for Gaitskell who was growing into the job of Chancellor and becoming much easier to work with. But he was not otherwise regretful about the change to a Conservative government in October 1951. He was feeling dissatisfied with government policy: the abolition of direct controls meant that budgetary policy would become the sole instrument available to manage the economy if monetary policy could not be used. He thought he might have more success in persuading the Conservative government to use monetary policy as well as fiscal policy. In addition he welcomed the idea of a Prime Minister whom he thought might intervene on important matters, instead of one like Attlee, who never seemed to stir a finger. For four years he wrote briefs for Attlee, who never gave Hall any idea of what he thought on any of the matters on which he had briefed him. Hall's briefs were never returned with any comments; nor did he ever see any sign in the Cabinet minutes that the Prime Minister had taken any notice of them. Attlee was not interested in economic affairs except in so far as he wished to socialise the economy. In Washington with Attlee for the rearmament discussions, on one occasion he went to see him alone in the Washington Embassy to give him reasons for thinking that Britain could stand the costs of rearmament, provided the American help expected was forthcoming. When Hall finished speaking, Attlee said, 'Thank you very much Mr Hall', and that was all he said during the whole interview.[13]

Among the other members of the Labour government, he was largely ignored by Harold Wilson who, as President of the Board of Trade, seemed to go out of his way to be rude to him. For Cripps however Hall felt a great loyalty. He thought him in all respects an outstanding man, wonderful for an adviser to work for; once convinced, he made much more of an adviser's arguments than the adviser himself. Hall felt it was Cripps who was entirely responsible for the development of demand management through the budget, in that he accepted Hall's framework of relating budgetary policy to the economic situation as a whole and not just the balance of government revenue and expenditure. If he had a weakness – or what Hall regarded as a weakness – it was his emotional belief in socialism and his consequent difficulty in preventing rises in government expenditure in response to the Labour ministers' extravagant aims for the welfare state.

Hall thought him a very good Chancellor; writing in 1961, he put Cripps as the number one Chancellor of the eight he had advised. Cripps would discuss with his officials his ideas about problems and argue with them. He backed up his officials and, if they made a mistake, he would take responsibility for it. His officials found him a most attractive man and far from as austere as was sometimes made out. He would occasionally take them out to dinner. Cripps as a vegetarian would have the most delicious-looking salads, while his officials would be offered something they found unpalatable like whale-meat. These were working dinners, but they were sociable occasions with light-hearted intervals. Hall also drew satisfaction from the thought that Cripps tended to take his advice. But he admitted that Cripps was the last man to be convinced in his

campaign to devalue the pound. This did not affect their relationship. When Cripps' health forced him to resign, Hall recorded his
belief that he would go down in history as one of the really great
Chancellors.[14]

In the later years of the Labour government, Hall received much
more support than he had earlier from his staff. In particular, he was
able to rely on Marcus Fleming and Nita Watts to make the running
on matters of external policy (even though he had reservations
about Fleming being too academic), to depend on David Butt to
take the lead in preparing and drafting the annual Economic
Surveys, and on Christopher Dow in preparing estimates for the
domestic outlook and to help prepare the budget judgment and
the budget speeches. Russell Bretherton, who came from the Board
of Trade, was a great help on more administrative matters, as well
as on raw materials and the defence programme. A number of new
staff had been recruited. John Jukes came from British Railways and
worked with him on the effects of defence, the cost of living, imports and exports; Fred Atkinson, joining the Section from Jesus
College, Oxford, with Jack Downie, also from Oxford, and Bryan
Hopkin, back from the Royal Commission on Population, provided
support on a wide range of problems. By 1949–50, he had enough
good staff to be able to send one member of the Section to Washington to the Treasury delegation there, and two others to Paris to
the British delegations to the OEEC and NATO. These postings
strengthened Hall's own position when he was representing Britain
at any of the meetings in these two cities.

The demands on Hall's time had increased even further with
Gaitskell as Chancellor. He leaned more heavily on the staff he
had, but he was inevitably under great pressure himself. Nor was it
only office hours that he devoted to meetings, briefings and discussions of all kinds. In his diary he recorded many lunches and dinners where policy and problems were discussed. There were a lot of
visiting Americans, both from the Administration and from the
press, who wished to talk to him and he always made time to see
them. He plugged away at people with his ideas and met many
members of the British financial press regularly, making sure they
understood the aims and objectives of government policy and
sometimes persuading them to write an article on a particular
topic. After one budget he felt apprehensive enough to call at the

offices of *The Economist* to reassure himself that they were taking a line which met with his approval. He also liked to keep in touch with the ideas of academic economists and he followed their work for useful research into the economic problems he was advising on. He attended the Political Economy Club in Oxford and gave an occasional lecture. In 1950 he spoke at the annual meeting of the Association of University Teachers of Economics – a small body in those days.

In the four years he worked under the Labour government, Hall's standing with ministers rose steadily. It is clear that he made little impact on Attlee, but in fact Attlee's understanding of economic questions was scanty and he took small interest in them. Relations with Cripps were a very different matter. Cripps called on his advice so regularly, that it was evident he thought highly of him. Gaitskell, too, made great demands on Hall and was very complimentary to him when he took leave of him. Hall records this in his diary, but modestly does not reveal what was actually said.

Some people thought the Labour government had been a disaster, but allowance should be made for the problems it faced. In economic affairs it groped its way through a series of difficulties. It inherited an economy which emerged from the war in 1945 in a very battered state, but with very ambitious aims. It was the first government to operate a macroeconomic policy, so there was no past experience to draw on. It started with an over-stretched economy but, as everyone did, mistakenly anticipated that there would be a deflation as there had been after the 1914–18 war. Instead the government had to grapple with continuous balance of payments problems, and with large debts incurred by the war. They received less help than they hoped for from the United States and when they responded to an appeal for help by the Americans over the Korean War they were badly let down over finance. After muddling through for the first few years their policies became more realistic and more effective. There is no doubt that the economy was in better shape for the government having paid attention to a good adviser.

Hall now faced not only a change of Chancellor, but a change of government also. His friends in the United States Administration expected to him to disappear from the scene, as would have happened under the American system of political appointments to key posts. They were surprised and delighted to discover that he was also to advise a Conservative government.[15]

It is fitting to close the account of these years with a note about his family life at Oxford at the weekends and on family holidays. He and his wife had many friends in Oxford and the Hall home had again become a very sociable one, especially at the weekends. There were parties which the girls found very glamorous. There would often be as many as twelve for Sunday lunch and more for drinks. Often there would also be people from outside Oxford and some-times visiting American economists. Hall always wanted to count the guests and lay the table accordingly; his wife was more relaxed and did not think it so important.

The family remember him taking them to concerts at Trinity. He was not particularly musical himself and had difficulty holding a tune. He told his daughters that as a child he had played the piano with his mother. On one occasion she made him play for guests, but he fluffed the piece and he refused to play again, regretting it in later life. But he enjoyed listening. He took a close interest in the books his elder daughter was reading and also read them all him-self. If he talked about them to her, she aimed to make him stay discussing them with her. If he took out a cigarette she knew he was interested. He always gave her a good reasoned answer to a question once he had slotted all the pieces in his mind.

For holidays, they went often to Gara Rock in Devon, where a packed lunch was eaten on the beach, and where there would be long walks with Hall leading the way through what their mother thought were dangerous places. There were also walks on the fells from Seatoller House in the Lake District, which Hall, Cox and Price were still renting from the Egremont estate. Hall had recov-ered his allotment in North Oxford and, from the mid–1940s until he left Oxford in 1967, he could be seen on Saturdays and Sundays cycling up to it. Sometimes it was a family outing and the girls were paid to pick the snails off the plants, while their parents sipped the cocktails they had brought with them. He regularly won prizes at the annual Treasury gardening society competition.[16]

CHAPTER ELEVEN

A Change of Government in 1951

In the event, the change of government in October 1951 presaged a year of tremendously hard work and frustration for Hall, and led to severe strains in his relations with the Overseas Finance Division of the Treasury and the Bank of England as a result of a scheme for the convertibility of sterling which became known as 'Robot'.

For the first few months business seemed to go on much as usual. Treasury officials took the view that the economic situation was very bad when the Conservatives took over, and wanted strong deflationary action to reduce the balance of payments deficit. Hall took a contrary view, arguing that it would be unwise of officials to put ministers into a panic and advise them to do bitterly controversial things. Hall's view at first prevailed and the advice presented to the new government was modified to proposals to raise bank rate, to introduce some import cuts and building restrictions, and to review rather than cut investment and public expenditure. In particular, Hall and Plowden pressed for a review of defence expenditure; since the approval of expenditure of £4,700 million over three years by the Labour government, some new burdens had appeared, including the loss of Iranian oil, a shortfall in exports of consumer goods and a shortage of steel.

Hall had long been in favour of using monetary policy as an instrument of full employment policy, without in any way changing his view that fiscal policy should be its main plank, and that monetary policy could play only a subordinate role. Recognising that the Conservative government would be much more sympathetic than its predecessor to using monetary policy as an instrument of full employment policy, Hall lost no time in advising in favour of an immediate rise in bank rate.

R. A. Butler made a good first impression as Chancellor, although to start with Hall was not completely sure that he would be tough enough. But he found that Butler had good sense and political judgment. Bank rate was raised – but only from 2 to 2½ per cent – and various ways of reducing the liquid assets of the commercial banks were put in hand. This increase sounds so low now that it is perhaps necessary to explain that the cheap money policy was not only a main plank of the Labour government; there is no doubt that everyone including the leading Conservatives, Keynes and the Governor of the Bank, expected interest rates to be low after the war. Hall himself thought the ½ per cent rise in bank rate was too small, arguing that odium would be incurred by any rise and not because of the actual rate adopted: 'it may well be represented as the act of a government willing to wound but afraid to strike'.[1] He reasoned that the psychological effects were likely to be greater than any direct disincentive effect. If the government was going to take action, it should act strongly. The Chancellor eventually got the message and bank rate was further raised to 4 per cent three months later. Nothing was done about credit restrictions for the time being, however, something else on which Hall wished to see action. Instead there was a series of cuts in the 1952 import programme and some pruning of government expenditure.

Towards the end of 1951, the inflationary trends provoked by the Korean War were no longer a problem, but as yet there were few signs of the recession in consumer demand which appeared in 1952. However both exports and consumption ceased to rise by the end of the year and in January Hall was pointing out that there were some signs of a move into a deflationary situation, with consumers' expenditure lower than a year earlier. In his view this indicated that there should be a mild budget. The official Treasury and the Bank argued for a severe one, as the only way to show that the government meant business and to stop the gold drain. But it was Hall's advice that won the day and the budget turned out to be almost a no change one – surely the right decision as it happened, given the recession that followed, minor though that was.

Work on the budget judgment and Butler's first budget speech was particularly exacting for Hall. Butler took to telephoning him in

Oxford over the weekends. Then he had him recalled to London to work on the speech over a Saturday and Sunday. This particular speech was altered more times even than usual – because the Minister of State, Sir Arthur Salter, changed it several times and it was then redrafted by officials. The Chancellor was still dissatisfied with it and Hall had to do another redraft. In the end almost all the calculations, which it had become customary to include in the speech, were removed just before the Chancellor spoke.

Hall had never known a budget speech to be finalised so late and to be redrafted so many times. This turned out to be only the first example of what was to happen many times over the next four years. Butler had the utmost difficulty in making up his mind on any course of action whatever. As Hall described it, Butler could not bear to take a decision which would remove from him the option of ever being able to take a different one. After a long meeting with him, Hall and other officials would think a problem had been settled and then, as they were leaving Butler's office, he would say, 'Now, mind, nothing's been decided.'[2] This was completely contrary to Hall's way of working. He disliked going back on matters which had been agreed. He thought the habit cowardly, and always wished to move on to the next problem as soon as possible. But apart from this one weakness, Hall found Butler had much personal charm and was very pleasant to work with.

Hall was disturbed by the attitude of the Treasury and the Bank to his advice that the economic outlook indicated that there should be a mild budget, because it reminded him too forcibly of the attitudes of the 1930s. So it was a relief to see a proposal for substantial panic cuts in food subsidies dropped. In a more considered discussion of public expenditure, Hall was all in favour of reducing food subsidies, but as part of a combined package of higher pensions and lower taxes, rather than as a panic measure. He thought at first that he had found an ally in the new Chancellor who refused to be bounced into hasty action by officials alleging a real reserves crisis. Throughout these crises and skirmishes, Hall remained outwardly calm and collected though furious at times and, for the most part, with unfailing confidence in his own judgment. But he did briefly become pessimistic about the budget, and went through a period of doubt about whether it was appropriate to the situation.

In the course of the budget discussions, a drastic plan by the Bank of England and the Overseas Division of the Treasury began to surface. The Chancellor said on several occasions that he was disquieted by the continuing loss of gold and dollar reserves and he would like to announce measures to deal with this in his budget speech. Hall understood that he was to be associated with a study on this subject, but he was not summoned to a meeting until 8 February, when a paper setting out the background was briefly discussed and sent to the Chancellor with Hall's agreement. Towards the end of the following week, he was shown a short note by the Governor of the Bank of England with an outline of a plan subsequently developed in a longer paper, which was discussed a few days later. There was only a brief discussion, with Hall and others feeling that further study was needed. When Hall saw the Chancellor, Butler appeared to agree with him that the plan was too drastic and inappropriate.

The plan which the Treasury and the Bank of England launched was to let the pound float within a defined range, at the same time making current earnings of sterling by non-residents freely convertible into dollars and gold, but blocking 80 per cent of the sterling balances held by countries other than the American Account countries (a group of Central American countries). This scheme, which was later christened 'Robot', was devised in the expectation that the loss of reserves would make it impossible to hold the sterling/dollar rate at above $2.30. The main arguments in favour of the plan, used by its authors, were that it would remove the need for intervention, take the strain off the reserves and replace it with movements in the exchange rate.[3]

When he first heard of the proposal, Hall thought it was worth examining. This was an attitude he invariably adopted to any proposal put forward seriously (the problems the government faced were too difficult to ignore or reject out of hand any proposal, and in any case it was not in his nature to do so), but he was very much taken aback when he discovered that the Chancellor was in favour of Robot and that the intention was to put it into effect in ten days time on budget day. The budget had been brought forward from early April to early March without any explanation (in fact in order to introduce Robot quickly at the same time). A meeting of the Chancellor, the Leader of the House and the Governor, with the Prime

1 Robert's mother and father after
their marriage in 1892

2 Robert aged about two with his
mother

3 The family home at Silverspur

4   Robert with his brother David and sister Helen in the garden at Silverspur

5   Railway bridge at Quart Pot Creek on which Robert delighted to stand

6   Robert on one of the Silverspur horses during the school holidays

7   With Edwin and Rita Cannan in the 1920s

8   Chopping wood

9   At Versailles

10 Golfing with his wife

11 Lighting a fire with one match

12 Happy parents with Felicity

13 Family holiday at Gara Rock

14   In Washington during the war

15   Hall with his mother aged
ninety-one at Silverspur in 1954

16   The Hall family in 1952

17 Hall at his desk in the Treasury in 1956

18 Talking to Richard Fry
(financial editor at the *Manchester
Guardian*) in 1956

20 With his sister, Margaret, at
    Toowoomba in 1967

19 Hall with his wife, Margaret, in
    Oxford in the 1960s

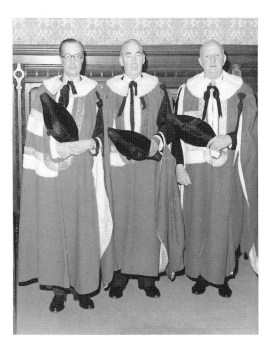

21 At the House of Lords, 1969, with sponsors
    Lords Plowden (left) and Cole

22   Hall with his second wife, Perilla, in 1968

24   Hall in his eighties

23   Making a garden in Cornwall,
1972

Minister, had decided that it would be wrong to introduce a budget giving the impression that no changes were needed, so the plan would have to be announced on budget day. Hall was dumbfounded and after a disturbed night's reflection he sent a memo to Bridges, which was followed by a discussion with the Chancellor. As a result it was decided to postpone budget day to 11 March to give a further week for studying the plan.

In Hall's view, the disadvantages of Robot had not been spelt out by the Treasury and the Bank. These were that the exchange rate would fall and the terms of trade worsen; that the cuts in imports needed would be much greater than those needed to eliminate the dollar deficit at the current exchange rate; that it would lead to a substantial increase in the cost of living, heavy pressure on wages, and then further inflation; that fiscal and monetary policy would have to be tightened to stop inflation and hold the rate, so threatening employment; and that there would be a loss of confidence in sterling with serious consequences for United Kingdom credit and a breakdown of the European Payments Union, which would be a serious blow to European recovery and to NATO.

After urgently considering all these consequences and disadvantages, Hall became strongly opposed to the Treasury/Bank scheme and set about trying to kill it. He used his usual method of mobilising opinion on his side. Plowden, his ally in such matters, was away in Lisbon for a meeting of NATO and he asked for him to be brought home, sending him a letter summarising the events and telling him his view. Before he returned, Plowden briefed Anthony Eden, the Foreign Secretary. Hall again saw the Chancellor to repeat his misgivings. Then he was sent for by Lord Cherwell, also a member of the Cabinet, who had been given a copy of the Chancellor's draft for the Cabinet. Donald MacDougall, working for Lord Cherwell, whom Churchill had brought back into the government as Paymaster General, was also strongly opposed to the scheme and actively working against it. He kept in touch with Hall and briefed Cherwell who felt sure of being able to hold up the scheme at the Cabinet meeting.

Members of the Economic Section had already begun working on alternatives. Paper after paper was urgently prepared by the mostly young members of the Section in an atmosphere of crusading excitement. Fleming, who had been so expert on such matters, had left some months earlier to go to Columbia University, New York. But the spate of papers included one by Nita Watts on 'What happens when the reserves run out?' which Hall included in his file of key documents. There were papers on 'The mechanics of sterling union' by Robert Neild; 'What should we do?' by John Jukes and 'A course of action' by Jack Downie. Peggy Hemming contributed two papers and David Butt five attacking Jukes's 'folly' and Downie's 'desperation', and outlining Butt's 'abortion'.[4]

Over a weekend, with the assistance of five members of his staff, Hall prepared a paper on external action, which described the plan by the Bank and the Treasury as a leap in the dark. He commented: 'the effect of making sterling fully convertible could be to increase the incentive for other countries to reduce expenditure on UK exports to earn convertible surpluses. Competitive import-cutting would therefore spread throughout the non-dollar world.' It would mean abandoning the whole attempt to adjust to the changes in world economic circumstances without resort to unemployment. It would result in a serious deterioration in the terms of trade. This in turn would damage the attempt to get some stability into internal prices and would set up a downward spiral of world trade such as there had been in the 1930s, with political consequences in many countries. The blocking of the sterling balances would be seen as a repudiation of debts and it was unlikely that those countries would then hold sterling again, thus forcing the break-up of the sterling area. Freeing the exchange rate, at a time when there was a world shortage of dollars, would lead to a depreciation of sterling, with a complicated train of effects on the cost of living, prices, production and employment.[5]

Hall proposed the consideration of an alternative, less drastic, version. The exchange rate should be maintained. The sterling area's balances should not be blocked, but the existing degree of convertibility should be modified and the countries asked to make drastic cuts in their dollar expenditure, with perhaps some limits on the amount that the deficit countries could draw. The non-sterling area balances could be blocked as proposed. Internal measures would also be needed.

Two days later Hall wrote a further paper for the Chancellor, elaborating some points that he did not think he had made clear. He also disputed the Bank's view that the reserves situation was worsening.

Plowden returned from Lisbon and produced a supportive note. By the time the Cabinet met, there were as many ministers against Robot as there were for it. The minutes record that, towards the end of the discussion, it became clear that many members of the Cabinet entertained serious doubts about the expediency of proceeding at once with so violent a change of policy. Ministers confirmed their wish to restore a freer economy with an ultimate goal of convertibility of sterling, but they were not satisfied that the moment was opportune, so it was decided not to go on with the plan without further study.

This was the second time in three years that Hall took a contrary view to the Chancellor on a major policy issue: *for* devaluation to which Cripps was opposed, and *against* Robot where Butler was in favour. On both occasions Hall's view, rather than that of the Chancellor, prevailed. It did not seem to mar Hall's relationship with Butler, any more than it had done with Cripps, and he did not seem to mind Hall's opposition, probably because Hall was so obviously honest and his advice always sincere, but perhaps also because Butler always acted like a grand gentleman and did not bear grudges. In fact, their association continued to come closer. Nor did Butler try to conceal Hall's views from the rest of the Cabinet.

The efforts by the Bank and Rowan to get the Robot scheme off the ground spluttered on, after a short lull, right through 1952, so that Hall renewed his opposition and this time he was able to convince Roger Makins at the Foreign Office that he should oppose the plan. Although the Bank made various modifications to the scheme, which they hoped would lead to its approval, Hall continued to dislike it, regarding it as still too violent a lurch towards 'one world' of sterling convertibility. He argued that the whole world was still short of dollars and the incentive for countries to discriminate against the dollar would be removed if they could convert their sterling earnings into dollars. This would mean a fall in British exports and unemployment in the export industries. He reiterated his view that the partial blocking of the balances would break up the sterling area and damage Britain's credit, and that it would lead to a downward spiral in world trade with far-reaching effects on the British economy.

Hall then initiated more work in the Economic Section which led to another spate of papers: Nita Watts on 'What has gone wrong?',

Jukes on 'Alternative policies', Dow and Downie on 'Present policy and targets', Butt on 'The pros and cons of the external sterling plan' and Peggy Hemming and Robert Neild on other topics. Drawing on all the various proposals, Hall then put round a paper on the future of sterling, which attacked Robot again, and then set out the features of a plan to work for a non-dollar trading area with no gold settlements, but wide credit margins. Rather than ask ministers again to accept or reject just one proposal – immediate convertibility and a floating pound or no convertibility – Hall's tactics this time were to suggest asking for authority to explore two possibilities, immediate convertibility and gradual convertibility.[6]

There was no enthusiasm for the Section's scheme in the Overseas Finance Division, nor in the Bank. Hall himself was aware that it was still open to serious objections; it let the exchange rate fall, making the problem of the UK dollar balance more difficult and it still did not solve the threat of a downward spiral of world trade. However it helped to stave off the more extreme proposals of Robot.

Gold then began to flow in, the danger to the reserves was passing and the Chancellor felt that it was his budget that had saved the pound. However, arguments among officials continued because the Cabinet, although it had rejected any immediate action on convertibility, had left open the possibility of later acceptance of Robot. The outlook for the dollar balance was still poor, the prospects for the reserves were still uncertain and failure to agree on Robot led the Economic Section into a number of conflicts with the Bank of England and the Treasury. It was partly a problem of personalities. Hall found Rowan a difficult and prickly character and he was disgusted with the way he and Clarke had tried to bulldoze Robot through. Hall named his file of papers relating to the scheme 'Operation Bolthole'. In his experience, no operation had been carried out so improperly, with Rowan and Clarke proposing a major change of policy, with no chance to discuss it – in fact with what looked like an attempt to short-circuit discussion.

The episode caused great bitterness inside the Treasury, with an attempt by the Overseas Finance Division to impose a sort of military discipline on the staff it controlled, which ruled out the normal interplay of argument and discussion among officials while it lasted. Hall described the attempts to steam-roller the scheme through ministers as scandalous. He put together a file of the most important papers and wrote a brief history of the events.[7] He was later rather ashamed of his history, because he was motivated in writing it by his extreme irritation with Bolton and Clarke for producing the scheme, and with Rowan for trying to push through something he did not really understand. However, as far as Hall could recall, it was the only occasion on which he was swayed to some extent by personal motives while he was the Economic Adviser to the government. He felt very passionate about it, as did his staff.

The Bank continued to complain that the measures taken so far to protect sterling were inadequate, and they predicted that confidence in sterling would soon be lost. There were further briefs to the Chancellor by Hall and to Lord Cherwell by MacDougall, both of whom felt that the Bank had itself done its best to cause a run on sterling by telling everyone that Britain would be ruined unless their scheme was adopted. This was as good as telling people to sell sterling.

It appears that the Overseas Finance Division of the Treasury and the Bank of England were carried away by their strong desire to restore the position of sterling as a world reserve currency – or perhaps, behind that, to restore a world in which external conditions became more like those of the prewar gold standard, under which the Bank was the judge of what policy these conditions dictated. This led to a fixation with the idea of rushing through convertibility and floating the pound, in most people's view long before it was appropriate, and when it could only lead to a general restriction of world trade and induce other countries to discriminate against Britain. The Bank's case became weaker as the reserves began to rise. Butler then became less enthusiastic about the scheme. It was rejected at a gathering of the main ministers at the end of June. A different version was put to the Commonwealth Conference in the autumn under the title of the 'Collective Approach', but it again met with little enthusiasm. Sometime later Butler minuted Bridges, saying that he had come to the conclusion that Hall was right all along.[8]

In considering the whole episode Hall found it odd that the Conservative government put a higher priority on sterling convertibility and non-discrimination than the Labour government had done, at a time when the increasing preoccupation of the United

States with the Russian problem made them less interested in these things. Hall's own preferred strategy remained all along for the more gradual approach, for example giving up discrimination against dollar goods where they were cheaper than other external sources and making out a case for a moderate tariff on other goods. He favoured the removal of restrictions on the use of sterling on dollar goods in individual cases before declaring sterling generally convertible – a policy which he described as 'testing the temperature'.

In fact the swing in the balance of payments of the sterling area far exceeded the most optimistic predictions made in the spring, and by the following year the dollar shortage was easing. Hall made out a strong case against the view that this meant no great harm would have been done if sterling had been made convertible in 1952. He argued that if sterling had been made convertible at that time, other countries would have accumulated gold and dollars at the expense of the United Kingdom's reserves. In fact, the swing in the balance of payments resulted from the reversal of stockbuilding and the terms of trade, which made 1951 such a disastrous year for the Labour government. Butler benefited from the reversal of panic buying and rising prices engendered by the Korean War.

One result of the whole exercise was a wavering in Hall's respect for the Chancellor and the Permanent Secretary. He felt Butler had behaved very weakly and that Bridges had been swept away by misplaced confidence in Rowan. Moreover, he greatly disliked the atmosphere of passion and prejudice which ran through the Treasury at the time, and thought that Bridges should have been able to counter that. The episode reinforced Hall's suspicions of all great new plans to set the world to rights – not because they were not needed, but because each needed at least six months to study before its merits and weaknesses could be clear.

At the end of this difficult year, 1952, the atmosphere quietened down when the Commonwealth Prime Ministers turned out to be so lukewarm about the 'Collective Approach'. In talks with the Americans it was decided to lay stress on caution and to emphasise the risks of a declining spiral of world trade if sterling convertibility were to be introduced too soon. It was a triumph for Hall when the Americans declared that they did not think Britain was strong enough to move to convertibility. He could then begin to feel that the outcome was a vindication of all he had fought for and acknowledged his debt to Plowden for the part he had played. As it was, under the guidance of Hall and Plowden and others, a whole year had passed without any rash steps being taken, and ministers decided that, in any future scheme, certain conditions, not in the original plan, would be introduced. Despite feeling triumphant, however, Hall also felt bitter about it all. The more he thought about it, the more incredible he felt it was that they had gone so far down a road wanted by neither political party, approved by no economist, and by no other OEEC country, nor by the Commonwealth, nor the United States. 'The sinister influence of the Bank of England in this is more like myth than reality', he wrote in his diary. It had been such an uncomfortable year for him that he felt he would be glad to leave the government service if he could find an alternative that attracted him.

It was a relief to turn to the 1953 budget discussions in the New Year. No-one disputed the Economic Section's conclusion that there was some slack in the economy and Hall put the case for some tax reductions to the Budget Committee. Hall's methods were by now well established, as this was the sixth budget in which he was involved. He would jot down his ideas on the basis of the report by the National Income Forecasts Working Party and then discuss them with one or more of his staff. Having satisfied himself about the figures which emerged from this working party, he was concerned about the slant and emphasis that should be given to the figures. He would say 'the time has come to do a draft – I think we should do it like this'. Then he would submit a first draft of the report to the Chancellor by the Budget Committee on the economic situation and the budget judgment. The budget speech itself would then go through about eight drafts. After about the fifth every change needed a strong justification. From then on Hall would strongly defend his draft using such phrases as 'No, you should not alter that; that sentence must stand' and, 'I'm sorry Chancellor, if you don't say that, you leave yourself wide open'.[9]

Hall advised the Chancellor that he should present his arguments in such a way that, if circumstances should change somewhat, he was still in a defensible position. He did not believe in hostages to fortune. Sometimes there would be a lot of heart-searching over one sentence. This happened in the 1953 speech when the Chancellor was concerned to explain why he had not foreseen the downturn in the economy in 1952. Hall eventually solved the problem and pleased the Chancellor by suggesting a positive phrase rather than an apologetic one: 'if we stand back and look at the developments of 1952 as a whole, we see clear evidence of the success of our disinflationary policies'. As usual the Chancellor hesitated and wavered at the last minute, but suggestions for small reductions in income tax and purchase tax were adopted, and the budget was well received.

The summer of 1953 was to prove a turning point for Hall. As a result of all the trouble Robot had caused, Bridges consulted Hall about the organisation of the Treasury and Hall sent him his suggestions for improving economic decision-taking, advising that the Deputy Secretary, the three Second Secretaries on economic affairs and the Director of the Economic Section should consult regularly. He reasoned that the economic system was a single organism and so the senior officials needed to work as a team. He expressed the view that the Director of the Section should not have life tenure like civil servants. He went on to comment on his own position. He pointed out that he had little private means and was 'a poorer man than when I came here' and 'I shall have to look for more remunerative work before long'. His daughter Felicity was about to go up to Oxford to read PPE as her mother and father had done before her and all the signs were that his younger daughter Anthea would follow her to Oxford. A further anxiety was that 'relations with OF [Overseas Finance] have been very bad for more than a year and more like a religious war than reasonable men trying to make a fair representation of a legitimate difference of opinion! I would not feel any sense of grievance at all if I, or anyone else, decided that my departure would be a contribution to a happier atmosphere.'[10]

Butler, when this was reported to him, saw Hall and then minuted Bridges: 'He feels he would do better at a university. I feel this is all very distressing and wrong indeed. The discrepancy between the salaries of Plowden and Hall is very wrong. Could you and Norman Brook handle this at once. Robert Hall wishes to stay and I intend that he should. You will accept that it is entirely because Robert is so gentlemanly a fellow that this has not been mentioned before. With him there is no need to make a fuss or bring me into it.'[11] As a result Hall's salary was raised, the Economic Section was moved to the Treasury from the Cabinet Office and Hall was given the title of Economic Adviser to the government and awarded a KCMG in the 1954 New Year Honours. There were also various staff moves in the Treasury, easing the friction which had worried Hall so much. The most notable of these was the transfer of Clarke from Overseas Finance to the Social Services division. Clarke was the one man who could make Hall lose his temper and his departure from the seat where he fought for Robot eased Hall's mind greatly. They then became allies in trying to reduce expenditure on the social services. Hall was surprised at the Chancellor's strong reaction to his suggestion that he should resign, and he found the great pressure brought on him to stay very flattering. It was a compensation too for the departure of Plowden, the loss of whose support he at first felt keenly as he found him very pleasant to work with and extremely loyal.

Plowden had decided to leave the Treasury late in 1953. He and Hall had worked very closely together for more than five years. Plowden was more forceful than Hall; he was decisive, persuasive and a good spokesman and, in this sense, more influential. Together they made a very powerful team. It was said after the second rejection of Robot that the Plowden/Hall team was the strongest force in Whitehall, since ministers would not accept anything that they strongly disapproved.[12] Plowden's departure was a great loss for Hall, though he later became as influential on his own as the two of them had been earlier.

The year 1953 closed with some warning signs on the industrial and wages fronts, and with the possible appearance of an American recession. It was 'a wait and see' budget in 1954 with few changes, the one expansionary innovation being an investment allowance, which exempted from tax 20 per cent of expenditure on plant and machinery and 10 per cent of expenditure on industrial and agricultural buildings. This was an attempt to encourage innovation and give a spur to economic growth, where it now began to be clear that Britain was lagging behind a number of other industrial countries.

The 1954 Commonwealth Finance Ministers Conference was held in Sydney and Hall seized the opportunity to take a few days leave after the conference to visit Silverspur to see his mother, and Brisbane and Toowomba to visit other relatives. He was very excited about it – he had not been to Australia since 1936, although his mother, sister and other relatives had visited England. Sadly for him his younger brother David, for whom he had never lost his very special feeling despite seeing so little of him, had died a few years earlier. But he was overjoyed to be back in his beloved Silverspur. While in Sydney for the conference itself, he contrived to meet old friends, sometimes for breakfast, and he had one glorious day sailing and swimming in the harbour.

It was around this time that he became concerned that the instruments of economic management were gradually being narrowed down. By the spring of 1954 nearly all the direct controls inherited from the war had been removed or were about to be removed. In some cases the controls had been used as instruments to reduce demand, for example import restrictions, rationing of food and other goods, and building licenses. As these were gradually eliminated, the remaining three instruments – the exchange rate, the budget and monetary policy – became more important. He was anxious that none of these should be abandoned and he recognised the possibility of an inconsistency between maintaining full employment and retaining sterling as an international currency.

A deterioration in the balance of payments early in 1955, together with a fall in unemployment and signs of incipient cost inflation, prompted Hall to call for the Chancellor to tighten credit, raise bank rate and reimpose hire purchase restrictions. These measures were all adopted in February. In normal circumstances the economic picture would have seemed to need a stiffer budget. However the senior Treasury staff, including Bridges, were sympathetic to the government's wish to reduce taxes in an election year, and did not discourage the Chancellor when he expressed his determination to reduce income tax. The politics of it all were not very clear, but the impression was given that a reduction in income tax was planned as part of a package, in which a cutback in payments to farmers and increases in coal prices and railway fares would offset the reduction in income tax, but none of these were approved.

It was clear to Hall that on economic grounds there should be no easing in the budget. If any changes were indicated, they were in the direction of some tightening, so that a budget which reduced taxation would be very difficult to defend, especially if the balance of payments deteriorated further. But the Chancellor had made up his mind to reduce income tax by 6d in the pound. Hall, after making his opposition clear, knew that any further argument would irritate Butler without shifting him, so he ceased to press his case. But he did voice strong opposition when suggestions were made for a larger reduction and he successfully called on Bridges to resist any such proposal. The consequence of these manoeuvres was that the budget speech became very woolly in an attempt to justify the tax reduction. Emphasis was laid on the need to improve incentives and to encourage growth and it was asserted that the tightening of monetary policy would provide some counterweight to the reduction in taxation. However, the budget judgment did not follow logically from the economic analysis. In fact it was an electioneering budget, even if not a very blatant one by later standards, and it was judged as such.[13]

Almost inevitably, disinflationary measures were needed during the year. Credit and hire-purchase restrictions were strengthened in July. But monetary measures proved insufficient to reverse the trends and an autumn budget followed. Purchase tax was raised by a fifth. For the next two years the emphasis of policy continued to be deflationary as the pressure of demand eased only slowly.

During 1955, the Bank once again became anxious about its ability to hold the transferable rate and started to press for some move to convertibility. Ian Little, who was in the Section for two years, likened the Bank's proposals to 'frightening the patient with threats of a heart attack, in order to get him to take a drug that will give him one'.[14] The Bank always acted when sterling was weak, whereas Hall's wish was to move from strength not weakness and then, when the economy was strong enough, he wanted full convertibility, not some halfway house.

The Governor's manoeuvres were unsuccessful, largely because the Chancellor became convinced that there was no possibility of the OEEC agreeing to them. However, rumours of impending convertibility led to renewed pressure on sterling in 1955 and the Chancellor had to make a statement asserting that the sterling rate would remain at $2.80. Butler had been advised by Rowan to also announce a wider spread in exchange rates of 3 per cent, or nearly 10 cents, either side of $2.80 (instead of the existing 1 per cent). To this Hall took strong exception and wrote an angry minute to Bridges.

It was to be another three years before convertibility was completely restored at the end of 1958. The timing of the move was initiated by Germany and it then applied to all the leading European countries. However, between 1955 and 1958, the Bank of England made a series of planned and less dramatic moves relating to the unification of the rates for transferable sterling, with official intervention if they should diverge. Members of the Economic Section continued to write papers debating the best course of action, none of them wishing to see premature convertibility. Hall was still anxious about the risks of going convertible as long as considerable discrimination still existed. The dollar problem was not yet solved, and the internal economy was fully extended.

Further calls for action were made by the Bank in 1956, 1957 and 1958. After a good deal of discussion in 1958, the Treasury, including Hall, agreed that a move should be made before the end of the year, Hall himself wanting it to be before Parliament rose for Christmas. Although at first ministers did not seem keen, the decision was taken to make the announcement on 27 December, with the Germans moving at the same time and the French devaluing the franc. As far as Hall was concerned, the move could not have been better timed. He noted in his diary that he was always against jumping out of a high window, and now they were walking out of a french window instead. As it turned out the operation went quite smoothly and the pound remained strong.

For a large part of Butler's chancellorship, Hall was heavily engaged in the internal quarrels which had convulsed the Treasury and these prevented him from making more progress on some of the fundamental problems created by Butler's full employment policy. But he had won an important victory, which delivered significant advantages to the economy. Blocking the adoption of Robot allowed the economy to grow throughout the 1950s, with a steady improvement in real incomes, a surplus on the current balance of payments in most years and a rise in the gold and dollar reserves. In addition, Hall's resistance may have had longer-term effects. It made it less likely, at least for a time, that there would be similar attempts to introduce a controversial policy without proper discussion. It certainly advanced his status in the government machine and it won him flattering recognition and the trust of the Conservative government as he had previously won that of the Labour government.

CHAPTER TWELVE

The Revival of
Monetary Policy under
the Tories

Butler's chancellorship had seen a revival in the use of monetary policy after the period of monetary inactivity under the Labour government. The cheap money policy pursued by Dalton from 1945 to 1947 can be seen as no more than an extension and intensification of the arrangements begun in the 1930s and carried on throughout the war. Cripps, though acquiescent in the retreat from ultra-cheap money, was equally anxious to keep down the cost of servicing the national debt, and so largely continued in the same vein as Dalton. Such arrangements were not peculiar to Britain. The United States Federal Reserve Bank of New York's rate remained at only 1 per cent from 1946 to 1948 and, even early in 1951, it was only 1¾ per cent. Interest rates in most of Europe except for Germany and Italy were also very low.

The maintenance of very low interest rates led to increased demand for credit and, in 1948, during the Labour administration, Hall and Jay initiated an attempt to restrict bank advances, but this was frustrated. Cripps wrote to the Governor in December 1947 asking for the limitation of credit facilities in certain fields – speculative, hire-purchase and building. 'I should be grateful if you would convey this request to the Banks and the Accepting Houses', he wrote. But this request was never implemented. The Bank of England wrote a memorandum on monetary policy which asserted that the proper volume of credit for the banks to make available should be determined solely by the bona fide demand for such credit. Fleming, minuting Hall, thought it showed that the Bank had learned nothing about credit policy during the past one hundred years. Other factors, which he argued should be taken into account, were the proper volume of bank money which should be created in the prevailing economic situation and the urgency of the demand for credit for government purposes.

There was also a move to raise bank rate during the 1950–1 rearmament episode but this was rejected by Gaitskell. Instead there was a general review of credit policy. The Economic Section was not prepared to concede that monetary policy should be allowed to work in a way that was contrary to the other elements of policy in the management of the economy. Policy should at least be made neutral and preferably have some positive effect in reinforcing physical controls and fiscal policy. Hall, minuting the Chancellor in January 1951, pointed out that he had constantly discussed the possibility of using selective credit controls with the Bank officials over the past two years and had always been told that the commercial banks could only cooperate if they were given precise instructions capable of being interpreted by branch managers. As it was impossible to lay down general principles about whole groups of activities without causing intolerable hardships, he had come to the conclusion that almost as large an official machine would be needed as for direct allocations or licensing. He therefore favoured a *general* tightening of credit rather than a *selective* one. The Chancellor pressed the Governor to restrict advances, again refusing to raise interest rates, and agreed that he would meet the bank chairmen himself in the autumn. This meeting never took place because the election intervened.

In Hall's eyes the revival of monetary policy by Butler had not been very satisfactory. The early years were bedevilled by the resistance of the Bank of England to the use of credit controls, and their insistence on cuts in government expenditure as the only remedy against excess demand. The success of their resistance showed the strength of the Bank's grip on policy, in spite of its nationalisation in 1946. The Economic Section conducted a post mortem on the part played by higher interest rates in bringing about the mini-recession of 1952. Their conclusion was that they were largely coincidental and the mini-recession could be explained by other events. Hall himself was more impressed by the correlation between monetary policy and the emergence of slack in the economy and kept an open mind, arguing that 'we don't really know a great deal about how bank rate changes work'. By 1953, the Bank was claiming some credit for the part played by the rise in bank rate in reducing the pressure of demand. But the mini-recession essentially represented the easing of the flood of excess demand that had taken five years to be eliminated and there were certainly other more immediate causes, in particular the end of the Korean War.

One problem that concerned Hall during the next few years was that Butler always treated the Governor of the Bank as his chief adviser on exchange and monetary questions, talking to him privately with no record of their discussions; and he never seemed to worry, and perhaps never noticed, if the Bank's advice was inconsistent. Cobbold, who had succeeded Catto as Governor in 1949, was concerned to preserve as much independence as the 1946 Act allowed. He did not want close relations with the Treasury; and he was a very successful stone-waller. But the Bank was not just resisting interference; it was on the offensive, trying to re-establish the dominant position it had held on policy before 1939.

Late in 1954, when Hall had reluctantly accepted the Chancellor's determination to reduce income taxes in the 1955 April budget, he advised some tightening of monetary policy to counter its effects. The Chancellor followed this advice in February and instructed the Governor to squeeze credit, in order to make room for his tax cut in the budget. But bank advances went on rising. When it became clear around the middle of the year that the control was not working, Hall, Gilbert and Brittain managed to obtain the agreement of the Bank to let the Treasury talk directly to the representatives of the clearing banks. It was evident at this meeting that the Bank of England had failed to convey the message that the government was serious about a reduction in bank advances as a means to reduce the pressure of demand. The banks thought that they had been doing what was expected of them, and admitted that they could do more. The Chancellor, who was outraged, himself then called on the clearing banks to make a significant reduction in their advances. The banks responded to this by agreeing to aim at a cut of 10 per cent by the end of the year.

Hall wrote a memorandum to the Chancellor on the lessons of this experience in attempting to bring about a restriction of credit.[1] Both he and Butler thought the delay in carrying out the government's wishes was one reason why he needed an autumn budget. He had reduced taxes in his 'election budget' in the spring and hoped to offset the effects by a tighter monetary policy. The overheating of the economy during 1955 exposed the Chancellor – and this meant Hall as well – to the accusation that he had taken risks with the balance of payments in order to influence the election. Hall felt that the whole episode had been highly damaging to Butler's reputation.

In the light of history, the significance of this episode has probably been exaggerated. The effects on demand pressure were relatively small and there have been worse mistakes in policy since. But there was enough truth in the charge of electioneering with the budget to make the criticism stick. Hall had pointed out the risk and Butler had decided to take it. The episode demoralised Butler who disliked having to have an autumn budget – though he handled the business well in the House of Commons. It made Hall rather restless and he again often felt like leaving, 'but I suppose not quite seriously enough'. He sensed that he did not know exactly what was going on and that no one else knew much more than he did.

The delay in imposing a credit squeeze in 1955 raised the question of whether and how far the monetary system could be made to work more effectively to support budgetary policy and check excess demand. Hall engaged in further skirmishes with the Bank and suggested an inquiry into the experiences of the past year. He was disgusted by the poor cooperation the Treasury had received from the Bank over economic policy: 'All the Governor does is to explain away the actions of the clearing banks and say that nothing but reduced government expenditure will help; yet he told me in 1953 that 1952 proved that bank rate was the dominant factor.' The inconsistencies were numerous. In the first half of 1955, the Governor kept telling the Chancellor that in a little while the credit squeeze would work, in spite of the fact that the instructions to the banks were inadequate. Then at the Mansion House dinner he said that it was a mistake to expect monetary policy to have much effect. Hall felt it was impossible to get any sensible assessment of its impact from the Bank. Probably the fact was that the Bank was not anxious to engage in serious dialogue with the Treasury officials, and especially not with Hall.

In December 1955, Butler ceased to be Chancellor and was succeeded by Harold Macmillan. The change was not altogether un-
welcome to Hall, as on the whole he felt Butler was a weak Chancellor and this had become more obvious during his last year. Macmillan
made a good impression and the 1956 budget was easier for Hall
than the 1955 one had been. It introduced only a small tightening
up. After the 1956 budget a small committee of Treasury and Bank
officials – Compton and Hall from the Treasury, and O'Brien and
Maurice Allen from the Bank – was set up to review the 1955
monetary policy generally. It produced an agreed report.[2] The tenor
of its conclusions are recalled in what Hall noted in his diary:

> While it is a bit too complimentary to the Bank over the events
> of 1955, it puts the whole thing in a much clearer and more
> intelligible light. I think their greatest fault was to allow RAB to
> introduce the 1955 budget which relied on monetary policy, with-
> out telling him that they thought it was not likely to do the
> trick...no one will ever convince me that they could not have put
> more pressure on the banks.[3]

At first Hall thought the report was a big advance, in that the
Bank had become more conscious of its responsibility to ensure effective monetary control. However he was not convinced the report
had made much impact on the Governor himself. Within a year,
Hall was again expressing grave doubts about monetary policy
and asking whether there was any control at all over the volume of
credit.

In the autumn of 1956 there were some important staff changes
in the Treasury and a reorganisation at the top, which had
considerable implications for Hall. The retirement of Bridges and
Gilbert meant the departure of the last senior Treasury officials
who were in post when Hall began. Bridges had been a man of
indomitable energy, a tireless worker with intense concentration
and stamina. But in his final years, because he took on too much,
he did not have time to act effectively as head of the Treasury on the
economic side. He moved in when there was a crisis but he had
many responsibilities aside from economic policy and, at the times
when economic matters were not at a critical point, he gave the
impression that his mind was on the next appointment he had to
make or the next Permanent Secretary of a department he had to
replace. He was by now sixty-four.[4]

It was Gilbert's retirement at the age of sixty-five that was the best news for Hall. He had been a thorn in his side because of his lack of action, particularly over monetary policy, which Hall thought would have developed very differently if Plowden had still been around the Treasury instead of Gilbert. Whereas Plowden had had ideas similar to his own and they had always supported one another, Gilbert's views on policy were often opposed to his; without support Hall was not always prepared to push hard enough. This was especially so over the 1955 budget, when Bridges had backed up Gilbert so strongly on the reduction in income tax.

Hall was confident that the new Permanent Secretary, Makins, would change all this. Makins returned to London from his position as Ambassador in Washington to become the joint head of the Treasury on the economic side, with Brook in charge of the rest and retaining his position as Secretary to the Cabinet. Hall and Makins had known one another for many years, liked one another and worked very well together. They talked the same language. Makins found Hall very reserved and reflective and with excellent judgment. In his three years at the Treasury he took Hall's advice and relied on him more than anyone else. It was a great change for Hall that he no longer had to deal with Gilbert and he found it a delightful contrast that Makins always had time to discuss matters. He was the personification of energy and action – just the opposite of Gilbert, whose functions Makins had taken over under the reorganisation of work following the retirements of Bridges and Gilbert. These changes meant that Hall became the longest serving member of the senior group of Treasury officials dealing with economic policy.

About this time talk began about the possibility of another public enquiry into banking and finance on the lines of the Macmillan Committee of 1931, of which Keynes had been a member.[5] Hall endorsed this proposal, one reason being that the circumstances had changed so much since the subject was last studied, but his more profound reason was his dissatisfaction with the Bank's operation of monetary policy. He thought an inquiry should have two purposes. Advice was required, first on the extent to which reliance should be placed on monetary measures in controlling the economy; and secondly, on the mechanism of monetary policy if it was decided to use it. The Governor, having opposed the idea for some time, was eventually persuaded that it was a good idea when the President asked for just such a committee in the United States. He then actually proposed it himself.

Before it could be set up there was another change of Chancellor following the Suez crisis and the resignation of Eden as Prime Minister. Hall was recalled from India where he had been invited to give advice to the government on long-term planning. Back in London he advised on the measures required to halt the speculative drain on the reserves sparked off by Suez. He noted in his diary: 'Whatever the outcome here, I cannot feel any doubt that our intervention in Suez has been a disaster from a political point of view. One hesitates to say that anything is an economic disaster for a country, short of a serious loss in productive facilities or in external income. But we have certainly lost a big slice of our external income as long as the Canal is closed and we must wait and see whether this is all there is to it.'[6] In the event, although the situation had looked alarming, the outlook rapidly improved.

Macmillan became Prime Minister when Eden resigned and Thorneycroft succeeded him as Chancellor of the Exchequer. Macmillan referred in his autobiography to the short time that he worked with Hall in the Treasury: 'Our professional economist, if one may use that term, was Sir Robert Hall, to whom I took an immediate liking. The fact that he was inarticulate was not altogether a disadvantage, for at any rate he was never dogmatic.'[7]

Under Thorneycroft things were to turn out very differently. He believed much more in the benefits of market decisions than the paternalistic Macmillan. At first he pursued a similar policy to that of Macmillan but, when sterling came under pressure in August in spite of a substantial current account surplus, Thorneycroft got it firmly into his head that it was all the result of too much money in the economic system; this was pricing Britain out of markets and leading to an increase in imports. Hall was upset when he discovered that Thorneycroft had preferred to take advice from Lionel Robbins of the London School of Economics instead. Robbins had by this time moved back nearer to what would now be regarded as the monetarist rather than the Keynesian school of economists – a position that Thorneycroft himself also occupied. Thorneycroft wished to restrict the money supply. He proposed that this should be done by fixing bank advances and by cutting down spending by the nationalised industries, government departments and local authorities, the main emphasis being on the latter.

The Governor fought back arguing that it was the wrong policy to prevent a rise in advances; he tried diversionary tactics, by proposing all sorts of measures other than credit restrictions, including improved monetary management. There was much to-ing and fro-ing, with the Chancellor pressing hard for further restrictions. A compromise was reached: there was to be a ceiling on advances and bank rate was raised to 7 per cent. Apart from this, restricting the money supply took the form of setting limits to forms of expenditure which could be controlled by the government.

In Hall's view, this was nothing more than deflation to increase unemployment in order to control wage inflation, although Thorneycroft could not be made to see it that way. For this policy to be effective, it was necessary for wages to be highly sensitive to the level of unemployment, which Hall doubted.

Thorneycroft expected his officials to tell him that there was only so much money available for the government to spend, so that he could tell his colleagues that this was all they could have. On hearing this, Hall thought he should resign, because everyone would know that such oversimplified advice could never have come from him, so it would be thought that his advice must have been ignored. He was persuaded by Makins to stay on the grounds that it would not be long before there was a new Chancellor.

When Hall had discovered that Thorneycroft had been consulting Robbins, he felt the Chancellor must have taken against him. Thorneycroft later expressed surprise at this reaction and denied that his consultation with Robbins implied such a thing; he did it only because he wanted another opinion. His opinion of Hall was otherwise favourable. In addition to describing him as a delightful man, he found him meticulously fair in his suggestions, always expressing his point of view clearly and simply. He admired his facility for setting out his arguments in a non-technical way.[8]

Nevertheless, as far as Hall was aware, he was the first Chancellor to go behind his back and Hall was extremely upset. He objected not only to the measures taken, but even more to the words chosen to announce the policy: they seemed to go too far towards committing the government to enough deflation to stop prices rising; in his view the measures announced would not produce enough unemployment to ease wage pressure during the winter.[9] In due course he noted in his diary that he and the Chancellor had patched it up 'for the moment'. After this Thorneycroft consulted Hall on several occasions alone, which he had never done before; Hall helped him to set out his economic arguments, and advised him it would be rash to commit himself to enough deflation to stop prices rising, since to achieve that extremely severe measures would probably be needed. Thorneycroft took this advice. He accepted that even if Hall did not wholly agree with his policy, he would still regard it as part of his job to make sure the Chancellor put it to Parliament in the best possible way.

Relations between the Treasury and the Bank suffered a setback with the attempt by Thorneycroft to tighten up monetary policy. There was even talk of dismissing the Governor, but the Chancellor was advised that under the 1946 Act of Parliament which had nationalised the Bank of England, he could dismiss neither the Governor nor the Court of the Bank; and even though the Bank was empowered to issue directives to the commercial banks, the Chancellor did not have the legal authority to direct the Bank of England to do so.[10]

Thorneycroft then set up a confidential working group on credit control, mainly of officials but including Robbins. Its terms of reference were to consider – in parallel with the Radcliffe Committee's deliberations – both how to control credit, and how to amend the law to give the Treasury the powers it thought it already had, namely to oblige the Governor to issue directives to the commercial banks. Hall collaborated with Robbins, who was a member of the group, writing a paper on which the report of the group was based.[11] The working group's report concentrated on the means of control and came down in favour of a prescribed liquidity ratio, plus something like Treasury deposit receipts to keep down the banks' supply of Treasury bills. The latter proposal eventually took shape as 'special deposits', then thought to be an effective means of control. The Bank agreed that this was practicable, but argued that it was unnecessary.

The Radcliffe Committee was set up in April 1957, an announcement about it having been made earlier in the budget speech. The fact that the membership suited Hall very well was no accident – he had been consulted about it. Members included Franks, Sayers,

Cairncross, Harcourt, Woods and Woodcock. Hall himself was given the main responsibility for writing the Treasury submission, which gave a critical account of recent years' events. He brought out the imperfect nature of official thinking on the subject, and the poor coordination on policy matters between the Treasury and the Bank. He argued that the question of what sort of interest rate policy should have been adopted had never been properly faced. Nor had it ever really been considered whether directives to the banks were needed as a permanent instrument. The paper went through six drafts, mainly because of objections to the inclusion of anything that implied criticism, either of past policies, or of the Treasury view. But he congratulated himself that he had been able to trace quotations from speeches by the Chancellor – most of which were written by himself – which illustrated all the main points he wished to see in the paper to go to the Radcliffe Committee.

When he appeared before the Committee, he tried to get across the point that in the period since 1951, when monetary policy was reactivated under the Conservative government, the policy had been experimental and no-one could have been expected to know all the answers. Privately he thought that the Treasury and the Bank were both to blame for their slowness in grasping that the funding of the national debt was an unpredictable operation and that control must be unpredictable also. The Governor had continued to argue that an overall budget surplus was the only course to keep down inflation.

A great deal of Hall's time during the second half of 1957 was spent on the preparations for the Radcliffe Committee.[12] He was fairly confident that the Committee would conclude that monetary policy had not been used firmly enough, as he thought himself. He was less sure about the conclusions they would reach on methods of control. He was beginning to believe that investment should be controlled more directly in a full employment economy. His main anxiety was that one of the difficult problems – the Bank's aversion to cooperation with the Treasury on internal monetary matters – would not be brought out clearly in the report. The Chancellor talked only in private to the Governor and Bank officials did not discuss their own assessments of the situation with the Treasury.

Hall wrote another note for the Radcliffe Committee with some final suggestions as to what its report should include. He proposed that the Committee should recognise that control over the supply of money had been lost and needed to be regained by the government. As there was no certainty that this could be done by conventional liquidity ratios, he thought alternative techniques were needed. Lastly he sounded some warnings against making the Bank of England independent of Parliament or the Treasury, an idea that had been tossed about by the Bank. When the report was published in mid-1959, it was more or less what he hoped, recommending that monetary policy must be part of the government's general economic policy, along with fiscal policy and direct controls. It should operate by changing interest rates, and the national debt should be managed in the light of this. The 30 per cent liquidity ratio should be made legal and variable at will.

There were also some interesting structural proposals in the report. It concluded that none of the Bank's functions should be regarded as separate and independent from the Treasury; and that there should be a standing committee to consider changes in monetary policy, with equal membership from the Bank and Treasury. All this suited Hall well and endorsed everything he had stood out for. He felt it was a triumph that the Bank had admitted that it was their responsibility to control the supply of money – a responsibility that now sounds self-evident.

In practice, Hall was never to place much reliance on monetary policy as an instrument of control. His scepticism had been reinforced in 1955, when credit restrictions failed to offset the effects of the tax reductions in the budget, even though this was partly because they were applied too late and were too mild. He also thought that interest rate policy could only be effective if ministers were prepared to make borrowing very dear indeed, in which case the main effect would be on investment, which might not be desirable. But he continued to think that credit controls should be used to support budgetary policy when the rate of expansion was judged to be excessively rapid. Credit controls are now out of fashion as a policy instrument and it is usually supposed that they are ineffective. Evasion became much easier in the 1970s after the introduction of a more competitive system in the banking sector. But in the 1950s there were fewer alternative sources of borrowing; the main lending was by the commercial banks so that in those days limits on bank lending were effective in curbing expenditure.

When the Radcliffe Committee's report was published, Hall used his influence to try to ensure that it would not embarrass the Bank.[13] He was anxious that the Bank should not repudiate it in public, knowing it contained things the Governor would not like. The Governor was urged to let it be known that he welcomed the report and took the recommendations as logical developments of current practice, rather than anything particularly revolutionary. Hall also briefed a number of the financial journalists whom he knew well, to encourage them to take the same line. In all this Hall was successful – although he then thought the Bank came out of the exercise perhaps rather better than it should have done.

After 1958 there was a notable improvement in Hall's relations with the Governor. When Hall wrote to congratulate Cobbold on becoming a Privy Counsellor in 1959, Cobbold replied:

If the Treasury and the Bank always took the same view, there would be no advantage in having the two institutions and, in my belief, the nation would be the loser. But if differing views are to be matched and to produce (at least sometimes we hope) a useful result, it requires that each should have the respect of the other. And that you have always had in full measure from us all here, and not least from myself.

After Thorneycroft's monetarist experiment in 1957/8, monetary policy fell back to the subordinate place that it occupied for almost all Hall's time as Director of the Economic Section. Policy was relaxed, restrictions removed and, in spite of this, inflation was very moderate – as indeed by later standards it was throughout 1948 to 1961. The attempt to introduce a 'monetarist' policy did not alter Hall's view that the traditional method of controlling the general level of prices through the money supply could only be effective through the circuitous route of higher interest rates, which would reduce demand for both investment and consumer goods; this would lead to a fall in employment. If the labour market operated in what economists called a 'perfect' way, then the resulting unemployment would moderate wage increases. But the labour market was not perfect and became less so in the 1950s as trade unions became stronger. Hall thought all along that an incomes policy would be less destructive and a much more effective instrument than monetary policies. But as the adoption of incomes policy was still uncertain, he thought it was helpful that it had been agreed that changes in interest rates and credit restriction would be used from time to time to support budgetary policy.

For example in January 1958, when Heathcoat Amory succeeded Thorneycroft as Chancellor, pressures on the economy were easing with the prospect of some slack later in the year. Bank rate was therefore lowered. By May unemployment was rising and Hall proposed to the Chancellor that expansion would soon be needed, but that there should be some warnings sounded about excessive wage increases at the same time. During the summer, after discussions with the Bank, credit restrictions were eased. This was followed by a relaxation of the hire-purchase restrictions which had been tightened in 1956, a doubling of the initial investment allowances and an increased allocation for housing repairs. Bank rate was then lowered further. Mastering the transition from Thorneycroft's deflationary policy to one of expansion was politically tricky, as the government did not want to make it too plain that they were reversing earlier policy.

In the final years of the 1950s, monetary policy was used only occasionally to support budgetary policy. In 1959 and 1960, the warnings were all that the economy was overheating and 1960 saw further calls to restrict credit. When in July bank advances showed a very large rise, Hall was especially annoyed because only a month earlier the Governor had claimed that he had everything under control. At Hall's instigation the Chancellor sent a strong protest to the Governor. Hall commented in his diary:

> It is one of the great disadvantages of monetary policy, compared to fiscal policy, that if you change taxes the revenue departments will go out and collect the money and be very unpleasant to the taxpayer if they do not get it. But if you try to tighten up on the money side, you get the Bank of England falling over themselves to soften the blow and to make all sorts of excuses for the bankers that they probably would be ashamed to make for themselves.[14]

Bank rate had been raised again in June 1960 and there was another call for special deposits. The Governor spoke sharply to the clearing banks and August advances were down. In spite of this, in September the Prime Minister was interfering and sending min-

utes to the Chancellor, complaining about how badly the credit
squeeze was working; expressing the view that relations between
the Bank and the Treasury and the clearing banks were very bad;
and wanting reassurance that the Governor would leave at the end
of the year as he said he would.

Hall then became caught up in the choice of a new Governor and
there is no doubt he was concerned that someone more coopera-
tive than Cobbold should be appointed. He hoped that Franks might
succeed him, but in the event it was Cromer who, when he was asked
to take it on, agonised about whether he could do it, until reassured
by Hall that he could.

The 1950s ended with the prospect of a more effective sort of
monetary policy. This was in no small measure owing to Hall's persistence. He had led criticism of the Bank whilst grappling with its
considerable evasion and obstruction. He had also devoted a great
deal of time to the preparation of evidence to the Radcliffe Committee which he hoped would lead to a more effective monetary
policy and a better relationship between the Treasury and the
Bank of England. None of this was because he believed in any al-
leged magical qualities of monetary policy. Rather he regarded it as
an instrument secondary only to fiscal policy but nevertheless
potentially useful. At the very least it should not operate counter to
the government's macroeconomic policy. As the 1950s advanced,
however, he became increasingly aware that neither fiscal nor monetary policy was sufficient to control inflation and had already begun to turn his attention to the consideration of additional instruments.

CHAPTER THIRTEEN

The Problem of Inflation

As this chapter will show, Hall was almost continuously concerned with the problem of inflation. Despite repeated disappointments, this concern took the form of trying to find an incomes policy that would work. Since his day, incomes policy has become unfashionable. Some look back on the attempts to use it as misguided; others, with nostalgia, are trying to revive a similar policy to the ones Hall favoured. Inflation is a problem still with us, the dilemmas Hall confronted are still with us, and it is interesting to see the strength of his concern and his unending efforts to persuade the governments he served.

Judged by the 1970s and 1980s, the rate of inflation in Britain in the 1950s was low. From 1947 to 1961 the average annual rise in prices was under 4 per cent. But at the time it seemed high and Hall was anxious about it. By the early 1950s it had become clear to him that neither the Labour nor the Conservative governments were willing to allow the economy to function at a lower level of activity. This was especially true of Macmillan: as the Member of Parliament for Stockton he had been strongly influenced by the unemployment there in the 1930s. When he became Chancellor in December 1955, the situation still seemed very inflationary and by early spring the size of the wage round looked particularly alarming. Consequently, just before the 1956 budget, the government issued a White Paper entitled *The Economic Implications of Full Employment*. This was the umpteenth version of a paper with which Hall had been involved for about six years, since Cripps first planned to publish a White Paper on wages in 1950.

Hall was not the first economist to come to the conclusion that full employment would lead to inflation, unless there was some policy to control wage increases, but he was perhaps the first at the centre of policymaking, who thought he had a chance to do something about it. The Economic Section had produced a number of briefs and papers on the subject after the publication of the White Paper on employment policy in 1944, which itself referred to this danger, but these had had little influence on ministers.

One of Hall's early tasks after his appointment as Director of the Economic Section was to write a paper for Cripps on the inflationary position. He observed that the only available remedy for inflation at that time was to deflate the economy, because the government was opposed to using a wage stop. Profits were easy and employers needed to retain their labour and avoid strikes, so that they had a strong incentive to pay more than the negotiated rates if necessary to retain their labour forces. Brooding about this in relation to future economic policy, Hall concluded that the government faced a real dilemma in preventing wages from rising too fast in full employment conditions. Wage restraint, it seemed, was the main condition for a successful full employment policy and so far any action which might have achieved this had been rejected.[1] Following this paper for Cripps, who disliked the idea of deflating the economy, there were two rounds of wage restraint in 1948 and 1949, as a result of negotiations between the government and the TUC but, though effective for a limited time, these were very temporary affairs. The wage freeze in 1949, following devaluation, broke down seven months later just as the Korean War began, in spite of the fact that it was supported by the TUC. This did not augur well for using this method in the future.

The subject was under discussion in the Economic Section and in 1949 members wrote many internal papers which ranged over various degrees of optimism and pessimism. There was agreement on the problem, but not on the solutions. These ranged from deflation and higher unemployment, state control over wages, a floating exchange rate and voluntary wage freezes, to a tax on employers who granted excessive wage increases. The Economic Section continued to wrestle with the problem, encouraged by Hall, but still without coming to any agreed solution. Ideas were increasingly based on the difference between demand inflation and cost inflation;

the latter seemed to Hall to have been neglected by economists outside the government.

In 1950, the government proposed to issue a White Paper on wages. Hall suggested it would be better to base it on employment policy, with the wages issue raised in that context, rather than to have a paper on wages as such. This advice was based on the sensitivity of the subject and Hall thought it could provide an opportunity to explain government policy, and the reasons for believing it was necessary to do something to contain wage increases. The Korean War caused a substantial rise in the cost of living, leading to even higher wage claims. Hall advised that the government should try to get across the message that such claims would in themselves lead to further rises in the cost of living. By this time Gaitskell was the acting Chancellor and he was convinced of the need for an incomes policy. Work was therefore renewed on the preparation of a White Paper, but that was as far as things went under the Labour government.

By the time the Tory government took over in October 1951, Hall was in a state of anxiety about the experiment in full employment being almost a failure, in the sense that the instruments used were inadequate to counter the strains and rigidities that full employment had imposed. These included the pressure on wages, the maldistribution of labour and a low rate of economic growth. He was increasingly concerned about the latter, as it became clear that the United Kingdom was falling behind its competitors in rates of growth. Butler himself returned to the two problems that caused Cripps so much worry: how to increase productivity and how to keep wages from rising faster than productivity. However, he did not wish to take any action which would lead to a more moderate level of employment, such as reducing government expenditure or increasing taxes. On these matters he was just as reluctant as the Labour Chancellors had been and unemployment remained very low while Butler was Chancellor.

Instead, Hall persuaded Butler to set in motion plans for a White Paper on inflation and the wages problem, as his predecessors had done. Hall himself regarded this as a matter of urgency, but the process of official and ministerial criticism whittled away his dream of speedy results. He had planned to write this White Paper himself, but other pressing problems and tasks made this impossible. In the meantime a visit to the United States intervened, so that in the end he put Downie on to doing a first draft. This was followed by a further five drafts but, in the end, all that happened was that Butler made a statement on wages to the National Joint Advisory Council. This statement had been written by Downie and others in the Economic Section, but it raised little interest and scarcely any debate.

Hall then tried a completely different and less orthodox method taking his ideas to the financial journalists and trying to persuade them to write on the subject. This also had little result, however. Then he encouraged economists in the universities and research institutes to do research on the problem but here again the results were not particularly fruitful. Over the next couple of years, he became disheartened about the subject, without however losing his conviction that the maintenance of steady prices in a full employment economy was a major issue.

Further versions of a possible White Paper on full employment and wages continued to be written by various members of the Section. However these did not help Hall very much. He did not know the answer and it continued to worry him. Instead he concentrated his efforts on trying to persuade officials of the need for effective monetary tightness and credit restrictions as anti-inflation measures. Then a sudden decision was taken by ministers to publish the current draft of the paper on full employment and wages as a White Paper. This appeared just before the 1956 budget, under the title of *The Economic Implications of Full Employment.*[2] This particular version originally contained five-year projections, which demonstrated that if wage behaviour was moderate the outlook was favourable, but that all this would be put at risk by cost inflation. The senior Treasury officials thought these projections were too optimistic and, as Hall was not prepared to 'fight to the death' about them, they were removed before the paper was published. The White Paper thus became just another exercise in exhortation and Hall regarded it as more or less useless. Moreover, he thought it was very badly timed. He was in the middle of pressing the need for some deflationary measures in the budget and he thought these should have been introduced before the White Paper was published. He did not think the steps which it proposed to restrain wages stood a chance with employment as high as it was then. There were also a number of government measures in the offing which would put up prices. Hall's proposal had been to carry all these through first, so that there would then be no more food subsidies to reduce, no need to increase indirect taxes and no early prospect of price increases in the nationalised industries. If a campaign were then launched, at least it would not be damaged by the government's own actions.

Macmillan, who succeeded Butler as Chancellor in December 1955, was the first really strong incomes policy man in the government. His basic priority was to avoid unemployment and he therefore leaned towards running the economy at full or over-full employment. This meant that he was sympathetic to the need to control incomes in other ways than by deflation. It was therefore not difficult for Hall to persuade Macmillan to put a paper to Cabinet, saying that the risk was grave and a firm lead must be given. The paper drew attention to the price increases still to come as a result of government actions, confirmed that there were no more in the offing and asked that an appeal be made to labour and employers to keep down prices and wage demands. If this were done then a period of price stability could be used to try to agree a long-term wage policy.

The Cabinet agreed the line in the paper, but did not agree to a published statement. Instead there were talks with the TUC and the employers' organisations. Hall was present at the meeting with the TUC – the only official allowed to be there – and he felt frustrated that ministers made little impact, and the press statements afterwards none at all. He was the first to admit that his policy might not have been much good; but it was the only thing like a policy, and it had gone off so feebly that he was depressed about it. However, as usual, he bounced back quickly, telling ministers they should expect strikes in the autumn and that they should face up to these and not give in to them, because it would be better 'to go down defending the pound, than to go down because they were afraid to defend it'.

Hall continued to press for ministerial statements in favour of wage restraint – with some success – in the summer of 1956. He took heart from hints that public opinion was gradually coming round to recognising the need for it. In the autumn, after one of his visits to the United States, he wrote yet another memorandum on a long-term policy for wages which was circulated to a committee on prices and wages. Some officials were leaning towards compulsory arbitration, but Hall was still in favour of trying persuasion for a little longer, although on more precise terms than those tried so far. He argued in favour of a policy which stated that increases should not exceed a stated percentage in any year, an idea which subsequently became known as the 'guiding light'.

These talks were temporarily interrupted by the Suez invasion. When things settled down again and the Treasury had a new Chancellor – Hall's sixth, this time Thorneycroft – Hall raised the matter of wages with him and wrote another paper on his by now familiar lines. However this time he argued, in addition, that the idea that the government should be impartial was wrong. The atmosphere in 1957 seemed to him altogether more militant than he had supposed:

for the first time since I have been in England – now more than 30 years – I am reminded of the atmosphere in Australia in the early 1920s. Full employment and prosperity seem to have roused the fighting spirit of the working man and the ingrained respect for the upper classes is probably being whittled away. It is therefore becoming crucial that the employers and workers should take productivity seriously, since we can only get on with a militant attitude if there are rapid increases in output.[3]

Hall's proposed strategy was to choose a time when there were no large price increases in the offing and then have a campaign to keep prices steady. Only then, with a reasonable prospect of price stability, should the government seek discussions with employers and unions on a long-term wage policy. He proposed that the government should decide the amount of the annual permissible increase in wages and then take effective steps to limit wages to this maximum. He still had grave doubts that the Cabinet would accept anything as drastic as he proposed, but his impression was that it was a bolder Cabinet than any since Cripps's time, so that it might just happen. He sensed that people were really tired of constantly rising prices and he hoped that a strong government and informed public opinion might result in some action. He was also encouraged to think that action might be successful, because the timing would be much better than at the earlier attempt. Unemployment was actually rising, so full employment might perhaps appear to be threatened. In fact the Chancellor made a number of speeches on this subject and Hall acknowledged his lead with gratitude.

However, his optimism again turned out to be misplaced. When Thorneycroft, as Chancellor, put Hall's proposals to Cabinet, the only consequence was the setting up of the Council on Prices, Productivity and Incomes. This independent body unfortunately turned out to sabotage Hall's attempts to establish a wages policy, chiefly because, as Hall put it in his diary, the economist appointed to it, Dennis Robertson, adopted a 'dogged look' whenever the words full employment were mentioned; and he would not budge from his conviction that price stability should be the sole aim, with no thought given to full employment. Hall had not anticipated that he would take such a line when consulted about the appointment. Consequently the early reports of the Council were useless from Hall's point of view, as they all put the blame for inflation on the government for running the economy at too high a level of demand.[4] After three reports in this vein, the personnel of the Council was altered. Robertson was succeeded by the more open-minded Henry Phelps Brown, who became convinced of the need for an incomes policy. The upward push on rates of pay figured as one of the causes of inflation in the Council's fourth report in 1961.

Some time before this, A. W. Phillips of the London School of Economics discovered a curve which illustrated a close historical relationship over the previous century between the level of unemployment and the rate of inflation. He sent Hall a draft of his article for *Economica*, and Hall took a good deal of trouble replying to him. Among other comments, he made the point that wages at a particular level of employment could be just as dependent on the extent to which trade unions used their bargaining power as they could on unemployment. To Hall the Phillips curve, as it became known, was much too precise an interpretation of an assumption which may have been true in the market economies of the past, but must have become a very uncertain relationship in modern conditions. Under collective bargaining, the trade unions were unlikely to be so impressed by unemployment, so that it would need to rise substantially before it influenced wages. Phillips's paper was published unaltered in November 1958.[5] It became famous among economists, politicians and commentators and had quite a vogue for a time, but it then became discredited as the relationship broke down in more recent years.[6] Later work showed that its findings needed to be put in a more sophisticated form.

At the beginning of 1958 the Chancellor became determined to get the public expenditure estimates down, so as to keep expenditure in 1958/9 the same as it had been in 1957/8. When the Cabinet was unwilling to agree to the last £50 million or so of the cuts he proposed, Thorneycroft resigned. Hall was altogether relieved as he thought the Chancellor was getting into a more and more rigid position, which was undesirable both from an economic and from a political point of view. When Heathcoat Amory succeeded him, Hall allowed himself to hope that he would get on better with him and that there would be no weakening on the wages front.

Heathcoat Amory shared with Hall the same sort of Keynesian attitude which was the basis of policy the whole time Hall was in the Economic Section, except for the short hiccup of Thorneycroft. Although he did not have any burning desire to reform anything, Hall persuaded him to consider inflation seriously, and to put some faith in incomes policy as an instrument for dealing with it. An official committee on wages policy was set up and Hall put in several papers to it. This committee decided to recommend to ministers Hall's 'guiding light' principle, that is the figure beyond which wage increases would be inflationary. Hall felt slightly triumphant because this was his doctrine which had been put to Cabinet by Thorneycroft six months earlier but in spite of this nothing was done.

The wage round went more slowly in 1958 than it had done in previous years, and the rise turned out to be a moderate 3½ to 4 per cent. By the end of the year the Chancellor was becoming concerned about the slowdown in economic activity. Hall, who liked government policy to look continuous and coherent, tried to reassure the Chancellor that business confidence at home was good – which should prevent any serious recession – and that the United States economy was picking up after a year of recession.

1959 opened with the economic situation much improved on a year earlier; the prospect was for a slow rise in output and unemployment steady, good conditions in which to make some progress on a wages policy. Output, however, was not much higher than it had been four years earlier. Hall wished to see a larger rise and thought some small stimulus in the budget would be appropriate but the Chancellor was alternately afraid of doing too much and too little. In the end it was an expansionary budget with reductions in taxation totalling about £350 million, which was more than Hall wished; he thought the economy could stand it but he wanted to go more gently.[7] It was, of course, to be an election year, which no doubt had some influence on the Chancellor and the Prime Minister.

Hall turned his attention to the prospects for the 1959 wage round, circulating yet another paper. Persuaded by Hall, the Chancellor then used the 2½ per cent 'guiding light' in a private meeting with city editors and hinted at it in both his Mansion House speech and his speech on the address. However, ministers then started to question the idea of linking wages with productivity, so that Hall almost despaired that they had become thoroughly confused. He spent some time together with Downie and Hopkin drafting a statement that might be made on wages, if ever it was agreed to try out the 'guiding light'.

He watched the economic situation closely throughout the year. A mid-term assessment showed that the situation was more inflationary than it had been in March and one worry was a sharp increase in bank advances, which were up by about a third on the year, for reasons not fully explained by the Bank of England. In a report to the Chancellor, Hall drew attention to the rise as one doubtful area. The election, which was held in October 1959, gave a further boost to confidence and led to a stock exchange boom. There was an increase in imports and the reserves fell, but the Prime Minister, Macmillan, would not allow any action which might check the recovery in investment.

It was not until early in 1960 that it became clear from the statistics that the general outlook appeared a good deal more inflationary than it had seemed three months earlier. In addition to a rise in Bank Rate, Hall advocated an increase in taxes in the budget, together with a curbing of bank advances. The Prime Minister disliked this advice, commenting that, following the 1959 budget and the election, a deflationary budget in 1960 would be 'either very foolish or very dishonest'. The Chancellor should therefore consider a standstill budget and, if deflationary measures were needed, the obvious weapon to use was 'special deposits' and 'if you like add hire-purchase to taste'. The Prime Minister had his way and the net tax change in the budget was negligible.[8]

Hall's view was expressed in a memorandum for a meeting of ministers. 'It seems to me that the Chancellor's colleagues would be taking a grave responsibility if they overrode his judgment on the situation. The Prime Minister said that if there was a strain on the reserves we could use them and borrow. This is all right if the situation would correct itself or if we were taking corrective action; not otherwise.' Hall's analysis proved sound. As subsequent statistics became available, they confirmed his view that the budget should have been less expansionary. It became necessary to introduce special deposits and further controls over hire-purchase terms. Hall drafted another statement for the Chancellor in case it was ever agreed to try out the 'guiding light' on wage increases. The new Permanent Secretary of the Treasury, Frank Lee, whom Hall had known since his Washington days, was finding out how difficult it was to get enough deflation to ensure steady prices, and he had become more interested in a wages policy.

Although, for most of the 1950s, Hall had found unhelpful the continued harping by the Bank of England on a reduction in public expenditure as the only way to cure inflation, he himself thought it was growing too fast. He came to realise that the pressure to increase it was very strong under Tory as well as Labour governments and concluded that better methods of control were needed. The existing system encouraged ministers to think only of spending by their own department, leaving the Chancellor to struggle with the aggregates and their implications for the whole economy. There was also always a delay in implementing decisions to alter spending, which made it an inefficient instrument for use in demand management.

There were several attempts to improve the methods of controlling government expenditure, but none of them were particularly effective. In 1959, a committee was set up under the chairmanship of Plowden to review the principles which governed the control by the executive of public expenditure. Plowden only agreed to chair it provided that Hall was a member. When it reported in 1961, it recommended that there should be regular ministerial appraisals of public expenditure as a whole, in relation to prospective resources, over a number of years ahead so that limits could be laid down well in advance; and that decisions once taken, should be observed. It argued that as far as possible short-term changes in public expenditure should not be used as an instrument of stabilisation policy. As a result, an official committee was set up to make regular surveys and forecasts for expenditure planning.[9] On the whole these recommendations reflected Hall's views, though he considered that room should be left for variations in public investment as an instrument for the control of economic conditions.

In July 1960 there was another new Chancellor, the fourth in five years. Selwyn Lloyd took inflation seriously and was a believer in incomes policy. He inaugurated a series of experiments. In 1961 he called for a temporary pause in pay increases while a more durable policy was worked out. He imposed the pay pause on wage increases in the public sector in the hope that the private sector would follow suit. Unfortunately the pay pause turned out to be a prolonged and rather ragged battle, with ground being gained in some sectors and lost in others.[10] During the pause the government, and the Prime Minister in particular, wrestled with the problem of providing a more permanent machinery. The policy which eventually emerged was on the lines proposed by Hall. It had three main constituents: a 'norm', a set of criteria by which wage claims were to be judged, and an independent body to pass judgments on particular cases. This institutional framework remained more or less unaltered until 1970.

Hall had retired from the Treasury in the April before Selwyn Lloyd introduced the pay pause in 1961. He was in an optimistic frame of mind about action on an incomes policy when he retired. He thought that by this time a large body of opinion was in favour of some form of incomes restraint, as an alternative to leaving incomes to free collective bargaining; and continued to believe it necessary if full employment and stable prices were to be combined. He was optimistic enough to think there would be some action under his successor.

One reason for Hall's lack of success on this issue was perhaps the lack of enthusiasm for it among officials in the Treasury. Towards the end of the 1950s, the Permanent Secretary was Frank Lee who was at heart a market man. Then the official Ministry of Labour hated the idea of interference in the wage process, because they thought it too complicated. If Plowden had still been in the Treasury, the powerful Plowden/Hall team might have won the day, and some machinery might have been set up, with sanctions as one of its features, but this is doubtful. By the time Plowden left Whitehall late in 1953, Hall was very much in the inner circle of policymaking. He no longer needed Plowden to help his cause and could achieve his objectives successfully on his own. However, persuading ministers to adopt a different approach on pay and prices was a very different order of problem from persuading them to adopt a particular macroeconomic policy. What Hall was seeking was a fundamental change in institutional arrangements, because he felt it must be wrong to have to deliberately engineer a recession in order to tame inflation. However this involved trying to alter long established attitudes, and persuading a very large number of independent decision makers to alter their behaviour, not necessarily in their own interests. The Conservative governments he served could easily have been accused of doing down the working class by urging wage restraint. For Labour governments, a pay policy was a contradiction of the role of the trade unions to get the best bargain for their members.

Some might argue that on this subject Hall misjudged the political possibilities and others would reason that it would not have worked even if it had been tried. Hall, however, refused to accept that it was beyond the wit of man to devise, or beyond the collective good sense of the nation to accept, a change in arrangements which would allow continued prosperity, without unacceptable levels of inflation. He knew the problem was not going to go away just because governments found it so difficult to arrive at a solution. Nevertheless, prompted by Hall's persistent efforts, the Conservative governments of the 1950s and early 1960s did make a number of sincere attempts to work out a way of moderating wage increases other than by deflating the economy. Hall felt that these were better than doing nothing. Slowing down the rate of inflation, even if only temporary in its effects, could have been helpful both at that time and for the future and might have made it easier to manage Britain's later difficulties more successfully. It was a serious policy, but never seriously enough applied to test it adequately. The 1960s experiments begun by Selwyn Lloyd were the most earnest attempts along the lines that Hall wanted, but in fact no progress was made towards any permanent modification of free collective bargaining. Hall continued to write on the subject after he left the government service and spoke a number of times on it in House of Lords debates.

CHAPTER FOURTEEN

International Economic Cooperation

Hall's role has so far been described mainly in terms of matters relating to developments within the British economy but he always had in mind the importance to Britain of developments in the world economy. He had lived through the recession of the 1930s and did not forget the effect a depression in the United States could have on the rest of the world. Moreover time had not stood still in Europe and Hall played a part in, or advised on, a number of events there. It is to international affairs that we turn in this chapter.

While Hall was in Whitehall, there were a number of exciting developments in international economic cooperation. Some of these had begun during the war or were a consequence of the war. In Europe the distribution of Marshall Aid and its consequences for European recovery provided a great boost to a new kind of European cooperation. There was the establishment of the European Economic Community, and the attempt to set up a rival Free Trade Area. As these new European institutions took shape, the British attitude was one of ambiguity, drawn as they were towards the special relationship with the United States and the belief that Britain was still an independent world power. In the United States there were the regular contacts which Britain regarded as part of the 'special relationship' between the two countries, while in the Commonwealth there were the attempts to hold the countries together through the formal conferences of economics ministers and finance ministers. In all these developments Hall, an Australian, as the senior economist in a civil service still with little macroeconomic expertise, and one who had been in close contact with the Americans during the war, played an important role.

In the early years Hall attended a few United Nations meetings and commodity study groups, but gradually these ceased to command his attention, though he continued to send a member of his staff to meetings of the Economic and Social Council and the Economic Commission for Europe. The developments in Europe and the United States also had implications for the organisation of work in Whitehall. More staff with some economic training were needed abroad and new committees were set up which absorbed a lot of time and energy both of Hall and his staff.

At the end of the war, the relationship between the United States and Britain was thought to be strong. The United States Administration was fully aware how much Britain had been weakened by the war, even though Congress probably had no real perception of it. As a result of the disruption in Europe and large parts of Asia, the rest of the world was abnormally dependent on the western hemisphere which had escaped the devastation of the war. Britain too was heavily dependent on the United States and hoped to remain the partner she had been during the war.

The belief that the Americans were still close allies suffered a series of setbacks, however, beginning with the abrupt ending of lend-lease. Confidence was further shaken by the stiff conditions imposed on the Anglo-American loan in 1945. The apparently generous offer of Marshall Aid swept away these doubts for a time, although it was clear that the territorial ambitions of the Soviet Union were not far from the minds of the State Department and the Congressmen who voted the funds. When Hall arrived in the Economic Section in 1947, it was gradually becoming apparent that the Americans had decided that a more integrated Europe would be better able to resist the threat of communism – as well as a third world war of their own making – and they appeared to be making efforts to push Britain into Europe, thus conflicting with Britain's own illusions that she was still a world power.

The immediate postwar period saw the beginnings of developments which were to draw the European nations into closer cooperation. This was something new in European history and in part the result of the two world wars which had both begun in Europe. Although the ultimate purpose of cooperation was political, its content was primarily economic. Hence the Treasury and the other economic departments in Whitehall were involved as much or more than the Foreign Office. It was therefore natural that the government economists should play a major role in developments as well as the established civil service. Hall became closely involved in these developments at an early stage, first through the distribution of Marshall Aid and then in advising the government on the economic consequences of the moves towards an Economic Community, beginning with the Schuman Plan.

In his first few years in the Section, Hall was deeply engaged in the affairs of the Organisation for European Economic Cooperation and British policy towards Europe. He was in Paris in the summer of 1948, helping Marjolin of France and Hammarskjold of Sweden in the first preparatory stage of the recovery plan to be submitted before Marshall Aid would flow. He was there again in the autumn to decide what to do about the replies to the questionnaire that had been sent to recipient countries. The need for a continuing organisation to progress the recovery programme, distribute the aid and foster cooperation had led earlier in the year to the establishment of this new organisation (the OEEC). At its head was a Council of Ministers, chaired by Spaak of Belgium and an Executive Committee chaired by Edmund Hall-Patch from the British Foreign Office. The Secretary General was the Frenchman, Robert Marjolin. A number of vertical committees were set up concerned with particular commodities or sectors of industry and there were a number of horizontal committees: on the balance of payments, inter-European payments, manpower and programmes. From the start therefore it was an elaborate organisation and throughout the succeeding years provided an area of increasing and effective liberalism in the world, when its original function of distributing Marshall Aid had ceased.[1]

The OEEC's aims were immediate and practical: European reconstruction, the efficient use of American aid, the progressive dismantling of protective barriers to trade and the eventual abolition of discrimination against the dollar. It led to a strengthening of the European economies. As such it was of immediate concern to Hall who, in addition to his own involvement, released a succession of members of his staff in turn to provide assistance with the reports and then others on loan to the organisation for a year. Members of the section also attended the committees and the country examinations from time to time.

   Throughout the 1950s, Hall continued to be very much concerned
with the developments in Paris at the OEEC. The success of
Britain's full employment policy was helped a good deal by the
increasing European prosperity over which the OEEC presided and
the economic collaboration which evolved there. Broad responsibility for their economies had been generally accepted by the
Western industrial countries, although there were some differences
of opinion about the relative importance of stable employment and
stable prices, as well as about the obligations of countries to one
another. The International Monetary Fund, after a brief flurry of
activity in 1946–7, was virtually out of the scene as long as incon-
vertibility lasted, and so was more or less inactive in the first half of
the 1950s. The scarce currency clause, which permitted the use of
import restrictions against a country whose currency was technically scarce, could not be invoked because the United States took
care to ensure that the fund was never short of dollars, while access to the resources of the fund was subject to very stiff conditions.
So far as the early postwar years were concerned, the fund might as
well not have been created. In these circumstances the focus of attention switched to the OEEC and it became the practice to discuss
macroeconomic problems amongst the industrial countries within
the OEEC. This body soon acquired a first class economic and statistical division in its secretariat, which gained the confidence of the
civil servants in member countries who provided most of the statistics and their own assessments of the outlook. Such a division,
collecting and grouping the statistics of sixteen West European countries to give a regional picture, was something new. It strengthened
the secretariat and provided both an overall appraisal and individual assessments which greatly assisted the discussions of the
committees. These assessments were used in the procedure under
which the countries submitted to mutual criticism in the light of the
wider objectives.
   Western European countries recovered quickly with the help of
Marshall Aid and, when it ceased in 1952, the OEEC became more
rather than less important. In 1960 its scope was enlarged by the
inclusion of the United States and Canada as full members and its
name was changed to the Organisation for Economic Cooperation
and Development (OECD). This was for potential donors of development aid and allowed for other industrial countries to be invited

to join. In practice, development was less important than the regular discussions on the world economic situation in a well-informed and reasonably confidential environment. The working parties filled the gap left by the inadequate coverage of the United Nations.

In 1954 Hall became the Chairman of the Group of Economic Experts which met regularly. He saw the meetings of this group as something quite exceptional for economists and something new in the history of the world. Their novelty lay in the smallness of the group and its informality. It was a high-level group; its seven, eight or nine members by and large were the chief professional advisers of the main Western governments. They all had the same sense of responsibility towards the presentation of facts about their countries and they all had similar professional training, in that they understood the forces operating upon the level of activity and the problems involved in maintaining it. They could discuss the economic outlook without committing their ministers. Hall valued these meetings which gave him a quick picture of developments in Europe and provided a forum for an exchange of views about such problems as inflation, the German balance of payments surplus, international liquidity, and the problems of the primary producers. Hall felt that the OEEC was doing the sort of job that the United Nations could not do.[2]

It was more than eleven years after Hall left the Treasury that Britain became a member of the European Community, but he had taken part in some of the postwar developments in European integration which led up to its establishment in 1958, and especially in the working out of alternative proposals for a European Free Trade Area, in the late 1950s.

European integration had begun in 1940 with Jean Monnet's idea that a union of France and Britain might avert the collapse of France and, although this did not succeed, Monnet's ideas became the basis of the movement towards European unity after the war. Monnet had been at the League of Nations in the 1920s and 1930s and during the war he was a member of the British Supply Council in Washington, where he and Hall had met. In 1946 he became head of the plan for the modernisation and equipment of France – *Le Plan*. Monnet's ideas had been given a boost by Churchill's speeches in 1946 when he was in opposition. At Fulton, Missouri and then in Switzerland, Churchill made an emotional appeal for a United States of Europe and a first practical step was taken with the formation of the Council of Europe in 1949. The British Foreign Office did not approve of these moves which it thought might prove embarrassing if they led the Europeans to think that Britain itself was to be part of this unity on the continent.

A separate strand in the story began with early initiatives by Ernest Bevin and the Foreign Office in January 1948. Believing that Russia wished to dominate the whole of Europe, the Foreign Office advocated the drawing together of the Western democracies to prevent such a disaster. Two months later the objectives were embodied in the Brussels Pact. This was a fifty-year pact of mutual aid and defence against any aggressor, between Britain, France and the Benelux countries. Permanent consultative machinery was set up as part of this crusade against communism. About a year later this led to the North Atlantic Treaty Organisation (NATO) in which the United States and Canada joined as well as other European states. This was strongly supported by Attlee and Bevin, in contrast to their former reluctance to becoming too closely connected with the Council of Europe.

Hall was disturbed by the negative attitude of the Treasury to Europe; it was not just neutral, but tended to be anti-European. He sensed that there were political interests in collaboration and perhaps, though he was less clear about this, economic interests as well. In the spring of 1949, Hall, Plowden and Hitchman (also of the Treasury) spent four days in Paris having talks with Monnet. Most of the economic problems of each country were explored, Monnet making suggestions for some form of cooperation which would catch the imagination of the American Economic Cooperation Administration – the ECA – and the French and British people. German recovery was getting under way and there was always a continuing fear of what the consequences would be when Germany's potential to make war was restored. Hall did not think that much progress was made at these talks, as the discussion was in very general terms. He thought about it all again from time to time and applied his mind in particular to Germany, searching to identify things that Britain, France, Germany and the other OEEC countries needed to do jointly. Monnet himself remained rather gloomy about the possibility of including Germany, taking the view that neither

Britain nor France really had any idea what could be done about that country, while there was a great need there and then for good Anglo-French understanding.

Britain, however, remained unenthusiastic and early in 1950 Monnet turned to West Germany instead, producing a scheme for integrating French coal and iron and steel industries with those of the Germans – the Schuman Plan. This plan was supported by the French Foreign Minister and the German Chancellor and was announced to the world in May 1950. Franco-German production of coal and steel was to be placed under a joint High Authority. It was open to other countries to join. At first this was cautiously welcomed by the Foreign Office and the defence departments, but its reception by the economic departments, especially the Ministry of Fuel and Power, was rather chilly.

Hall and Plowden were convinced by Monnet that Britain ought to back the scheme and to join if the conditions were suitable.[3] Their stern resolve to persuade ministers of this was scarcely needed, as ministers themselves decided on more or less the same line. Unfortunately things did not work out that way, because Monnet decided that agreement to join must come first, with the details being worked out afterwards by experts. Otherwise, he argued, its adoption would founder on the details. Hall would probably have gone along with this, feeling that whatever the economic disadvantages they were nothing compared to the possible political gains. At this stage he was mainly concerned that the economic advantages should not be exaggerated. However ministers could not accept the surrender of sovereignty in this way, committing the country irrevocably to Europe, unless the extent of the commitment could be measured. Britain delayed her reply while assessing the pros and cons. The French became impatient and, in effect, issued an ultimatum. This was communicated on 1 June and required an answer the next day, which led to Britain's refusal to join. The Europeans were not going to wait. Relations were changing rapidly and they gave up counting on British leadership. The Coal and Steel Community was thus set up without Britain.[4]

Hall accepted that the Schuman Plan was rejected by Britain because the Labour government did not wish to be as closely knit to continental Europe as the plan implied. Attlee and most of the Labour leaders were functionalist rather than federalist in their approach to European unity. Attlee wrote that as a general proposition he thought closer cooperation was desirable, but he recognised the practical difficulties and commented that Britain could not enter engagements to the full extent possible to the continental powers. Gaitskell, then Minister of Fuel and Power, did not think it was in Britain's interest to join, because she had more and better coal than the other countries. The Treasury, representing the economic side, recommended that Britain should not join, but should establish close relations with those running the plan. In fact Britain had a strong team sitting in on all the negotiations leading to the 1952 Treaty of Association.

From his various talks with ministers, Hall understood that the Cabinet was still thinking in terms of the British and Americans having won the war; and they were still hoping that Britain would remain the partner she had been then. Ministers remained conscious that Britain's main interests lay outside Europe and so dragged their feet on moves towards European integration. Arrangements like the Coal and Steel Community were suitable for continental Europe, but would interfere with Britain's independence and her world role. As late as 1962 Gaitskell said that to have joined would have meant turning our backs on a thousand years of history. Not unnaturally Hall, as an Australian, did not go along with that, but he recognised that a lot of people felt that way and he certainly did not believe in trying to argue about it with ministers who were opposed to it, when the economic benefits were not obvious.

At the start of the discussions on European integration, most civil servants saw immense difficulties in carrying through a scheme like the Schuman Plan and Hall shared this view. He was not surprised when the government refused to accept the plan before any details were worked out. When the French decided to go ahead without the British, Hall saw no option but to wish them luck. He took the view that, at least in theory, most of the potential advantages of integration were obtainable anyway by an advanced economy the size of Britain, provided international trade was free enough to exploit them. He thought that if British firms had the will to do so, it was open to them to take advantage of greater competition; and an incentive in the form of European integration would be no more likely to stir them up. He was not therefore very perturbed when the government refused to join the Schuman Plan. At that time he thought that the British economy would probably benefit more from closer cooperation with complementary economies rather than with European ones, which were so like Britain in many respects.

The change in government and Churchill's return to power in 1951 was hailed in Europe as likely to mark a new approach to European questions. Churchill was the figurehead of the so-called European Movement and he had lent his immense prestige to the founding of the Council of Europe in 1949. He wanted to play a part in uniting Europe, and he was impressed by the arguments of the federalists like Monnet and Spaak; but he never saw Britain itself as part of a federal Europe. When the Conservative Cabinet reconsidered participation in the Schuman Plan, therefore, it was again rejected. Hall at this time was too taken up with domestic matters to be closely involved in the work on these European matters.

During 1951, Hall had a talk with Marjolin, the Secretary General of the OEEC, and he agreed with him that there were various things that needed attention in Europe, which might be approached jointly. These included tax reforms, the control of inflation and the introduction of a number of social reforms. But Hall and his staff were busy on more immediate problems and were unable to devote as much time as they would have liked to the longer-term issues.

The most important of all postwar events which was to dictate Britain's destiny was soon to come. This was a meeting which took place in Messina in Sicily in 1955. It was here that the foreign ministers of the six countries, which had tried but failed to establish the European Defence Community with an integrated European army, met to explore a new direction for European unity. They issued an invitation to Britain to take part on any terms and conditions she wished. One suggestion put forward was the formation of a European common market. Hall and Little prepared an analysis which found comparatively little gain or loss in economic terms, a conclusion which led to the comment that Hall thought the economic arguments were about fifty-fifty.[5]

However, Hall did advise that access to a larger market was bound to be of some real value. In the first place, his experience through those years gradually convinced him that there was not much prospect that there would be a successful attack on the things which were wrong with the British economy. These included the slowness of industrialists to adopt the most up-to-date methods, the general resistance by both sides of industry to improving productivity and the trade union pressure for wage increases which were in fact inflationary. He began to believe that younger people might be more adventurous in the context of a common European market.

He became convinced that it would be easier to bring about a successful policy for stable prices and solve the balance of payments problem if Britain could secure a faster rate of economic growth. Hall was one of a number of people who had been brooding for some time about the causes of growth and the part that the government could play in helping to accelerate it. The Labour government of 1945–51 had been interested in planning for growth, setting up the Economic Planning Board with membership to include government, employers and trade unionists, and Stafford Cripps had run a campaign for higher productivity. These efforts had not had much success. The Conservative governments of the 1950s were less interested and the Planning Board fell into disuse.

Hall perceived that it was not changes in industrial structure that were needed, so much as a shift from the less efficient to the more efficient units right across the board. The need to quicken the pace of industry generally appeared to be a stronger argument for entering a common market than that drawn from an increase in the international division of labour itself.

Secondly he gradually came to the conclusion that there was little hope of making rapid progress, either to a worldwide elimination of tariffs, or to closer trading arrangements with the Commonwealth. Nearly all the Commonwealth countries were protecting their own industries against Britain. He still thought that the less developed countries needed the protection of commodity agreements, as well as continuing aid, and access to the American and European markets for their newer manufactures. But these were all matters which could only be sorted out in an international context and if Britain really wished to take part, she could do it better inside a common market than she could outside it. All this meant that he became more sympathetic to Britain joining the European Community. However, because he knew that what Monnet really wanted was a political pact, he felt that it was up to ministers to tell their official advisers what their 'political will' was; they would then operate within that framework.

However, complacency had set in in London and in particular

at the Foreign Office, where Eden – who had succeeded Churchill as Prime Minister – was advised to decline even to send a
representative to Messina lest this raised hopes that Britain did not
intend to fulfil. The six governments were France, Germany, Italy,
Holland, Belgium and Luxembourg, and it was the Belgians and the
Dutch who had wanted the door to remain open for Britain. Unlike
the preconditions of commitment with which Britain was confronted
over the Schuman Plan five years earlier, there were none in the
Messina invitation. There was therefore much less reason to refuse
it. The treaty was drafted at Messina without British involvement.
There followed six months during which the so-called Spaak committees worked out the design for what became the Common Market. From July to November when the committees were working
away in Brussels, the British sent Bretherton, who had been a Deputy
Director of the Economic Section under Robert Hall from 1949 to
1951 and was now an Under Secretary at the Board of Trade, as
a representative.[6]

Hall played little part in the discussions and briefings on Messina
and the events in Brussels. He did however attend a meeting of officials in October that recommended that the United Kingdom should
not join the Common Market. But he was not at the meeting of the
Economic Steering Committee which discussed the subject, and
not present at informal meetings held by Clarke on a fresh initiative.[7] Having observed the extent of ministerial opposition, he did
not devote too much time to the subject, when more immediate
problems were demanding his attention. Butler was convinced
that Britain should not join, at any rate for some time to come.
Churchill wished to keep out of the far-reaching schemes of Brussels,
while Macmillan was also opposed to it in 1955; he thought it
would fail to strengthen Europe, undermine the future of European cooperation and set up a discriminatory bloc which would be
contrary to Britain's own interests. Thorneycroft, then President of
the Board of Trade was also against it.[8]

Bretherton's brief was to be helpful, but to make no commitment. The Foreign Office thought little would happen in Brussels.
But Bretherton's advice that the chances of an agreement were
greater than ministers thought led to a change of attitude. A study
was laid on in London of the economic advantages of joining in
with a customs union, and the disadvantages that might follow if

there were one of which Britain was not a member. The study, in which the Economic Section took part, concluded that, while it was probable that Britain would gain from going in, the balance of economic advantage was insufficient to compel any rethinking of the policy that had already been decided.[9] Hall himself stood by his view that the issue should be decided on political rather than economic grounds.

After the series of meetings in Brussels came to an end in November, the negotiations took a different form. Only a small group, consisting of the heads of delegations and one expert each, varying according to the topic under discussion, was to be present. On this arrangement the British delegate could not take part with the instructions he had been given and he therefore withdrew. The subsequent negotiations were often on the brink of failure, but determination eventually led to success and the Treaty of Rome was ready in May 1957.

Well before the Treaty of Rome was ready, it had become clear that the negotiations were probably going to be successful and it therefore became essential for Britain to work out a policy towards this new institution. Officials, including Hall, became busy with what was known as Plan G, a British proposal for a free trade area which would embrace both the Six and the rest of the OEEC countries in Europe. The proposal was confined to manufactured goods and excluded all agricultural products. The aim was to reconcile free entry for Commonwealth food and raw materials into Britain with the preservation of access to European markets for British manufactures. The general Whitehall view, with which Hall agreed, was that the changes that this scheme would promote were very like changes that the British economy needed anyway. Under this plan, they would all be made that bit more quickly and on a slightly larger scale. One implication was that there would be no way of sheltering a particular industry by tariffs. Hall also sensed that the political consequences of closer relations with Europe and looser ones with the Commonwealth would be acceptable to ministers, because by this time the ties between Britain and the Commonwealth were loosening anyway.[10]

Nevertheless, it was clear that there might be trouble when the scheme was disclosed to the Commonwealth, the Tory Party and Parliament. A first discussion with the Commonwealth took place at the Bank/Fund meetings in Washington while Hall was there. He gained the impression that no one there was in a position to react one way or another. There was intense interest back in London and in the press generally and it became known that Macmillan, by this time Chancellor of the Exchequer, supported it.

However, early in 1957, the proposed free trade area ran into difficulties because the French had persuaded the Messina countries to include their colonies on a preferential basis, so that their exports to the Common Market would have preference over competing products from other countries. This would be a blow to some members of the Commonwealth and to the British colonies. In spite of this, a European free trade area (EFTA as it became known) was still thought to be the best guarantee against any excesses by the Six. There followed attempts to sell the idea to the Commonwealth and Hall took part in these.

The EFTA negotiations were suspended in 1958, after French officials declared their opposition to it, reasoning that members of the French Assembly would be able to claim that their government would be committing itself to another treaty which gave fewer safeguards than the Treaty of Rome. In addition they might argue that it would endanger the ratification of the Treaty of Rome. Things were in rather a mess, but Hall did not find the skirmishes very interesting and predicted that some compromise would be reached eventually. In 1959 a separate smaller EFTA was established with the Scandinavians, Switzerland and Austria. It became a purely commercial arrangement, establishing free trade in industrial goods between the parties, but allowing existing tariffs to stand against other countries.

Following the failure to interest the Common Market countries in the EFTA, the British government reconsidered their attitude to the Common Market. Officials advised that in the new circumstances there were strong foreign policy reasons for joining. Inside the Community, influence in world affairs would be enhanced as the right to speak independently would be retained to some degree as well as being part of a bloc. On the economic side, there now seemed to be some grounds for hoping that commerce and industry would benefit and there would be gains from large-scale production, specialisation and higher efficiency; but these would only be achieved if Britain was fully competitive and maintained appropriate policies at home. It was emphasised that joining the Community meant accepting the institutional arrangements and joining in any developments towards closer political integration.

Before Hall left the Treasury, in the spring of 1961, he had a talk with Macmillan, then Prime Minister, about the European question. He pointed out that the original drive towards integration had been political and Britain had rejected membership on political grounds. At an early stage Hall had been sympathetic to the idea, seeing it as the best safeguard against future wars in Europe. Believing that nationalism was the curse of the age, he reasoned, like Monnet, that if the parts were so scrambled together, the countries would not be able to disentangle themselves sufficiently to go to war with one another. As the ultimate object was political unity, he always felt that the economic issues should be kept in perspective and argued that what the country could afford as the costs of entry depended to a large extent on the value that was placed on this wider objective. So he felt that fears about the cost of living, or the effects on agriculture and the balance of payments, should not be the deciding factor. In the case of the balance of payments, he thought even a small improvement in Britain's growth rate would outweigh the costs of entry. He advised Macmillan that it was unlikely that Britain could enter the Common Market on any special terms but that, if the government were willing to accept the political implications, some compromise should be possible on the two major difficulties – namely Commonwealth free entry and the British system of agricultural support. This time he was over-optimistic. It was to be another twelve years before Britain entered the Common Market and she then had to accept major changes in her arrangements on both these issues.

Throughout these events in Europe, Britain attempted to keep alive the special relationships with the United States and the Commonwealth. Labour and Tory governments were both motivated mainly by political considerations and the desire to maintain British prestige as a world power; but it was the economic relationships which interested Hall. Although the wide issue of relations with other countries was primarily the responsibility of the Foreign Office, that body had no economists and Hall was not satisfied that they could keep him well enough informed about the economic situation in the United States – at that time by far the most important foreign influence on Britain. At that time Britain still retained some political strength, though economically very weak and heavily dependent on the United States.

Hall therefore continued to visit Washington at least twice a year, meeting the officials in the United States Treasury and the Council of Economic Advisers. He also made friends at the Federal Reserve Board and the Federal Reserve Bank of New York. In this way he found out at first hand the views and expectations of those at the centre of affairs, so that his advice to the Chancellor could reflect any changes in the situation very quickly. At the same time he was able to provide to the Americans an up-to-date assessment of the situation at home which was greatly appreciated, many of them feeling that they obtained a much better understanding from him than from their other sources of information, as Hall always had the whole situation at his fingertips. He had a large circle of friends and was in great demand when he visited there. There were a large number of economists in the Administration and many welcomed a talk with him. Among his friends were the Alsops, Joe and Stuart, who were political commentators and authors of the column 'Matter of Fact' in the *New York Herald Tribune*. They and a number of their friends, including Paul Nitze of the State Department and Bill Martin of the Federal Reserve Board, dined together on Sunday evenings. Hall was invited when he was in Washington. He had many helpful discussions about Britain's problems and returned refreshed to deal with them.

Although gradually coming to accept that Britain should join the Common Market, Hall was one of those who throughout the 1950s tried to keep alive the special relationship with the United States which was being gradually eroded, as it began to look as if it was only called upon when it suited the Americans. The ups and downs of this relationship, especially around the time of the Korean War, did not mar Hall's relations with his friends there.

On his travels Hall also came into contact with many policymakers and advisers in the Commonwealth countries and many of them also visited him in London. His visits to those countries were rarer than to Europe and the United States, but he attended Bank/Fund and Commonwealth conferences and he kept in touch especially with Canadian and Australian developments. He visited Australia twice – in 1954 and 1960 – and regularly attended the Anglo-Canadian

Continuing Committee, which gave him an opportunity to discuss points of common interest. Although these trips were sometimes tiring, he found them very valuable and they gave him a breathing space from Whitehall during which he was able to stand back a little way from immediate day-to-day problems. In the late 1950s, Britain was tending to become isolated in international economic affairs. The ideas of the old Commonwealth as a free trade group based on sterling as the key currency were clearly obsolete. The older dominions were going their own way: Canada was leaning towards the United States; and Australia and New Zealand were heading in the direction of autonomy. India had become a member of the third world and the rest of the colonial empire was being dismantled.

The world was settling into groups, to none of which Britain belonged, unless one counted the EFTA, which carried no assurance of political unity and held little promise of great economic advantage. Economic forces had weakened the British position in the Commonwealth and Hall tried, in his own way, to maintain contacts in the governments and central banks in those countries and to prevent Britain's relationship with them deteriorating even further. As the only senior economist in Whitehall during these years – a situation that was to change in 1964 – he was in a unique position to play the role of roving economic ambassador. That he enjoyed doing this is clear from his diaries. The remarkable thing was that he managed to make time to do it.

CHAPTER FIFTEEN

London, Oxford and Cornwall

Hall retired from the Treasury in April 1961 when he reached the age of sixty. This was normal retiring age for civil servants, but Hall was under no compulsion to leave, because he was not an established civil servant and, as with all members of his staff other than those on secondment from other departments, he was pensioned under university arrangements, not civil service ones. He was on very good terms with the Permanent Secretary, then Frank Lee, who tried hard to persuade him not to resign, but he did not like the idea of staying on when he was aging – he had seen too many stay too long and he did not want to be one of them. He made up his mind to go while he was still wanted. Hall had been 'in post' for nearly fourteen years and he had served eight Chancellors. This was a long time in that sort of job.

Hall had no great regrets at leaving the Treasury. He had already been approached by George Cole at Unilever and Edwin Plowden at Tube Investments and after he left he became an advisory director at Unilever and an adviser at Tube Investments. He had made many links with business throughout his career and he thought that one of the main uses of the professional economist to businessmen was to present them with a coherent view of general economic developments, something he was accustomed to doing for the government.

Hall had always enjoyed the mixture of life in London and Oxford, so that he was pleased to be able to continue this with jobs that would demand his presence in London two or three days a week. He therefore spent nearly as much time in London as he had before. He was able to boast to his sister that he had no less than three offices and could call on three secretaries. Margaret was spending some time as a visiting professor at the Massachusetts Institute of Technology, so that Hall's weekends in Oxford were mainly to look after the garden and allotment. He did not find the advisory posts very demanding and he enjoyed the contacts. He was clearly very useful to the companies. Ernest Woodroofe, then the Deputy Chairman of Unilever, described Hall's role as very much that of an elder statesman.

He was meticulous about attending Unilever Board meetings and was a regular contributor. Drawing on his wealth of experience and his innate wisdom, he gave us his interpretation of political and economic developments throughout the world, but particularly in the United Kingdom, and the significance for Unilever. He did not confine himself to these spheres, but undoubtedly this was his major contribution. In order to review major policies, the Unilever Board took itself off for a long weekend every eighteen months to some place in the Netherlands or Britain, away from the distraction of the telephone and day-to-day responsibil-ities. These were, and still are, occasions when the advisory directors made a major input to the thinking of Unilever. Robert Hall was always very much on the ball at these discussions.[1]

Hall's role at Tube Investments was slightly different in that he was not formally a member of the Board, but did attend Board lunches. His advice was more often given directly to Plowden, the Chairman, who discussed many matters with him. One of his main recommendations was that the cycle division should be sold off, and so it was, to the benefit of the company.[2]

On his departure from the Treasury, Hall had time to do some writing. *The Economist* invited him to write two articles on a subject of his choice and he took the opportunity to write on Britain's economic problem. This he identified as 'to combine price stability, or at any rate as much price stability as is enjoyed by our competitors, with a high level of employment'. He pointed out that for short periods in 1950, in 1953–4 and in 1958–9, this had seemed to be within our reach. But all hopes proved illusory. In advocating a rational policy for prices he set out two targets. The first was a determination by governments to avoid the temptation to overload the economy, as a result of the relentless pressures to increase government expenditure and to reduce taxation. The second target should be a clear statement about the rate of increase in money wages which would be consistent with reasonably stable prices. In elaborating on the conditions necessary for a successful policy, he proceeded to a study of the need for a faster rate of growth. Parts of the articles seem rather dated thirty years later, for example on the hoarding of labour and over-full employment, but his conclusions still seem appropriate:

No one can deny that we have had rising prices, that our productivity does not increase as fast as we think it could, or that anti-social action is found in all classes of society, and not only in the privileged classes of the past. Unless we are willing to think out afresh the problems of our own day, our descendants will have to deal with them. While we wait, our weaknesses will get worse and our prospects in relation to other countries will get worse too. We do not want to be regarded as the somewhat discreditable life tenants of what we received as a great estate.[3]

Within two months of leaving the Treasury, Hall also wrote on the role of the economist in government, a subject which he had written about before on several occasions.[4] He felt there were a number of departmental problems which needed more economic analysis than they were getting and was concerned that the Economic Section was not big enough. It had always been short-handed, in the sense that it could have used more people if it had them. Hall observed that, by the time he left, the original prejudice in the Treasury against economists was much less than it was when he arrived but there was still some prejudice in the Establishment Division and also in the First Division Association (the trade union of top civil servants) against improving the tenure or pay of economists and against giving them posts which would block promotion for the administrative grade.

Hall advised a more attractive structure, with some senior economic posts in several departments and better pay and prospects. He thought it would be best to begin by enlarging the Economic Section, since the training there was very good. Then there could be more interchange between departments. In addition, the system of secondments from universities which Hall had fostered should be encouraged. There were two further recommendations. First the Economic Adviser should be given a general responsibility for economists in the public service, not for hiring and firing, but the right and duty to keep in touch with them. Secondly, a fairly senior government economist should have a definite responsibility to study and supervise staffing problems. Hall's ideas eventually emerged with the creation of the Government Economic Service. But he did not foresee the size of the expansion in the number of economists which took place after 1964, when the new Labour ministers recruited large numbers of economists to their own departments and a new department of Economic Affairs was created. Although that Department only lasted about five years, by and large the increase in economists has remained as part of the civil service.

At about the same time he wrote a more general note on the organisation of the civil service and its responsibilities, which commented on a proposal to introduce 'project directors', in order to strengthen the civil service. Hall concluded that there would be an undoubted advantage in bringing in men and women of proven ability to work in Whitehall, subject to certain limitations. But he felt that the real threat to efficiency in government was not the civil service system, nor its members, nor its lack of experts or lack of knowledge. Rather it was the inability or unwillingness of ministers, often for wholly understandable political reasons, to take the necessary hard political decisions. It was an illusion to think that in the British political system more experts or better information were a substitute for political decisiveness, judgment and courage.[5]

Throughout 1961–2, Hall remained a member of a number of public committees, including the Plowden Committee on public expenditure which reported in July 1961, and a working party on the economy of Northern Ireland. He was also a part-time Economic Adviser to the Ministry of Transport until 1964. He spent a lot of time too responding to appeals for comments on writings by others and, when asked, providing ideas and briefs for politicians.

Outside Whitehall, the National Institute of Economic and Social Research became a greater interest for Hall when he was invited to be the Chairman in 1963. His support for the work of the Institute had originated several years earlier. In the 1950s he was concerned that the methods and results of the macroeconomic studies in Whitehall could not be made public, so that the only criticisms of them were internal. He was conscious that, although the methods had been improved, they still suffered a good deal from lack of staff and inadequate statistics and from the need to produce the results quickly, in order to decide on the action that was needed.

Prompted by two members of his staff on leave from the Treasury – Bryan Hopkin, then Director of the National Institute and Christopher Dow, then researching there on the management of the British economy – Hall pressed the Executive Committee of the Institute to undertake the functions of a Konjunktur institute, on the model of those institutes in some other European countries. This would mean publishing regular economic analysis and forecasts, reporting periodically on the state of the economy, and, to underpin the work of the current assessments, allocating much of its resources to research into the behaviour of the economy. He convinced the Committee that a separate unofficial set of forecasts was needed to reinforce or to criticise those that were being made by his own staff. He felt that too much power was in the hands of a few civil servants, because, at that time, there was no body outside the government with the expertise to put forward a well-informed independent view on the state of the economy and its prospects.

There were many problems to be solved before the Institute could take this radical step. Money had to be raised, staff recruited and a method of work agreed. But it all went forward and the first issue of the *National Institute Economic Review* was published in January 1959. By the time Hall became Chairman of the Institute in 1963, the *Economic Review* was four years old and an established publication.[6]

Hall was an active Chairman, although it was the practice at the Institute for the Director to have a great deal of independence over the management of the research programme and for the Secretary to be in a similar position with all the business side. Hall did not interfere, but he was greatly encouraging and supportive. In addition to his interest in the economic assessments and forecasts of the Institute, he was also concerned with the other part of the research programme and produced many ideas for new projects. For example he took great interest in a series of studies on growth and wished to launch more industrial research, including a study of the effects of mergers on profitability. He also helped to publicise the Institute's work. The Institute has never had any kind of endowment and he provided advice and help with raising the necessary funds.[7]

In 1964 he took on two new tasks. First he was appointed the head of Hertford College, Oxford and secondly he served on the Franks Commission on Oxford University. He found the Franks Commission very exacting. The Commission was appointed in February 1964 and reported in March 1966. It met on 189 days, 144 of which were for private discussion and 45 were for taking oral evidence. Moreover Franks was rather a hard taskmaster and expected his members to research and write papers for him. Hall had known Franks for many years. They were contemporaries at Oxford in the 1920s, spending a holiday together at Banyuls-sur-Mer in the south of France one summer. There had been many contacts during and since the war, so Hall was prepared to make a major contribution to the Commission. His main input to the report related to the financial problems of the university.[8]

As head of Hertford College, he and his wife moved out of Banbury Road where they had lived since 1932 – apart from the war years – and into the college lodging. The only condition Hall made when he accepted the appointment was that central heating should be installed. In the short time he was the head of the college, he initiated a number of developments which raised its status. First of all, he set up a sub-committee of Fellows to consider the academic standard of their undergraduates. The Fellows accepted its recommendations about the recruitment of exceptional candidates from secondary maintained schools and subsequently resolved to encourage the entry of able candidates who lacked the full period of sixth-form education.

His other innovations related to the facilities of the college. He was very keen that the library facilities should be improved and the Fellows proceeded with a library extension and the appointment of a library clerk which they had never had. Hall also negotiated with Merton College to acquire the Bath Place site adjoining it, which enabled Hertford to build new rooms and so expand the capacity of the college. Another development while Hall was head was much appreciated by the Fellows. This was the introduction of sabbatical leave of a maximum of one year in seven.[9]

Hall resigned when his marriage ended in the second half of the 1960s, much to the regret of the Fellows who tried hard to persuade him to stay; and shortly after he and Margaret were divorced he went to Australia, visiting his sister and other relatives, and making a nostalgic trip to Silverspur. He gave a paper at a conference on economic policy arranged by the University of Queensland. His previous visit to the university had been in 1960, while still in the Treasury. This was at the time of the university's centenary celebrations, when the degree of Doctor of Science, *honoris causa,* was conferred on him. He gave the address as the 'distinguished orator'. In his vote of thanks the Vice-Chancellor commented: 'there is obviously something to be said for starting as a scientist and finally settling to be an economist by way of a study of engineering and philosophy'.[10]

In 1967 when he resigned as head of Hertford College, Hall left Oxford after the breakup of his marriage and moved to London. The following year he married Perilla Nowell-Smith. Then in 1969 he was made a life peer, taking the title of Lord Roberthall of Silverspur in Queensland and Trenance in Cornwall. Trenance was where Perilla owned a holiday cottage and where Hall set out to make a garden on a steep slope down to the shore.

During the 1970s Hall spoke in most of the economic debates in the House of Lords and in others too from time to time. Like many retired senior civil servants, he found the House of Lords an agreeable place. His most interesting interventions in the debates related to his continuing concern about incomes policy and reflected his developing views on the subject. But he also spoke in most of the economic debates and his interventions showed that he was still seeking ways of improving Britain's rate of growth. He continued an interest in European Community affairs, chairing a sub-committee on this subject and airing his doubts about the European Monetary System and the Exchange Rate Mechanism.

He supported the Counter-inflation Bill in 1973, while regretting the long delay in the conversion of the government and giving a brief resumé of the history of wage policies, emphasising the realisation, since the election of the Labour government in 1964, that some strong lead and possibly a compulsory policy was needed. Hall still thought that there were three fundamental conditions for a successful policy: the government should state a 'norm', there should be a mechanism for adjustments and, in the end, there should be some form of sanctions.

In a debate on economic policy in 1974, Hall doubted very much whether the enormous amount of writing about growth over the last thirty years added much to what was already known. He bemoaned the fact that all efforts to increase productivity had failed to achieve a higher rate of growth than the little over 3 per cent average of the 1950s. 'The most sinister thing for me was the dash for growth by Barber.' Accepting the value of more investment, better equipment, more ideas and their quicker adoption, Hall addressed himself to willingness and motivation, with illustrations from agriculture, the 1974 three-day week and education on the relationship between productivity and the national income.

In 1975 he became very gloomy and felt the country was on the brink of disaster, but by the end of the year he was more encouraged by the recent events and thought the trade unions were at last beginning to realise that power also carried with it responsibilities. When the breakdown of the Bretton Woods system with its fixed exchange rates was debated in the House of Lords at the end of 1975, Hall took the view that the strain was caused by the failure to deal with inflation; this caused rates of exchange to get out of step. After struggling for so long with devaluations, the United States finally gave up.

By 1976 Hall was arguing that any future policy must be a combination of both monetary and incomes policies. It was a great disappointment to him that incomes policies had collapsed, commenting: 'it is a sad day for me to see it, if not in ruins, in a very shaky state ... nobody knows the amount of unemployment necessary to give a particular degree of price stability ... This government has not the power to have an incomes policy and this is a great political weakness.'

Hall felt that the actions of the 1975–9 Labour government were a setback for incomes policy. He regretted the changes in the employment law in the mid-1970s which he regarded as 'a consistent tilting in the law in favour of the trade unions against employers and a change in industrial structure which has made it easier for a small number of people to inflict great damage'. He had grave doubts about a proposal that workers' representatives should join company boards on the grounds that it might give them more ammunition for use in other struggles. Moreover, he believed that the trade unions exercised their power in a way which worked to the disadvantage of workers. While he recognised that it was natural for them to use their power as hard as possible, he did not think it was necessary for the Labour government to continue to strengthen their legal position. It all made it more difficult to overcome the opposition of the unions to some form of incomes policy and it made it more difficult for managers to make changes. The TUC made admirable statements but were not able to 'deliver the goods' as a result of the new situation. The new employment acts made it even more difficult to reach agreement on an incomes policy.

By this time Hall was forced to admit that all attempts to introduce an incomes policy had not worked and he thought the government had no option but to turn to the alternative of deflating the economy to reduce inflation, although he predicted that the cost of monetary deflation would be a good deal higher than was thought at the time by the monetarists.

In the debate on the Queen's speech in November 1978, he made some apt comments on the European Monetary System which the government was contemplating joining. The comments he made would have been just as appropriate in 1992:

> I do not think it would help the EMS at all if we joined as an act of faith and were forced to leave it soon afterwards because we could not carry out the steps necessary to enable us to remain in it ... if you are committed to a fixed rate and you are not behaving in a way which will enable you to maintain it, you will get a flood of speculation against you; and you are on a hiding to nothing and will end up leaving the rate, having lost a lot of reserves and incurred a lot of debts at the same time.

The 1981 budget seemed to Hall to be an example of the 'worst kind of monetary dogmatism, looking only at a particular set of indicators which, as we know, are extremely uncertain both in their content and in their interpretation, and not looking at all at other things'. During that year, Hall joined the SDP and 'left the quiet waters of the cross benches to plunge into the turbulent ones'. He found sitting as an SDP peer and speaking for them on economic affairs more satisfying than being an independent, where there was no feeling of camaraderie and all the members reserved the right to differ as much as they pleased. As one who had spent fourteen years in government service working towards agreement on policy, he preferred to be part of a group. He explained that he could not be a real party man as he did not wish to commit himself to late nights, except on special occasions and he intended to spend half his time in Cornwall. He was accepted on this basis.[11]

Hall spoke strongly in the House of Lords against the policies of the Conservative government: 'If you wanted to argue that an incomes policy made things very much worse statistically you could put up a very good case. Now we can see that monetary policy has not worked either. It is clear that the cost of bringing down the rate of inflation ... has been very much greater than was expected.' He agreed that people who are on the verge of losing their jobs moderate their wage claims, but:

> The expectation theory behind monetary policy, so far as I can understand it, was that people would notice what was going on and would moderate their own claims. I do not think that those people who are not expecting to lose their jobs are in the least affected, even if they understand the argument, by the thought that they might be putting somebody else out of work. We now have the worst of both worlds – high unemployment and high inflation ... The objective of high employment and reasonably stable prices was a fine objective. I still believe in it. I think it is worth fighting for.

During the 1980s, Hall spent less and less time in London and more and more in Cornwall. His final contribution to a debate in the House of Lords was on monetary policy in 1986. Sarcasm was not a weapon that Hall often used, but on that occasion he did so, when he asked if we were now to accept that, since the government could no longer identify money, they had lost all control over the monetary system.

In all his speeches and lectures throughout the 1960s, 1970s and early 1980s, Hall set out his theories on the control of economic conditions, drawing on his experience, but also pressing new ideas and responding to the changing economic conditions of the 1970s and 1980s. The problem of inflation was a recurring theme. He also frequently took up the subject of economic growth, although more tentatively; he wrote about the obstacles presented by resistance to innovation by both management and labour and the problem of leadership in a community which does not seem to know what it wants – neither socialism nor capitalism. Hall's own experience with full employment led him to ask whether democracy as a form of political organisation was decadent – a painful question to one who had been fully committed to democracy as found in Britain and the old Commonwealth. He knew that whether Britain has a stable price level or an adequate growth rate are very minor matters compared to whether humanity will destroy itself with a nuclear war, be faced with mass starvation because of its inability to control the growth of population, or destroy the environment through its reckless exploitation of the world's natural resources. However, for any time horizon with which he was concerned, these questions turned on an ability to deal with political problems; he always argued that it was much easier to think of ways of bringing about a desired result if the political will was there, than it was to arrange a successful marriage between politicians and technicians and the political restraints were never far from his mind.

CHAPTER SIXTEEN

Economic Statesman

Recent years have demonstrated how difficult it is for governments to manage the economy, to maintain price stability and growth at the same time, and to manage the exchange rate and prevent a large deficit in the balance of payments. This was also true in Hall's time although the problems were different. Less was then known about the causes of rising prices, how monetary trends affected the economy, which policies could raise the level of industrial investment (to promote growth) and the factors influencing stock changes. Then, there was much greater emphasis than now on the aim of a high level of employment in a growing economy. It was accepted that the state should use its own revenue and expenditure as a balancing force, to offset either a deficiency or an excess of effective demand; but it was also expected that there would be a tendency to a deficiency of demand once the pent-up needs created by the lack of goods during the war had been satisfied.

However the expected deficiency of demand did not appear and for a number of years after the war direct controls were retained to restrain the excess demand: rationing, building licences and import restrictions were relaxed only gradually. In the event, for most of the 1950s employment tended to be too high rather than too low. In spite of this, in the years in which Hall was the government's Economic Adviser, inflation averaged only 3 per cent, the worst year being 1951 as a result of the Korean War when retail prices rose by 12 per cent; the economy grew by an average of 3 per cent a year and the balance of payments was in surplus for ten of the fourteen years with a large deficit in only two of them.[1] Hall's role in all this is not so easily identifiable as that of an academic economist who always publishes his work and advice. His work was embodied in the official machinery of the government service and at first we only heard a little about it when his name was mentioned by others in their memoirs – Butler, Jay and Macmillan. But within the last five years his own diary has been published and the public records have been released. These have enabled us to identify his role more clearly and all the evidence shows that he had great influence.

At the start of his appointment, he was not at all confident. Various aspects of the work continued to worry him throughout the fourteen years. This was not surprising; it was a very demanding job. But Hall had a satisfactory defence mechanism: when he had had enough, he took himself off to bed. Reading was a great relaxation. He once read the whole of Proust's *À la recherche du temps perdu* in French in order to take his mind off economic problems.[2] Although occasionally frustrated, he was never bored with the job. Since the 1930s, his overriding interest had been in the functions of the state and especially in the use of the state's powers to prevent a return of unemployment, which had been such a nightmare in the period before the Second World War. There could not have been a better post from which to practise this interest.

During the whole of these fourteen years 1947 to 1961, he was the only economic adviser at his level – a very different situation from that after 1964, when the Labour government brought in several others and also created the Department of Economic Affairs. Hall was involved in all aspects of economic policy, both domestic and external economic policy, and his impact and that of his Economic Section were very evident. As well as working with ministers and senior officials in all the departments, this brought him into close contact with officials in the United States and the countries of Western Europe, where he won equal esteem and respect.

One of the first challenges he faced was to discover the techniques and know-how of employment policy. He needed to find out what the actual results of applying a particular measure would be and to estimate the interval between using it and the emergence of its effects. There was no experience to help him. There had been no such policy before the war, and the theory itself had been worked out with only very simple models. He knew that the application of such a policy was also likely to run into difficulties, because both fiscal and monetary policies would have political effects. He did not know how ministers would react to these, but he was aware that they were likely to restrict the freedom to choose between the various options.

He learnt quickly and, as experience was gained, it became increasingly apparent that in the conditions of the 1950s it was comparatively easy to maintain a high level of employment. But it was much more difficult to prevent it becoming too high; and increasingly difficult and intractable problems were presented by what Hall called the side effects of the policy. In addition, as he had anticipated, politics intervened, creating complications from time to time. The most intractable problem was the rise in wage rates, both in its effects on the domestic price level and on the balance of payments. The danger of cost inflation was regularly stressed in public by government spokesmen as early as 1948. But the hope that the trade unions would cooperate in any sort of long-term policy to restrain wage increases died slowly, partly because on several occasions stability was attained for short periods by temporary pay freezes, so that the government was misled into thinking they were being successful.

The domestic political complications of policy occurred when governments wished to raise expenditure or lower taxes, at a time when the indications were that the economy was already fully extended. The most notable of these were Butler's spring 1955 budget and the 1960 one, when Macmillan ruled out a deflationary budget. However, the implications of these were relatively unimportant beside the major external political complication of the Korean War and the lesser one of the Suez invasion. The Korean War turned out to be a costly venture which temporarily upset the balance of the economy. The size of the defence programme and the deterioration of the terms of trade caused inflation. Such events complicated attempts to maintain steady growth in the level of activity. Nevertheless, the 'stops and goes' of 1947 to 1961 were relatively minor affairs.

It has been argued that the economy was run at too high a level in the 1950s. Hall's advice to ministers contained many warnings about overloading the economy but he was realistic about politics and tried not to irritate his Chancellors by continuing to give them advice they did not want and he knew they would ignore. Many of his briefs on the economic situation contained warnings about the high level of government expenditure and suggest the need for restraint in the social services and defence programmes. On the two occasions the government decided to reduce taxes, when economic trends reasoned against such a move, he was concerned that the reductions should be designed to provide incentives to industry and exports, which might at least stimulate long-term growth of the economy about which there was growing concern. However Hall was not always successful and his warnings that the economy was being driven at too high a pace were largely ignored by ministers anxious to maintain a high level of social services and a large public investment programme, together with a defence policy commensurate with Britain's role in the world, which governments still regarded as a leading one.

What Hall did achieve was the establishment of a practicable macroeconomic basis for fiscal policy. He ensured that national income analysis became the foundation of the modern budget, which was used as an instrument to maintain the balance of the economic system. It is a commonplace amongst economists that everything involves everything else; the forces of economic change are very complicated and the relationships complex. Hall succeeded in persuading ministers and senior officials that this applied to their decisions and that any action they took on one variable would have an effect on all others. The level and balance of economic activity should therefore be regarded as a single problem requiring a simultaneous solution.

He found that his attention often had to be directed to one particular objective. But other objectives could never be neglected, because progress to one objective had implications for all the others. Moreover, his economics training had taught him always to consider the interrelationships of the particulars without losing sight of the general – and at the level of practical choice, the interrelationships can be very complex. He himself sometimes felt that constructing a budget was like designing a house. Even if all the bits in the plans were satisfactory, one could not be sure that the house would stand until the whole had been completed.

What was often required from Hall was an analysis of the whole situation, which would lead to a conclusion about which total situation was to be preferred to any of the alternatives open. In the senior ranks of the Treasury in 1947, he found that no one understood these matters very well. Hall had to educate his senior Treasury officials to recognise and accept such heretical notions that, for example, consumption levels could be raised by increasing investment, if there were unused resources and the idea that the best way to curb excess demand might sometimes be to allow prices to rise.

One of his many tasks therefore was that of an elucidator. Ministers were very much concerned to understand the forces of economic change, in order to decide whether to acquiesce in, promote, mitigate, or prevent change. In his contacts with ministers, Hall tried to identify all the forces at work and to measure the cost of as many as possible in money terms. This did not in itself yield a clear-cut answer every time, but it was almost always helpful. Clearly, Hall helped ministers and senior officials to a better understanding of the working of the economic system. Douglas Jay, when he was Economic Secretary, discovered that Hall was also very practical in another way: he found him a good person on whom to try out his ideas and felt that Hall always helped him to a better perspective.

As an elucidator and teacher he had that rare knack of sizing up what his audience – in many cases a minister – could take in. He knew how to respond to a minister who asked to be put in the picture on the general economic scene, so that the minister would comprehend. It was rather as if the minister was in the position of a pupil being taught by his tutor. In one-to-one discussions, he had an imaginative grasp of the capacity of the person he was briefing, which enabled him to find the right level of technicality. What ministers seek is technical and expert advice that is intellectually rigorous and does not duck inconvenient questions. This they received in good measure from Hall.

At the larger occasion he was less good – some thought him hopeless. In committees he did not shine. His hesitant manner did not help. He knew this was a handicap and he had to compensate for it by working outside the committees to have as many officials as possible lined up on his side, so that he did not have to press his own case in the committee – others did it for him. In the early days it was chiefly Plowden, but later there were many others. On the other hand he sometimes lectured well. He made sure he had completely mastered his subject and then would expose himself to questions, which he handled most skilfully, especially if they were debunking ones.

With hindsight, it seems likely that the success of economic management in the 1950s led some people to overestimate what macroeconomic policy could do. The experience of this time did not reveal the full range of instability that was to emerge later. But Hall never became complacent about it. He wanted further progress on reducing the area on which he had to rely on intuition or trial and error, or on such direct approaches as investment intentions surveys, which were always subject to revision. He was not content with the statistical information available, even though it had been much improved as a result of his encouragement. He recognised that it would always be a struggle between the economist who wants everything now, the statistician who wants everything right and the unfortunate supplier of the statistics who has to fill up the form. He left the Treasury before the development of the fully computerised models of the economy. Under his direction some functional relationships had been worked out. He believed these should not be over-complex, sensing that models used for short-term forecasting should remain simple.

Some have labelled Hall 'an old-fashioned Keynesian'. Certainly he was a Keynesian in the sense that he took on board Keynes's theory of effective demand, believing that it was the state's responsibility to improve on the economic situations yielded by *laissez-faire*. To a practical man like Hall, the Keynesian revolution was essentially the acceptance of budgetary and monetary policy as instruments for correcting excesses and deficiencies of effective demand. But he thought insufficient attention had been paid to methods to deal with cost inflation and this led him into many attempts to persuade the government to introduce some kind of incomes policy, when there seemed to him no other way of remedying it, other than by a massive increase in unemployment. He was only one of many who favoured such a policy in the 1950s and 1960s but, unlike some, he applied his practical mind to working out ways of implementing it.

Hall liked to make sure that his successive Chancellors were provided with the means to give a coherent public explanation of their policies. For example, in budget and other speeches he always supplied the rationale behind their decisions – decisions which involved direct action on economic variables. He did not merely write briefs or advise ministers on the need to behave differently.

There were two policies for which he carried great responsibility: first recognising the need in 1949 for devaluation and seeing through its acceptance at a reasonably well-based rate and secondly preventing a premature move to sterling convertibility in 1952, and then helping to reach a more sensible timing of such a move from a stronger position. Such decisions were taken on the advice of a small number of officials around the Chancellor, on the basis of discussions and argument. In the matter of convertibility, there was in-fighting and an attempt to steamroller it through without proper consultation. From his own diaries and the official papers, the part he played has become much clearer. His main failure was over incomes policy. In spite of all his efforts and those of his staff, he was unable to see established what he thought at that time had become essential for the successful execution of a full employment policy: that is a policy for restraining rises in wages and salaries.

Hall was continually searching for better policies, better ways to carry them out and ways of bringing about change. He encouraged research both within his own section and elsewhere, inside and outside Whitehall. He received many letters and research papers from academics and others and always took pains to answer them. He was invariably cautious about discouraging any ideas, rather tending to stimulate further work if he was interested in the problem, even though he was not very hopeful that this would be productive. He was conscious that he was the representative of the economic profession and felt this responsiblity keenly. He took every opportunity to discuss matters with the many academic colleagues in Oxford and elsewhere and with the many economists he met on his overseas visits.

He gave some thought to the organisation of the civil service and economic advice. He disapproved of anything like secret talks between a minister and any of his staff except the Permanent Secretary. He himself always had access to the Chancellor if he wanted it, but he was on such close terms with all three Permanent Secretaries he worked under – Bridges, Makins and Lee – that he always showed them any minute which he thought he should send directly to the Chancellor. When there was a disagreement between the Economic Section and other parts of the Treasury, the Permanent Secretary would usually present an agreed note to the Chancellor showing what the differences were. The Chancellor himself would then have a meeting. Hall thought this worked well, and the only time he ever felt excluded from decisions was near the end of Thorneycroft's time as Chancellor.

From his own experience, he came to the conclusion that there should be a close connection between those who formulate policy and those advising on its technical aspects and that it was an advantage if administrators had some economics training and economists some experience of administration.

He took the initiative in moving some of his staff abroad, both to the United States, and to the OEEC and NATO in Paris. Together with H. C. Coombs of the Commonwealth Bank of Australia, he organised an exchange of young economists between the London and Canberra Cabinet Offices in the early postwar years, although this ceased when Canberra refused to accept a woman.

Hall's attitude to the financial journalists was an interesting innovation. He regularly saw them to talk about the latest developments, to interpret policy to them and answer their questions. There is no doubt that he was much more open than any previous Treasury official had been; and that this did much to develop economic journalism to the high standard that it has achieved. Richard Fry, the financial editor of the *Manchester Guardian*, always found him very serious, speaking in a fatherly way, very clearly. They had friendly arguments which Fry enjoyed because Hall did not pretend to know everything as the politicians always did, although Fry did not always appreciate what he thought was over-precision in the statistics. Hall sometimes suggested questions for inclusion in Fry's industrial inquiry. He was always aware of the importance of press comment on government policy and went to some lengths to see the journalists and provide guidance where necessary on its interpretation. Although standard practice now, forty years ago this was an unusual thing for an official to do. Maurice Green of *The Times* was someone he lunched with occasionally. He also saw Wilfred King, the editor of *The Banker*, and Geoffrey Crowther, the editor of *The Economist*, whenever he thought it would be helpful.

Hall's speciality was the practical application of economics to public policy. In the 1950s his reputation in Whitehall grew steadily. He was referred to later as a great Treasury figure. He never fought on minor matters. In some cases, where there was a possibility of action, it was not at all clear what the objective ought to be. In his approach to such problems, Hall was influenced by his philosophical training. He agreed within limits that the question of what society wants, or should want, was not within the professional competence of economists, so that when his advice was asked on what an objective should be, he understood that he was being asked as the 'whole man', not only as an economist. Otherwise, where there was agreement about the objective, he understood that he was being asked, as the economist, about the means of achieving it.

However, he felt it was an illusion to imagine that the economist engaged in the practical world could be dispassionate, and he certainly was not. It has been argued that economists should stop at analysis. One view is that because politicians have to take all the responsibility, civil servants should not advise about actual decisions. Hall thought that where the right course is not at all obvious in difficult cases needing nice judgment, then the government economic adviser ought to take part, if asked to do so, in discussions about policy. But in these cases, he must try to put himself in the place of those who will bear the final responsibility: 'he ought to be an expert in an administrative setting'.[3]

In carrying out this intention, for example, he did not stand aside from the awkward political decisions raised by the Korean War and rearmament. He believed there was a real threat of a third world war, and he was convinced by his American friends that it was essential to resist the Soviet Union's expansionist plans. He was a man of deep emotions and had an idealistic approach to his work. He cared greatly about Britain, and he was subject to the turbulences, doubts and distresses of all who feel strongly. He, along with Plowden and Franks, felt that the time had come to resist the extension of communist control.[4] If the Americans did not do it in the Far East, then the Russians would think they would meet no American resistance in Europe. Britain needed to stand with the Americans over Korea because, as their most dependable ally, they would not understand it if Britain did not fight with them. The United States did not like acting alone when in trouble. She wanted other allies. Hall noted in his diary that it seemed probable that the defence programme might have been smaller if he and Plowden had not said the economy could stand the increase proposed by the Ministry of Defence. The size of this programme and therefore Hall's advice has since been held responsible by some historians for putting too heavy a burden on Britain, setting back recovery and even being responsible for Britain's relative industrial decline.[5] In the event the defence expenditure programme was never achieved and forty years on, after much research into the causes of Britain's slow growth, the effects seem at most to have been temporary.

Part of Hall's success lay in the way he dealt with people. This applied not only to ministers, senior officials and his staff, but also to academic colleagues, financial journalists, the Americans and the Europeans with whom he came into contact. He had a great gift for friendship and those who worked with him were quick to appreciate this and become on easy terms with him. Among ministers, both Butler and Macmillan in their memoirs have paid tribute to his influence and judgment. In a personal note on Hall's retirement, Butler wrote that he sensed they both had the same approach on the human side and he sent his warmest thanks for the past. While Macmillan, who used to describe Hall as the farmer – 'Let's see what the farmer thinks' – wrote 'I can never be sufficiently grateful to you for all the help you gave me when I was Chancellor of the Exchequer, and this sense of confidence in your wisdom and experience has continued to be of support to me since I became Prime Minister.'[6]

A number of his senior colleagues also wrote to him to say how deeply the country was indebted to him for saner and better economic policies than Britain would otherwise have had. Lord Franks described Hall as

> the architect of a complete revolution in the traditional conceptions of the place and function of fiscal policy, with sureness of judgment of the trends of the economy and the international influences upon it; and you have brought intelligence, experience and flair to bear on the practical issues, which at times approached divination. Your grip on reality has been outstanding.[7]

Nevertheless, he had to overcome some scepticism among senior Treasury officials. At first, when he referred to the gross domestic product, he was thought to be using jargon and such phrases as 'productive potential' and 'rate of growth' cast him as a mad technician and too clever by half. But they also found him very likeable and easy to get along with, so that his relations with them became more harmonious. Even those whom he found most difficult to work with seemed in the end to regard him as a friend. In spite of numerous disagreements with Rowan, the latter wrote Hall a very friendly letter when he left the Treasury in 1956. Rowan hoped the severance would be exclusively official and went on to say:

> We first really met in 1947 when I joined Stafford and since then working with you has been one of the few things which has helped me to feel that our system is worth working for. You have had a very difficult part to play so often and you have played it very well. I do hope that what you are now striving for will not be upset by hasty decisions; I hope too, though it does not lie in my mouth to say so, that you will be there for some time to guide and direct – I can see no replacement.[8]

It is interesting to note that Hall was in his special role in the Treasury longer than any other of the senior officials. He worked with three Permanent Secretaries and the Second and Third Secretaries had a similar rate of turnover. By the time he left he had provided a continuity in policy advice that was rather rare in a civil service which believed in moving officials round a great deal. Economic advice involves looking beyond the current situation. In the conditions of the 1950s, when Hall was the only government economic adviser in Whitehall, he felt that if he could not take a view and give advice on the basis of that view, then he should make way for someone who would be braver. In fourteen years of advising the government he never felt the need to make way for someone who would be braver.

Hall explained his own skills when he identified the reasons for the effectiveness of the Economic Section: 'Its effectiveness, like that of all economists in large organisations, depended on its professional competence, but also on its ability to understand what was administratively and politically possible; and on its own powers of working with non-economists and persuading them of its competence and realism.' No doubt Hall owed part of his success to his staff. He believed in recruiting first-rate staff, and he had a flair for selecting them. Although many stayed only a short time in the Section – the secondments he arranged from the universities and other departments were usually for two years – there were a number who made very successful careers as economists in the public service, working in other organisations as well as in the Treasury. The record of those who worked for him is impressive.

Hall won the respect and affection of his staff and inspired a great sense of loyalty among them. They all wanted to do their best for him. Most of them appreciated his determinedly pragmatic approach and his undoubted great integrity, and the fact that he did not impose any doctrinal views on them. Others, less pragmatic, thought him insufficiently zealous in pursuit of his, or their, first preference and some younger staff inevitably felt neglected. But even those who did not see much of him felt his presence. The Economic Section was Robert Hall and his team. They knew that his common sense was the hard-won kind and there was nothing superficial about it. He was rock solid in a crisis. He was very wise. A first-class draughtsman himself, he could be very patient, for example with redrafting, even though a document might go through many versions with no real difference in the sense. In one of the Economic Surveys, one sentence went through sixteen versions. For several years the Economic Section had an annual competition in forecasting the main magnitudes in the economy. The forecasts were sealed up for a year. Hall's were always the best, to the great indignation of the rest of the Section.[9]

On a more personal level he was very good company away from the office. He occasionally dropped into the 'local' for a drink with colleagues after work. On a few rare occasions a member of his staff went with him on official visits abroad, generally when other senior officials were also taking an assistant with them. All who had this experience greatly enjoyed being with him, travelling with him and perhaps occasionally dining with him. Those who had been posted abroad greatly looked forward to his visits.

On his retirement from the Treasury Hall did not lose touch with his colleagues and staff, many of them remaining his friends. A number of them visited him in Cornwall and saw him happily engaged in his favourite hobby in his windswept garden. Kit MacMahon has referred to one of his happiest memories of Hall as sitting in his old clothes with his wife Perilla, surveying the Quarry garden and the sea, with a gin and tonic in his hand. Life, as he himself said, stripped down to its bare luxuries.

APPENDIX A

Members of the Economic Section under Robert Hall

Note: Several of those listed below also worked in the Section either before Hall took over or after he left. Years spent on secondment away from the Section are included here.

Abramson, S. 1948–50
Atkinson, F. J. 1949–61 (later Sir Fred)
Butt, D. B. 1947–9
Bretherton, R. F. 1949–51
Brown, Miss M. P. 1959–61
Brunner, J. 1958–61 (later Sir John)
Day, A. C. L. 1954–6
Dow, J. C. R. 1947–54
Downie, J. 1948–61
Fearn, J. M. 1947–8
Figgures, F. 1955–7 (later Sir Frank)
Fleming, J. Marcus 1947–51
Fleming, J. Miles 1952–4
Forsyth, Miss J. M. 1947–9
Franklin, M. D. M. 1952–5 (later Sir Michael)
Godley, W. A. H. 1956–61
Grieve-Smith, J. 1949–54
Hemming, Mrs M. W. B. 1947–55
Henderson, P. D. 1957–8
Hopkin, W. A. B. 1948–61 (later Sir Bryan)
Howell, D. A. R. 1959–60
Howell, Miss K. 1947–60 (Mrs Jones)

Jefferies, G. P. 1947–9
Jones, D. J. C. 1950–3
Jukes, J. A. 1948–54
Keane, J. W. P. 1947–52
Kelley, Miss J. 1949–54
Kennedy, M. C. 1956–61
Lawler, P. 1952–3 (later Sir Peter)
Le Cheminant, P. 1950–2
Licence, J. W. V. 1948–52
Little, I. M. D. 1953–5
Mackintosh, A. S. 1957–61
McMahon, C. W. 1954–7 (later Sir Kit)
Neild, R. R. 1951–6
Nove, A. 1956–8
Opie, R. G. 1958–60
Richenberg, L. 1955–7
Ross, C. R. 1952–5
Sadler, J. S. 1954–6
Scammell, W. S. 1956–8
Scott, M. F. 1953–4
Shackle, G. L. S. 1947–9
Stamler, Mrs H. 1954–6
Stewart, M. J. 1957–61
Swan, T. 1947–9
Troup, G. W. 1957
Wannan, Miss G. 1956–8
Watts, N. G. M. 1947–55
Watts, P. E. 1954–9

APPENDIX B

Economic Trends 1947–61

Year	GDP(a)	Ind. prodn.	Retail prices	Wage rates	Unem-ploy-ment	Current balance	Change in reserves
	% change on previous year		4thQ on 4thQ %		%	£mn	$mn
1947	1.0	6.0	2.4	4.1	1.6	-381	-152
1948	3.5	8.0	5.9	4.2	1.5	+ 26	- 55
1949	4.5	6.5	3.3	1.9	1.5	- 1	- 3
1950	3.5	6.5	3.0	3.4	1.5	+307	+575
1951	2.5	3.5	11.8	10.7	1.2	-369	-344
1952	0.0	-3.0	6.7	6.7	2.0	+163	-175
1953	4.0	6.0	1.4	3.2	1.6	+145	+240
1954	4.0	7.0	3.4	4.7	1.3	+117	+ 87
1955	3.0	5.1	5.9	7.0	1.1	-155	-229
1956	2.0	0.5	3.3	7.6	1.2	+208	+ 42
1957	1.5	1.7	4.4	5.7	1.4	+233	+ 13
1958	0.0	-1.1	1.5	3.6	2.1	+350	+284
1959	4.0	6.0	0.5	1.2	2.2	+164	-119
1960	5.0	7.7	1.5	2.7	1.6	-237	+495
1961	3.0	0.0	2.9	4.1	1.4	+ 35	+ 87

Sources: CSO *Economic Trends Annual Supplement*, 1992; CSO *Annual Abstract of Statistics*, various issues.
(a) at constant prices.

APPENDIX C

The Mine at Silverspur by Robert Hall

The centre piece of the mine was the shaft itself above which the engine room buildings had an air compressor with a huge fly-wheel and the winding gear, its drum like an enormous cotton reel, which had wire ropes leading to the poppet heads from which the cages were suspended over the shaft. A small steam engine at each side drove the rods which rotated the drum and lowered one cage while the other moved in the opposite way. There was also a lower platform with an ingenious arrangement for bailing out the water which collected in the shaft.

Beside the engine room was a store room, which to a child was an Aladdin's cave with treasures of boxes of candles and lamps and all kinds of tools for miners. Next came the blacksmith's shop where I was allowed to blow the bellows as I got older and then to wield the sledge hammer on the spot indicated by the lighter blow of the master's hammer. I learnt to manipulate wrought iron and mild steel, although to my regret I never learnt to temper steel.

The ore and the rock which had to be cut away to get at the ore veins came up in little trucks which were wheeled away by an attendant, the ore to the rock-breaker and the rock to dumps which were out on the flat plain which extended four or five miles up the river. Then came the calciner, the huge oven with three fire-boxes on each side and on which the ore, by now finely crushed by the rock-breaker, was spread out and heated in order to extract as much of the sulphur and zinc as possible. A large smoke-stack carried away the gases. Huge rakes ran on an endless wire rope over the ore. Finally there were the two reverberating furnaces in which the ore was smelted, each manned by a shift consisting of a

197

captain and a first and second mate. The engine room, the oven and the furnaces were surrounded by large woodpiles cut from the woods which grew on the nearby hills, and which were brought down in wagons mostly drawn by five horses, though sometimes by twelve bullocks.

The last piece of the mine complex was the mine dam, fed from long ditches on the hill-sides if there was any rain and topped up from the mine-water. This was the local swimming pool where I remember the triumph with which I first swam the 40 feet across, all out of my depth. The whole complex of mine buildings and the processes of extracting and treatment of the ore – breaking it, roasting it, and smelting it, were a continuous source of interest and fascination to me.

APPENDIX D

Minute to Sir Edwin Plowden (PRO T 171/397)

BUDGET COMMITTEE

I do not know whether this committee meets throughout the year, or whether it takes a rest in the earlier stages. But it seems to me that there are a number of problems about the general place of the Budget in the national economy which could profitably be discussed at more leisure than we have had in recent months.

In particular I have in mind the present levels of total expenditure and the question of whether our present tax structure provides an adequate incentive to that part of the national economy which depends on private enterprise. It could be argued that we are trying to put altogether too heavy a load on the economy and that this will produce a continuous tendency towards inflation which can only be checked by taxation so severe as to dishearten the community. There is, indeed, something to be said for appointing a new Royal Commission on the lines of the Colwyn Committee to study the whole matter, but, whether this is done or not, I feel it would be very helpful if we could find time for some talks on questions like those I have mentioned. It might well turn out to be the case that the Revenue Departments and the Home Finance Section of the Treasury have also got matters which they would like to consider without feeling that they must produce results at short notice.

[Signed] Robert Hall
19 March 1948

Minute to the Prime Minister (PRO CAB 21/2245)

THE DOLLAR SITUATION EPC(49)72

1. The country is now facing a major crisis and it will ask how this can come about when production and exports are both at record levels, and the fundamentals of prosperity, the productive employment of our resources, apparently never so well assured. The paper by the Chancellor of the Exchequer sets out to explain this paradox and to suggest remedies.

2. Our difficulties in the end can be reduced to two. We have been trying to do too much at home, and we have been trying to support an over-valued currency. The first has shown itself in the high levels of investment and of Government expenditure, combined with a determination to maintain our standard of living. This results in a continuous tendency towards inflation, which we have only held in check by severe Budgets and by the White Paper policy on wages etc. But the full employment, which has enabled us to progress at unprecedented rates despite our strained condition, has in the inflationary context made it impossible to prevent a gradual rise in our costs and this has brought to the forefront the over-valuation of our currency and the serious threat to our reserves which is the immediate problem. The American recession has made the situation worse but it would be an illusion to think that this is the cause of our troubles. For even before it affected our position, we were making very slow progress in closing the dollar gap and we have needed about one billion dollars a year from the Americans to sustain our position.

3. Recently, of course, we have been doing much better than this suggests as we have been making large 'unrequited' exports to soft currency countries. They have not got the supplies we must have to maintain our economic system, and economic and political necessity both require that we should substitute dollar earning exports for those for which we are now getting nothing but a reduction in our sterling debts. This must entail some loss, as we are unable to sell our surplus exports for dollars at their present prices; but it ought not to require changes so painful that we cannot face them. There ought to be some possible solution for our troubles. And this must be in the direction of reaching a better dollar balance. It is an illusion to think that we could reach a satisfactory situation by doing without North America: the supplies are simply not available in other places.

4. It follows that the solution must be found first in taking some strain off our own system, and secondly in finding conditions in which we can hope to expand rather than contract our dollar earnings, so that we can live without U.S. help as this is reduced.

5. There is however an immediate problem. The loss of dollar earnings has brought a loss of confidence in sterling and all those who can avoid holding it are doing so. It is not easy to get out of sterling against our exchange control but it is being done. That is why it is so important to take measures to restore confidence as soon as possible. If this is not done, our reserves will fall below the danger level and there will be no alternative to a number of unpleasant adjustments, since we shall only be able to import what our current earnings plus American help allow us to do.

6. The Chancellor proposes to reduce the strain on our system (a) by reducing dollar imports; (b) by reducing Government expenditure. The measures to improve the dollar earning potentialities are (c) to intensify existing policies on limitation of personal incomes, etc; (d) to give some preferential treatment to exporters to the dollar areas.

7. He also proposes to persuade Commonwealth countries to make further economies in their use of dollars; and to approach the U.S.A.

to try to reach some agreement with them about improving and maintaining the position of sterling.

8. In my opinion, these measures will not in themselves be enough to restore confidence in sterling and to stop the run on our reserves. Nor do I think that they will form a satisfactory basis for an approach to the U.S.A. There are a number of things which the US ought to do to help the situation and in some circumstances they might even be persuaded to support sterling. But they will certainly want to know what we are going to do to help ourselves before they give us any more help. And they could only support sterling on condition that we undertook to control our expenditure and our monetary policy, and to improve our cost levels. It would be very bad for our relations with them if they had to impose such conditions on us. And it is much better for our negotiating position with them that we should make up our minds beforehand about what we are going to do.

9. I am one of the officials [referred to in Appendix A] who consider that we should devalue sterling in the very near future. It is agreed that our costs are too high for the North American market and that we must get them down somehow. I do not believe that there are any measures other than devaluation which will do this in time to be of any use. I think it is very likely that this step will be forced upon us from the loss of reserves unless we take more drastic measures than those proposed; and I think it is much better to do something while we are in control of the situation than under duress. I do not think that it is practicable to subsidise exports to the dollar markets: we have pledged ourselves not to do this and it would annoy the Americans when we are appealing to them, and lead them to impose anti-dumping duties. It would also add to our Budget difficulties when we want to lessen them. I think therefore that devaluation is the course most likely to reverse the present trend to falling dollar earnings, and that it would convince the Americans more than anything else that we intended to stand up to our own problems.

10. I think we should also adopt measures to halt the increase in Government expenditure. But I am not at all happy about the pro-

posal to reduce food subsidies by £100 millions and would much prefer to cut the cost of the health services. A reduction in food subsidies would make it extremely difficult to reinforce the policy of the White Paper, which we need to do. Finally I think that we should adopt some moderate restriction of credit, for the reasons set out in paragraph 33 of the Chancellor's paper. I do not think the increase in interest payments to holders of the floating debt is nearly so important as a general realisation that monetary policy in future is going to move in support of Government policy generally. At present the policy of very cheap money is contrary to the disinflationary policy of the Budget and to the policy of holding down investment.

11. In this way, it seems to me that we would be taking measures which would have the best chance of holding and improving our position. The great dangers now are that we shall not do enough, and lose control of the situation with incalculable results; or that we shall take deflationary measures which are too severe, causing a loss of production and probably severe industrial unrest, which would be bad in itself and economically. The measures proposed with the addition of devaluation seem to me to be positive and with the hope of avoiding both dangers.

12. There is no doubt that all the benefits of devaluation would be lost and all the disadvantages secured, if it were followed by an immediate increase in wages and costs which would put them back to the present relation to the dollar. It is not likely that the immediate effect of devaluation would be a marked rise in the cost of living. All the measures proposed in the paper require that we should be able to prevent costs from rising. The atmosphere of devaluation would be that best calculated to enable a general appeal to be made to the country. But in addition, if we devalued we could face some moderate increase in wages with equanimity, since we would have a considerable margin. The alternative policy requires that they be held firmly where they are, which it seems almost impossible to expect at present.

13. Those who oppose this course seem to think that we can go on as we are with the very moderate measures proposed, until we

have seen the effect of those measures, and had our talks with the Americans. The main differences that I feel with them are (a) I do not think that the situation will wait for us; (b) I do not think the measures suggested give us enough for satisfactory talks with the Americans.

14. Summary
(i) The country is facing a very critical situation due to the loss of dollar income and the loss of confidence in sterling.
(ii) This requires firm measures which will convince the country and the world that we are going to deal with our troubles.
(iii) I do not think the measures proposed will meet the situation.
(iv) I support these measures with the exception of export subsidies.
(v) I think that these measures, with an early devaluation of sterling, would be sufficient.

[Signed] R. L. Hall
29 June 1949

Brief for the Prime Minister (PRO T 171/400)

BUDGET POLICY C.P.(50)35

This paper was prepared on the instructions of the Chancellor of the Exchequer at the suggestion of the Prime Minister. It arises because of doubts felt by the Lord Privy Seal about the wisdom of our policy of having large Budget surpluses.

2. The subject is intensely difficult to understand and, though the paper is put in simple language, it is rather doubtful whether in the end there will not have to be an act of faith.

3. On the merits of the case, I feel personally convinced that all economists would agree that our present policy is not only right, but that it would be very wrong to adopt any other. The last Government adopted in 1947 and 1948 a revolution in British practice, when they took responsibility for maintaining full employment, but avoiding inflation. It is the best argument in favour of this policy that the revolution passed almost unnoticed. The policy was accepted as the right one both in this country and abroad, except perhaps in countries like Belgium which have gone back to laissez faire and are making use of unemployment as a method of economic regulation.

4. There is perhaps room for argument about the application of the policy at any moment. Many critics would say that we were not being severe enough, while on the other side there is a natural

leaning towards maintaining expenditure and reducing taxation because in the short run such a course is pleasanter for everyone.

5. But there can surely be no danger that the present Government will deliberately push deflation too far and produce unemployment. Quite apart from its general policy, the Chancellor of the Exchequer has deliberately drawn attention to the need for flexibility in his Budget speeches.

6. The real danger is, therefore, that we shall be too weak, have too much inflation, and thus put difficulties in the way of our export trade and produce a new balance of payments crisis. The Government has taken the very drastic step of devaluation of the currency. All the results so far justify the decision, but only on condition, which was publicly accepted by the Prime Minister and the Chancellor of the Exchequer last October, that we hold inflation in check.

7. It is therefore my considered opinion that it is the plain duty of the Government to support this policy. Any serious departure from it would be rightly regarded as an abandonment of the principle of planning, and would, in my opinion, do great harm to the cause, both here and abroad. I feel no doubt that this view would be supported by the great body of economists outside the Government as well as in it.

[Signed] Robert Hall
16 March 1950

APPENDIX G

Note for the Record (PRO T 236/3245)

A short account of the matters covered by this folder may be of historical interest.

2. In the course of January, the Chancellor of the Exchequer said on several occasions that he was disquieted by the continuing loss of the reserves and that he would like to be able to announce further measures in his Budget speech to deal with this. I got the impression that Sir Leslie Rowan was responsible and that I was to be associated with the study. I did not, however, hear anything further until Doc No. 1 [Emergency Action by the Treasury – no mention of Robot] was produced on 8th February. This was briefly discussed at a meeting taken by Sir Leslie Rowan and sent to the Chancellor, with my agreement. I do not know what happened to this paper after it reached the Chancellor.

3. Towards the end of the following week, I was shown a short note by the Governor of the Bank of England on the lines of the plan subsequently developed. This note is not on the file, but this was the first information that anything else was considered. This was followed by the meeting attended by Sir Edwin Plowden and me, held by Sir Leslie Rowan on the afternoon of 19th February, which discussed Doc. No. 2 [Plan for Overseas Sterling] which I understood to have originated with the Bank of England. There was a very brief discussion at which my impression was that we all felt that

further study was needed and that there would be time available for this. We saw the Chancellor later that evening and it appeared to be agreed that the internal consequences of the plan were too drastic. Sir Edwin left that night for Lisbon.

4. The Chancellor of the Exchequer, the Leader of the Government in the House of Commons and the Governor of the Bank of England dined that night with the Prime Minister, and I understand that there was some discussion of the proposal and that the view was taken that if any drastic changes were decided on in principle, it would be wrong to introduce a Budget in which the Government gave the impression that they had no knowledge of the change in view. The deduction was drawn from this that if the new plan were to be put into force it would have to be done on Budget day, 4th March. I first heard of this at a meeting on the afternoon of 20th February, when the first of the two papers at Doc. No. 9 [Modified Plan of Action by Treasury] was put before us. I was dumbfounded at the idea that such drastic steps were to be taken in such a short time, and after a night's reflection sent Sir Edward Bridges the minute at 6A, which I discussed with him and the Chancellor of the Exchequer on the morning of 21st February. They both agreed with my view [that more time was needed to consider the proposals] and I gather that they then decided to recommend that Budget day should be advanced to 11th March.

5. On the morning of 21st February, Sir Leslie Rowan had a meeting at which were present Mr Clarke, Sir George Bolton, Sir William Strang, Sir Percivale Liesching, Sir Hilton Poynton, Sir Frank Lee, Mr Hitchman and me. The heads of the other Departments present were then shown the fuller paper at Doc. No. 9 and were told that the situation of sterling was so bad that Ministers might well decide to adopt this plan on 4th March. They were asked to consider in the course of the day what they would have to do if this decision was reached, and to come to a meeting later in the afternoon.

6. At the afternoon meeting, they gave their views. No analysis of the results of the action had been provided, the views were mostly a statement of the action which their Departments would have to take. The only people who expressed any doubts about the

scheme were Sir Frank Lee, Mr Strath and me.

7. During that day I had seen the draft memorandum for the Chancellor, done by Mr Clarke at Doc. No. 8 [External Action] and this was looked at very briefly at a meeting which the Chancellor of the Exchequer took that evening. I understood that he was proposing to circulate it to some of his colleagues the next morning. I said that the action proposed would have such drastic and complex results that I was not yet in a position to give a considered view. During the night the document was duplicated in the form appearing at Doc. No. 10 [External Action]. I saw the Chancellor of the Exchequer early on the morning of 22nd February and asked that Sir Edwin Plowden should be brought back to consider it. I also expressed my misgivings at the general developments.

8. That afternoon I was sent for by the Paymaster-General and we had a short discussion of the plan. I had by that time come to the conclusion that it was not likely to be successful except at very great cost and I indicated my views very briefly to Lord Cherwell on these lines. There had been a meeting of a small group of Ministers that afternoon at which they had been given copies of the Chancellor's draft memorandum. I understood that at that stage only the Paymaster-General was opposed to the action.

9. On Saturday 23rd February, I prepared, with the assistance of five members of the Economic Section, a memorandum at Doc. No. 12 [External Action – Memorandum by Mr R. L. Hall] and gave copies of this to Mr Armstrong for the Chancellor, Mr Strath, and Sir Leslie Rowan with a copy for Sir George Bolton. Copies were given on 25th February to Sir Edward Bridges and Sir Edwin Plowden.

10. During the weekend I was again sent for by the Paymaster-General who showed me the draft of a note which later became his memorandum at Doc. No. 14 [objecting to the plan]. I understand that this was circulated to a small group of Ministers on about 28th February, though it was in the hands of the Chancellor on 25th February.

11. On 22nd February it was decided to send Sir Herbert Brittain and Mr Berthoud to Lisbon to explain the proposals to the Foreign Secretary, and on Sir Edward Bridges' invitation I sent Sir Edwin a letter with a copy to Sir Leslie Rowan. On 22nd February also I was authorised by Sir Edward Bridges to consult Professor Lionel Robbins, which I did that afternoon at 6 p.m. His views were very much the same as mine, though he thought that we might be driven to some such plan as that of the Bank in the end. But he felt very strongly that we would be much condemned by the world in adopting so drastic a plan without taking further steps ourselves before then, and in particular, without putting up the bank rate.

12. Sir Edwin Plowden returned on the night of 24th February and he and I saw the Chancellor the next afternoon and later produced the note at Doc. No. 16 giving our own views about the action required. This was followed by the revised note at Doc. No. 18 [Alternative to Bank Proposals] on the 27th. On that day I also sent the Chancellor the minute at Doc. No. 19 [re-emphasising his reasons for objecting to the plan], with copies to Sir Edward Bridges, Sir Leslie Rowan, Sir Edwin Plowden and the Minister of State for Economic Affairs.

13. Sir Edwin Plowden and I saw the Minister of State at his request several times between 26th February and 28th February and discussed with him the difficulties we felt about the plan.

14. I understood that Ministers finally decided against the plan, at any rate for the time being, on the morning of 29th February, and that they considered the alternative proposals, based on Doc. No. 18 on the afternoon of that day.

15. In my view, the main difficulties arose because of the decision reached on the evening of 19th February to try to get the plan through before the Budget. As telegrams would have had to go to Commonwealth countries about a week before, this left an impossibly short time for discussion to put the Budget a week later.

16. I myself felt, however, throughout the discussions that the procedure was quite different from anything to which I had previously

been accustomed. The Bank draft made no attempt to discuss the methods by which the necessary adjustments would in fact take place. Mr Clarke's draft paper, which attempted to do this, was a tour de force but was written under great pressure and without any opportunity for consultation among officials. The meeting of Permanent Secretaries held by Sir Leslie Rowan on 21st February was given no analysis at all of the proposals, and anything that they were able to work out during that day must have been by the light of nature, as it is out of the question for anyone who is not a professional economist or banker to deduce the consequences from the bit of paper which they had.

17. Throughout the proceedings, there was never any real attempt to prepare a considered view representing Whitehall or even Great George Street opinion. I do not know the exact circulation given to the memorandum by the Chancellor or when each Minister received it. I am strongly of the opinion, however, that Ministers had had no time to get a real grasp of what it was they were discussing or of what consequences might be expected to follow from the action recommended.

[Signed] Robert Hall
[undated, probably summer 1952]

APPENDIX H

Extract from 'The Future of Sterling' (PRO T 236/3242)

OBJECTIONS TO THE ROBOT PLAN:

(i) The Exchange Rate and the Terms of Trade

It is suggested that the immediate effect of freeing the exchange rate and establishing convertibility would be a sufficient capital inflow to hold the rate near its present level. But such speculation in favour of sterling and any borrowing that may be possible could not long offset the depressing effect on the rate of the sterling area's current deficit with the dollar area. The rate would therefore fall and our terms of trade worsen. This fall would widen the deficit; supply limitations would prevent a quick increase in exports, while the essential nature of our imports (and the large part of national expenditure which is on public account and therefore not immediately sensitive to price changes) means that the demand would not fall without very large price increases. The increase in the deficit would drive the rate down still further and this fall would then be intensified by the speculative movements which free rates encourage. In the absence of Government intervention, the rate would not be stabilised until substantial quantities of essential food and raw materials had ceased to be imported because they were too dear for people and businesses to buy.

In practice it would be impossible to avoid official intervention to support the rate, in the first place by Exchange Equalisation account operations and then by direct cuts in imports. The loss of gold involved in holding the lower rate would be greater than that needed to hold the present rate, and the cuts in imports would be far greater than those needed to eliminate the dollar deficit at the present exchange rate.

In fact the attempt to use convertibility as a drastic cure for the imbalance of world trade would only operate if the exchange adjustments were in fact of a drastic order, and the balance of payments problems would not be solved by Robot unless the rate went down much further than the initial fall suggested in the Treasury paper.

Only so would reliance on the price system alone be sufficient to bring world trade into balance and as shown below the loss of trade and output would be high.

(ii) Downward Spiral of Non-dollar Trade

The establishment of convertibility of all external sterling into gold and dollars in a situation of general dollar stringency caused by the need for essential supplies, which can only be got from the dollar area, would prove a new incentive to other countries to earn dollars from us by restricting their imports from us. The remedy suggested, in paragraph 31(ii) of the Treasury paper, is that if any other country imposed discriminatory restrictions on imports from us we should react with great vigour by withdrawing OGLs from the country in question and treating it as dollar-hard. This is, however, a course which would almost certainly do more damage to us than to the other country (since on the whole our exports tend to be less essential to other countries than our imports are to us) and seems more likely to intensify than to alleviate the downward spiralling of non-dollar trade which it was designed to avoid.

(iii) Internal Implications

It follows from the preceding paragraphs that the effect of the new system, which would throw our own dollar shortage and that of other countries on to movements of the exchange rate, would be to cause after some delay a substantial increase in the cost of living and a fall in living standards. This is because we cannot come into balance until the rate falls far enough to bring about the necessary reduction in imports and expansion in dollar exports. It seems likely that this would lead to heavy pressure on wages which would push

up prices again and further depress the rate. This would not make
for confidence in sterling. There would also be heavy unemployment from the loss in exports to the non-dollar world. This
would act against the tendency for wages to rise.

There would undoubtedly be heavy pressure on the Government
to take corrective action which would involve a return to the direct
controls which Robot is designed to dispense with. It is difficult to
see how the Government could withstand such pressure. But the
size of the problem would be far greater and the means available
for dealing with it far weaker than at present. In short, Robot
would not remove the need for deliberate cuts in food, housing
and defence but would increase the size of the cuts needed.

(iv) The Effect on United Kingdom Credit

The extensive blocking of sterling balances accumulated in good faith
by both sterling and non-sterling countries could not but have a
serious effect on United Kingdom credit, and would certainly
effectively discourage any of these countries from supplying us
with credit by accumulating sterling balances in future. Moreover
this, together with abandoning our IMF commitment to fixed
exchange rates, would go against our chances of borrowing from
international institutions.

(v) Relations with Sterling Area

It appears from the Treasury paper, that the sterling area countries
would themselves have discretion in the transfer of sterling from
internal to external accounts for the purpose of acquiring foreign
currencies. This means that any expenditure by the United Kingdom
in the sterling area would be a potential pressure on the exchange
rate. We should still have to rely on sterling area cooperation to
minimise this danger. But we should greatly have reduced the incentive for them to give such cooperation. They would have no financial inducement to exercise any discrimination against expenditure
outside the sterling area (within the limits of their total resources)
since the only effects of increasing expenditure would be to depress the exchange rate. Since they are important exporters of
primary commodities to the dollar area (the price of which is fixed

in dollars) this would in fact tend to improve their terms of trade with us, while it would worsen those of the United Kingdom with them. Thus in place of the present system under which the Rest of the Sterling Area has little positive incentive to discriminate in our favour the Robot plan would offer an incentive to them to discriminate against us. This might become a disruptive force inside the sterling area.

(vi) International Political Implications

The new system involves the breakdown of the European Payments Union, and is, for that reason at least, a blow to European recovery. This would be regarded as an unfriendly act by both the United States and the European countries. The United States would also consider that we had dealt a serious blow to the International Monetary Fund by adopting a free exchange rate. The blocking of the sterling balances, which could hardly be regarded as a friendly act, might have serious effects on our political relations with the non-sterling area. The effect on the sterling area itself is uncertain. More generally, the unemployment, rising prices, and contraction of trade which would follow throughout the non-dollar world from such an attempt to force it into equilibrium with the dollar area without the benefit of discrimination could not help but lessen both the strength and cohesion of the free world.

25 March 1952

APPENDIX I

*Brief for the Chancellor of the Exchequer
(PRO T 230/384)*

TOP SECRET

MONETARY POLICY

I said that I wished to put in writing my views about what we have learnt from our recent experiences in attempting to bring about a restriction of credit. I consider that this experience has shown two important weaknesses in our system. These are:

(1) the relations between the Treasury, the Bank of England and the clearing banks,

(2) the mechanism for controlling the supply of money.

It is probably true that as a result of our experience the first of these will work better in future, and it is mainly a question of organisation. The second is of fundamental importance.

(1) It is not necessary to go into too much detail to show that a restriction of credit has been a fundamental part of our policy for many months. The first assessment of the economic situation made for the Budget Committee in December 1954 pointed out that 'there is very little room for tax reductions' and Sir E. Bridges conveyed to the Governor of the Bank of England at about that time that a tighter credit policy would be helpful. The outlook became more uncomfortable from then on and on 24th February, the Chancel-

lor announced that Bank Rate was to be increased to 4½% with a view 'to moderate excessive internal demand'. This was certainly widely understood to mean that there would be a restriction of credit.

Finally, the Chancellor made it clear in his Budget speech that he intended to offset the increased stimulus which would be given by tax remissions by a tighter monetary policy. This was a perfectly defensible position. From then on it was mentioned on numerous occasions at office meetings and elsewhere that monetary policy seemed to be taking a long time to work but we were always given to understand that it was working though it would take some time.

At the beginning of this month the Treasury became so worried that a number of conversations took place, not only with the Bank of England, but with representatives of the clearing banks. These conversations can be summarised by saying that the clearing banks considered that they were doing all that was needed, but that if the Government was really serious and prepared to face complaints, e.g. about local unemployment, then the banks could do more: but they would need a plain statement of the Government's intention in order to have something to show their customers. This is well put in Sir E. Boyle's note of 7th July about the lunch of the Chancellor with Lord Aldenham and Mr. Robarts at the Bank of England, 'If the Government really wanted a deflationary policy to be set in motion, and were prepared to accept the consequences, then the banks would certainly fall into line.'

No doubt in such a situation it is dangerous to blame anyone and I think in retrospect we were all to blame. But the consequences of our failure to grasp the situation have been embarrassing to the Government and particularly to the Chancellor, and have been serious from the national point of view.

The Government is certainly made to appear to have been weak and dilatory in carrying out its own policy. It is always a confession of weakness to say that one's major instrument needs to be used more toughly, and especially if this has to be said in the last week before the summer recess. The Chancellor is exposed to widespread suggestions that he took risks with the balance of payments in his Budget in order to influence the election. This could not have been said if credit policy had in fact been working strongly between 24th February and 26th July. From the national point of view we have

lost a good deal of valuable time. We could not say in advance
how sharply the restrictions would act nor how efficacious they
would be. But surely we were right to suppose that by now there
would have been some evidence on the subject. All we have is a loss
of reserves.

The control of credit has to be carried out by the Bank of England
and it needs clear evidence before Treasury officials can say plainly
that they are not satisfied by the result. It seems to me quite clear
either that the Bank of England did not understand that the policy
was meant to be serious or that they failed to tell us that it would
not work properly unless there was some statement such as that of
yesterday. If they did not understand our policy then we were all
wrong in thinking that it was quite evident from the statements of
24th February and of the Budget. If they knew what we wanted but
did not tell us that we could not get it unless there was a stronger
statement of Government policy, then they ought to have told us.
In either case, the channels of communication are inadequate and
the Government and the country have suffered as a result.

I hope that the arrangements Sir E. Bridges has now proposed
to the Chancellor, and the latter has accepted, will put this right but
I think it is most unfortunate that recent events were needed to
show us where we were wrong. And in retrospect I consider myself
very much to blame for advising the Chancellor to put so much
confidence in credit policy without taking proper steps to satisfy
myself that everyone concerned understood what was wanted.

(2) In the course of the discussions we have had with the clearing
banks in recent weeks it has become clear to me that it is their business to make advances to credit-worthy customers unless there is
a clear indication to the contrary from the Government. This
pernicious view (which was called the Banking View) is supposed to
have been disposed of in monetary controversies after the Napo-
leonic wars. When prices are rising, the demands of the business
world for credit automatically increase and the security offered
appears better and better. The additional accommodation feeds
the inflation which will only stop when the credit expansion is
stopped. If it was not stopped earlier, it was stopped in the old days
by an outflow of gold which cut down the cash base of the credit
system: the demand for gold would in the end have ruined the

banks. Today we also have an outflow of gold but we have insulated the banking system from this, so that they cannot be ruined because their depositors ask for gold.

The accepted doctrine therefore became that it was the duty of the Central Bank to control the total lending powers of the clearing banks. I do not for a moment suppose that the Bank of England do not understand this and in fact it is evident from the figures that the Bank has succeeded in cutting down the total of the deposits. But the clearing banks have offset this by selling securities and increasing their advances. This is very inconvenient for the Government as the securities they sell are short Government paper and this adds to our difficulties in financing the floating debt. The request to the banks to reduce the total of their advances is in effect an admission that orthodox measures of control were operating too slowly.

We have therefore been placed in the position of having to ask the banks as a favour to do what they ought to have been compelled to do because they could not afford to lend any more. Mr S. C. Leslie in his note to Mr Petch of 27th July quotes Sir Oscar Hobson as saying 'that after 45 years in the City he had absolutely no confidence in the banks' readiness to operate the squeeze as long as they had money to lend...the success of the squeeze depended wholly on how far the Treasury and the Bank would go in putting the screw on the banks themselves.'

The banks have no divine right to lend as much money as they see fit. It is their action which determines the total of the money supply and it is the inescapable duty of the Government to regulate the quantity of money.

There is no lack of power to do this. Probably the simplest course would be to prescribe the liquidity ratio and I gather that the Governor himself would like a liquidity ratio of 32%. This would be simpler than having to ask the banks to restrict their advances unless we would like to be able to give them guidance or direction as to how they should do the restrictions. But there are other possible methods on which I could submit a note if desired. The technical details should, of course, be better known to the Bank than to us. Apart from export business, I do not myself think that we ought to give them any guidance. We ought to see that they can only lend a certain amount so that they can tell their customers that there is no more in the till.

I think therefore, that we should now find out from the Bank of England exactly how they consider the system works and whether their powers are sufficient to enable them to control the total lending by the banks and if not what extra powers are needed. It would be very helpful if the Bank would write a paper on these subjects to be discussed with the Treasury under the new arrangements. We ought to make it clear that in future the Government will expect advances to be limited because the banks cannot lend any more without departing from their cash and liquidity ratios.

This is a professional matter and I would be very glad if the opinion of any economist who is a recognised authority on money and banking were taken to confirm or qualify my views.

[Signed] Robert Hall
28 July 1955

APPENDIX J

Extract from 'Economic Outlook for 1960' (PRO T 171/506)

BC(60)14.

8. General Assessment. The economy as a whole is at present about as fully employed as we would wish it to be. Even at present, it would be preferable if more output were going to exports. The forecasts of expenditure suggest that during 1960 there will be a tendency for the pressure of demand to increase moderately. If these forecasts prove exactly right, then at the end of the year the pressure of demand would be rather higher than is desirable. Allowing for the uncertainties in the forecasts, the prospect may be defined as follows. If expenditure turns out lower than forecast, the pressure of demand in the labour market would remain constant: an actual slackening does not seem to be on the map. But if expenditure increases more than is forecast, the pressure of demand might prove seriously embarrassing, with damaging effects on the balance of payments and strong pressure on wages and prices. Thus the danger is of too much demand rather than too little.

9. The case for taking some action to damp down demand is reinforced by the considerations that already in the present wage round the likely pattern of settlements is on a scale sufficient to cause prices to rise, and that the balance of payments is somewhat less than satisfactory.

10. In considering action to reduce demand the following points are relevant:

(i) fixed investment by manufacturing industry has been declining and we do not want to discourage the increase now beginning.

(ii) this does not apply so much to non-manufacturing industry, while anything that would discourage house-building (especially in the private sector) would be welcome. This raises the question of credit restriction.

(iii) public sector investment has been rising rapidly and there is a case against any further expansion.

(iv) forces already in operation are likely to slow down considerably the increase in expenditure on consumer durables, other than cars. Presumably we do not want to check the expansion of investment by motor-car firms in development areas. Thus there is not a very strong case for hire-purchase restriction.

(v) there is a case for restricting consumer purchasing power generally.

R. L. Hall
9 December 1959

APPENDIX K

Brief for Prime Minister (PRO PREM 8/1428)

FRANCO-GERMAN STEEL AND COAL AUTHORITY

A paper is being prepared on the economic implications of the French proposals. This will state that the effects of carrying out the proposals would be negligible for the UK for the next few years. But after that the proposals would almost certainly improve the efficiency of Continental steel and coal production, and to that extent would worsen our own prospects for these particular industries.

2. It seems to me that it would be out of the question for us to oppose publicly proposals designed to make the industries of other countries more efficient. We are continually urging our own industries to do this, and we could not possibly say that we were against the same remedies for other countries.

3. The issue should, of course, be looked at on the widest basis. There are immense practical and administrative difficulties in carrying through any scheme of this kind. But if it were in fact carried through, the important factor for us would be the change in the whole European picture which would be implied by the fact that France and Germany had proved themselves willing and able to take a step of such importance. If we really think that they are likely to do this, we ought at once to examine the implications of the step for the whole of our policy, in economic as in other fields.

4. My own view is that we have no option but to welcome the move, and to wish for luck. Meanwhile, we ought to make a much more detailed examination of it than has been possible in the time available. I feel that we would look very much of a dog in the manger if we appeared to disapprove of the proposal, though we are in no way obliged to state our own attitude towards participation until we have had much longer to think about it.

[Signed] Robert Hall
11 May 1950

Notes

CHAPTER 1

1 There is a list of those who worked in the Economic Section during Hall's directorship in Appendix A.
2 Annual figures for 1947–61 are in Appendix B.
3 For example Cairncross (1985); Cairncross and Watts (1989); Dow (1964); Fforde (1992).

CHAPTER 2

1 This chapter and chapter 3 draw heavily on Robert Hall's notes for an autobiography and the quotations are from these notes.
2 Lowe returned to England in 1850 after practising law in Sydney, where he sat in the Legislative Council for New South Wales. He became an MP in 1852. Unlike Hall he was an able and eloquent speaker. In 1868 he joined the Cabinet for the first time when he became Chancellor of the Exchequer and introduced five budgets. He moved to become Home Secretary in 1873 and his official life ceased with the defeat of the Gladstone Ministry in 1874. He became the first Viscount Sherbrooke. His best speeches were made during the Reform Bill debates in 1866–7 (information from the Dictionary of National Biography).
3 Hall's own description of the Silverspur mine is in Appendix C.

CHAPTER 3

1 Allsop, Joseph Henry, *A Centenary History of the Ipswich Grammar School 1863–1963*.
2 Information from Bill Kerr.
3 Ipswich Grammar School, Queensland, records.
4 Joan Kelley has remembered this incident.
5 These events are recorded on the Honours Boards in the old school hall at Ipswich Grammar School which is now a museum.
6 Queensland University Library has a record of these events.
7 Professor Kathleen Campbell Brown recalls how she danced or sat out every dance with him at one Commem. Ball. The following year he was in love with Kitty Hasler.
8 Letter to Margaret Boyce 22.11.1922.
9 There were six Rhodes scholars from Australia. Early scholars received £300 a year, having reached Oxford without financial assistance. From this they paid their fees and living expenses.

CHAPTER 4

1 Letter to Margaret Boyce 11.11. 1922.
2 Letter to A. J. Brown 18.11.1985.
3 Letter to Margaret Boyce 26.11.1923.
4 Letter to Edgar Hall 6.6.1924.
5 A detailed account of Hall's friendship with Stephensen is deposited in the Fryer Library at Queensland University. See also Munro (1984).
6 Letter to Margaret Boyce 6.10.1924.
7 Letter to Margaret Boyce 10.3.1925. In Australia 'throw sevens' means 'have a fit'.
8 See Lindsay (1962).

CHAPTER 5

1 The description of economics at Oxford in the 1930s is drawn from Brown (1988) and Lee (1981).
2 Letter to A. J. Brown 18.11.1985.
3 Letter from A. J. Brown to the author 2.2.1992.

4 Letter to Margaret Boyce 6.11.1929.

5 Letter to Margaret Boyce 6.11.1929.

6 Letter to A. J. Brown 18.11.1985.

7 See Chester (1986) and Lee (1981).

8 See A. J. Brown (1988).

9 The other original members of the OERG were Maurice Allen, Russell Bretherton, Roy Harrod, Hubert Henderson, James Meade, Redvers Opie, Henry Phelps Brown and Charles Hitch.

10 Henderson (1938).

11 Hall and Hitch (1939).

12 Wilson and Andrews (1951).

13 Hall (1934). One of a series of which the General Editor was Dr Kenneth Kirk, then Chaplain of Trinity, but later Bishop of Oxford.

14 Hall (1937).

15 Durbin (1985).

16 Letter to Rose Hall 23.1.1933.

17 Information from Michael Maclagan, Henry Phelps Brown and Bruce Wemham.

18 Bruce Wemham provided these descriptions.

19 In 1946 they let the house to Mrs Cockbain. During the 1950s Seatoller House came into the hands of the Treasury in lieu of death duties. The following is an extract from the Seatoller House Day Book: 'When the Treasury came to sell the house, it was handled by Lofts and Warner who advertised it for sale. They accepted John Cockbain's offer (through Claud Bicknell's firm, Stanton, Atkinson and Bird) at the advertised price. After a long delay they informed Bicknell that a higher offer had been received. Bicknell insisted that his offer had been accepted and made sure that the Treasury Solicitor's dishonourable action was made known. His complaint was passed up through the civil service by Robert Hall, Sir Thomas Padmore and Sir Roger Makins, and the matter was finally settled at a Cabinet committee. Sir Edward Boyle wrote to Bicknell that his offer was accepted by the Chancellor of the Exchequer, and the sale went through and Cockbain became owner. (Ref. Lord Roberthall, Claud Bicknell, Sir Stuart Milner Barry, 1982'.)

20 Trinity College Handbook.

21 Information from Sir Lees Mayall.

22 Information from Bruce Wemham.
23 This story came from Sir Kit MacMahon.
24 Information from Michael Maclagan.
25 Letter to Margaret Boyce.

CHAPTER 6

1 The sources for this chapter are very helpful notes from K. H. Huggins who worked for Hall in Washington; History of the RMD in PRO SUPP 14; Hall, H. D. (1955); Hall and Wrigley (1956).
2 Hides and Skins Control Memo by R. L. Hall in PRO SUPP 14.
3 Letter to Margaret Boyce 26.4.1940.
4 Letter to Margaret Boyce 26.1.1941.
5 PRO CAB 111 Allied Supplies Executive.
6 Hall, H. D. (1955).
7 Margaret Hall to Margaret Boyce 30.5.1942.
8 Robert Hall had a staff of seven.
9 The description of the machinery owes much to Huggins's notes.
10 Hancock and Gowing (1949).
11 Huggins's notes.
12 PRO AVIA 38/1148.
13 Letter to Rose Hall 27.1.1943.

CHAPTER 7

1 The main sources for this chapter are the PRO files CAB 123/145; CAB 78/6, 9, 14; BT 11/2167, 3196, 3351, 3925; T 230/30, 31, 32.
2 Scammell (1980).
3 Cairncross and Watts (1989).
4 PRO CAB 123/145.
5 Richard Law's report is in PRO CAB 123/145.
6 Howson and Moggeridge (1990).
7 Scammell (1980) provides more detail on these events.
8 The papers of these discussions are in PRO CAB 78/14.
9 PRO BT 11/2167.
10 PRO BT 11/3351.
11 PRO BT 11/3196.
12 PRO BT 11/3925.

CHAPTER 8

1 For the early history of the Economic Section see Cairncross and Watts (1989); A list of those who worked for Robert Hall is in Appendix A.
2 Letter to Margaret Boyce 10.4.1947.
3 Hall's miscellaneous notes.
4 Note to Fleming in PRO T 230/277.
5 For a more detailed account see Cairncross (1985).
6 See Cairncross and Watts (1989).
7 *The Roberthall Diaries 1954–61,* ed. Cairncross (1991), p.117.
8 A detailed description of these and subsequent budgets is in Dow (1964).
9 Hall's miscellaneous notes.
10 Hall comments on the senior officials from time to time in his *Diaries.*
11 *The Roberthall Diaries 1947–53,* p. 21.

CHAPTER 9

1 This paper was probably by Dow.
2 PRO T 171/397 reproduced in Appendix D.
3 See Scammell (1980) for a more detailed discussion.
4 Fforde (1992) has a number of references to Hall's activities seen from the Bank's point of view.
5 PRO T 236/2398.
6 The report is in PRO T 269/1.
7 PREM 8/1178 EE Bridges Economic Situation 26.7.49. Hall's brief for Attlee is reproduced in Appendix E. An earlier attempt by Hall to explain the situation (not one of his best efforts) was marked by Attlee: 'I do not think much of this paper.'
8 *The Roberthall Diaries 1947–53,* ed. Cairncross (1989), p. 71.
9 Plowden (1989) relates how Bevin and Cripps did not meet for the first three or four days of the Atlantic crossing because Cripps rose at 4 or 5 a.m. and went to bed at 4 or 5 p.m., while Bevin did not rise until after that time. Officials had to persuade Cripps to stay up a little later one day so that they could speak to them together.

10 The papers and briefs prepared in the Economic Section on the effects of a devaluation and the choice of the new rate all assumed that most of the non-dollar world, particularly the sterling area and most OEEC countries would devalue their currencies with the pound and by similar amounts. See for example memoranda by Hall and Fleming in PRO T 269/1. This assumption proved more or less correct. In the sterling area only Pakistan did not devalue and in Western Europe only the Swiss franc remained at the old parity.
11 For a more detailed account see Cairncross (1985).
12 Plowden (1989).
13 When the October cuts were finally announced, *The Economist* described them as a fleabite. Hall writes in his diary that *The Economist* made a mistake in their calculations. This annoyed him and he wrote to Crowther, the editor, complaining and then organised a letter to *The Economist* from economists at the Oxford Institute of Statistics drawing attention to the error.
14 Hall's note is reproduced in Appendix F.

CHAPTER 10

1 Minute by R. L. Hall to R. W. B. Clarke on The Fall in Stocks PRO T 230/177.
2 The papers are in PRO T 230/208.
3 ES(50) 4 in PRO T 230/208.
4 Also in PRO T 230/208.
5 PRO T 171/403 'The General Budgetary Situation' in 1951.
6 The Nitze exercise was a multilateral process in which the economic burden of rearmament was to be shared out fairly and tolerably among all the NATO countries including the US. See Plowden (1989) and Jay (1980).
7 Their report is in PRO CAB 129/44, 'Chancellor of the Exchequer, Economic Implications of the Defence Proposals' 19.1.51.
8 See Cairncross (1985) for a discussion on this point.
9 Information from Lincoln Gordon.
10 These papers are in PRO CAB 134/489 and 492.
11 Plowden (1989), pp. 125–33, 'Operation Wise Man'.
12 Possibly Attlee thought Gaitskell and Morrison would be opposed to holding an election at this time.

13 British Oral Archive of Political and Administrative History, Interview with Lord Roberthall, 23.4.80.

14 As note 13.

15 Information from Paul Nitze and Paul Samuelson.

16 One of his specialities was sweet corn and for many years he won the 'any other vegetable' class with it. But there were many other successes. He once confessed to the author that he put his apples in a very slow oven for a short time to bring up the bloom; and that the timing of this operation was crucial – a moment too long and the apples went soft.

CHAPTER 11

1 PRO T 230/469.

2 British Oral Archive 23.4.80.

3 There have been several detailed accounts of Robot – see Cairncross (1985), Fforde (1992), MacDougall (1987) and Plowden (1989). In addition I have drawn especially on Hall's diaries and the Treasury papers which are in PRO T 236/3242, 3243, 3245 with Hall's 'Note for the Record' in PRO T 236/3245, reproduced in Appendix G.

4 All these papers are in PRO T 230/389.

5 This paper is in PRO T 236/3245.

6 'The Future of Sterling' 25.3.52 in PRO T 236/3242. There is an extract in Appendix H.

7 Hall's 'Note for the Record'.

8 In his autobiography Butler maintained that in the long term the decision not to free the pound was a fundamental mistake. But Hall had observed earlier Butler's tendency to reinterpret the past. (*Roberthall Diaries 1947–53*, p. 255).

9 William Armstrong (*Roberthall Diaries 1947–53*, p. 275).

10 Information from C. R. Ross.

11 PRO T 273 Senior Appointments.

12 As note 11. Hall's salary did not reflect the influence he had. Before he moved to the Treasury in 1953, his salary was £2,750 compared with Plowden's £6,500 (considerably more than Bridges' £5,000 but Plowden received no pension contribution). After his move to the Treasury, Hall's salary was raised by £1,000 to £3,750, still only about halfway between the rates of pay for

the Third and Second Secretaries.
13 The 1955 budget papers are in PRO T 171/453 and 464.
14 PRO T 230/ 394, 11.2.55.

CHAPTER 12

1 Reproduced at Appendix I.
2 The papers are in PRO T 230/472.
3 *Roberthall Diaries 1954–61*, p. 68.
4 Both Bridges and Gilbert had been appointed when the civil service retiring age was sixty-five. Those in post when it was lowered to sixty had the option to go when they wished between the ages of sixty and sixty-five.
5 Committee on Finance and Industry: *Report, Cmd* 3897, HMSO, 1931.
6 *Roberthall Diaries 1954–61*, p. 86.
7 Macmillan (1971).
8 Thorneycroft to the author.
9 *Roberthall Diaries 1954–61*, p. 126.
10 *Roberthall Diaries 1954–61*, p. 127.
11 Report of the Working Group on Credit, PRO T 230/337.
12 In the midst of the Radcliffe investigations, an inquiry was set up following allegations of a leak before the increase in bank rate the previous September. Hall made a statement, as did many others including the Chancellor, but no one suspected the Treasury officials and the report cleared them all. The inquiry found no clear evidence of a leak, but from then on the Court of the Bank was not informed of interest rate decisions ahead of the rest of the market.
13 Committee on the Working of the Monetary System: *Report, Cmnd* 827, HMSO, 1959.
14 *Roberthall Diaries 1954–61*, p. 243.

CHAPTER 13

1 In PRO T 171/392.
2 *Economic Implications of Full Employment, Cmd* 9725, HMSO, 1956.
3 *Roberthall Diaries 1953–61*, p. 107.

4 Council on Prices, Productivity and Incomes, *Reports 1–4*, 1958–61.

5 Phillips (1958).

6 See Knowles and Winsten (1959) and Lipsey (1960).

7 The 1959 budget papers are in PRO T 171/496.

8 The 1960 budget papers are in PRO T 171/506. An extract from Hall's paper for the Budget Committee on the economic outlook in 1960 is at Appendix J.

9 *The Control of Public Expenditure, Cmnd* 1432, London, HMSO, 1961.

10 See Blackaby (1978) for a discussion of the administration of the pay pause.

CHAPTER 14

1 See *A Decade of Cooperation*, OEEC, 1958.

2 *Roberthall Diaries 1954–61*, p. 35.

3 Hall's brief to Attlee on the Schuman Plan is in Appendix K.

4 See Plowden (1989) for a more detailed description of these events.

5 Information from Cairncross. Paper not traced.

6 Bretherton's description of these events is in Charlton (1983).

7 See PRO T 234/181.

8 See PRO T 234/182.

9 See PRO T 234/183.

10 The papers are in PRO T 230/336.

CHAPTER 15

1 Letter to the author from Sir Ernest Woodroofe.

2 Information from Lord Plowden.

3 *The Economist* 16 September 1961 and 23 September 1961.

4 There is a copy of this note among Hall's miscellaneous papers.

5 Letter to Edward Heath among Hall's papers.

6 *National Institute Economic Review*, November 1969.

7 Jones (1988).

8 University of Oxford (1966).

9 Information from Neil Tanner and Richard Malpas.

10 Hall (1968).

11 Letter to Margaret Boyce 18 March 1979.

CHAPTER 16

1 Annual figures are in Appendix B.
2 Hall must have read widely in French literature. Christopher Dow remembers him paying an informal call, picking up Martin Turnell's work on the French novel and leafing it through. On reaching the chapter on *Les Liaisons Dangereuses*, 'Marvellous book', he said, and added 'Don't take it as a practical guide though, as a friend of mine did – with a disastrous result.'
3 Hall (1955). The Sidney Ball lecture was given in 1954. This was exactly thirty years since Keynes gave the Sidney Ball lecture in 1924 on 'The End of Laissez-Faire'.
4 Franks wrote to Attlee on 15 July 1950 on aspects of sending token ground forces to Korea as they affected Anglo-American relations. He concluded 'Thirdly a considerable and influential section of the American people and many high officials in Washington think of Korea as the defence of the United Nations. They believe in the United Nations: they are certain that unopposed aggression in Korea would have broken its usefulness; they are proud that the United States should be able and willing to undertake the lion's share of the burden. But they feel that the contributions of other countries are essential to the UN character of the operations and are also a test of the faith of other countries in the United Nations.'
5 See Cairncross and Watts (1989) for a discussion on this point.
6 Letter among Hall's miscellaneous papers.
7 As 6.
8 As 6.
9 Hall disallowed Grieve-Smith's win in 1950, because of the Korean War.

Sources and References

PUBLIC RECORDS

PRO AVIA
11 Ministry of Supply: Private Office Papers
12 Ministry of Supply: Unregistered Papers
22 Ministry of Supply: Registered Files
38 North American Supplies

PRO BT
11 Board of Trade Commercial Department: Correspondence and Papers
131 Board of Trade: War Histories (1939–45) Files
213 Board of Trade: Commodity and General Division Files

PRO CAB
21 Cabinet Office Registered Files
78 War Cabinet Committees, Miscellaneous and General Series
92 War Cabinet Committees on Supply Production Priority and Manpower
107 War Cabinet Coordination of Departmental Action in the Event of War with Certain Countries
110 Joint American Secretariat: Secretary's Files
111 Allied Supplies Executive
115 Central Office for North American Supplies
123 Lord President of the Council: Secretariat Files
128 Cabinet Minutes 1945–60

129 Cabinet Memoranda 1945–60
134 Cabinet Committees: General Series 1945–67

PRO PREM
  8 Prime Minister's Office: Correspondence and Papers 1945–51

PRO SUPP
 14 Ministry of Supply Files

PRO T
171 Budget and Finance Papers
172 Chancellor of Exchequer's Miscellaneous Papers
229 Central Planning Division
230 Economic Advisory Division
233 Home Finance Division
234 Home and Overseas Planning Staff Division
236 Overseas Finance Division
269 Devaluation 1949
270 Bridges papers

OFFICIAL REPORTS AND PAPERS

Ministry of Reconstruction (1944), *Employment Policy, Cmd 6527*, HMSO.
HM Treasury (1956), *Economic Implications of Full Employment, Cmd 9725*, HMSO.
— (1957), *A European Free Trade Area, Cmnd 72*, HMSO.
— Committee on Working of the Monetary System:
    (1959), *Report* [Radcliffe Report], *Cmnd 827*, HMSO.
    (1960), *Minutes of Evidence*, HMSO.
    (1960), *Principal Memoranda of Evidence*, HMSO.
— (1961), *The Control of Public Expenditure* [Plowden Report], *Cmnd 1432*, HMSO.
OECD (1961), *The Problem of Rising Prices* by W. Fellner *et al.* Paris.

UNPUBLISHED SOURCES

Robert Hall, notes for an autobiography

Robert Hall, letters to Alec Cairncross
Robert Hall, letters to Mrs Margaret Boyce and Mr and Mrs E. Hall
Robert Hall, notes about P. R. Stephensen 1918–32, Fotheringham
    Papers, Fryer Library University of Queensland, Brisbane
Robert Hall, miscellaneous letters and notes
Lee, F. S., Interview with Lord Roberthall, May 1980
Munro, C., Interview with Lord Roberthall (1980)
Comments on Hall by students provided by F. S. Lee
Miscellaneous letters to the author

PUBLISHED WORKS

Allsopp, J. H. (1963), *A Centenary History of the Ipswich Grammar School 1863–1963* (published by the school).
Attlee, C. R. (1954), *As it Happened*, Heinemann.
Blackaby, F. (ed.) (1978), *British Economic Policy 1960–74*, Cambridge University Press.
Boyle, Lord (1979), 'The economist in government' in Bowers, *Inflation, Development and Integration*, Leeds University Press.
Brittan, S. (1971), *Steering the Economy*, Harmondsworth, Penguin Books.
Brown, A. J. (1988), 'A worm's eye view of the Keynesian revolution', in Hilliard, *J. M. Keynes in Retrospect*, Edward Elgar.
Butler, Lord (1971), *The Art of the Possible*, Hamish Hamilton.
Cairncross, A. (ed.) (1989 and 1991), *The Roberthall Diaries 1947–53 and 1954–61*, Unwin Hyman .
— (1985), *Years of Recovery. British Economic Policy 1945–51*, Methuen.
Cairncross, A. and Watts, N. (1989), *The Economic Section 1939–61. A study in Economic Advising*, Routledge.
Cairncross, F. (ed.) (1981), *Changing Perceptions of Economic Policy*, Methuen.
Charlton, M. (1983), *The Price of Victory*, British Broadcasting Corporation.
Chester, Sir Norman (1986), *Economic, Political and Social Studies in Oxford 1900–85*, Macmillan.
Cole, M. (1971), *Life of G. D. H. Cole*, Macmillan.
Cooke, C. (1957), *The Life of Richard Stafford Cripps*, Hodder and Stoughton.

Dow, J. C. R. (1964), *The Management of the British Economy 1945–60*, Cambridge University Press.

Durbin, E. (1985), *New Jerusalems*, Routledge Kegan Paul.

Fforde, J. S. (1954), *The Federal Reserve System 1945–49*, Oxford, Clarendon Press.

— (1992), *The Bank of England and Public Policy 1941–58*, Cambridge University Press.

Hall, H. D. (1955), *North American Supply, History of the Second World War*, HMSO and Longmans, Green and Co.

Hall, H. D. and Wrigley, G.C. (1956), *Studies of Overseas Supply, History of the Second World War*, HMSO and Longmans, Green and Co.

Hall, R. L. (1934), *Earning and Spending*, Centenary Press, London.

— (1937), *The Economic System in a Socialist State*, Macmillan.

— (1955), 'The place of the economist in Government', *Oxford Economic Papers*, vol. 7, no. 2 (Sydney Ball Lecture, 1954).

— (1957), 'Some current economic problems', *Society of Business Economists*.

— (1959), 'Reflections on the practical application of economics', *Economic Journal*, vol. LXIX, RES Presidential Address.

— (1961), 'Britain's economic problem', *Economist*, September 16 and 23.

— (1962), 'Commodity prices and the terms of trade', *Lloyds Bank Review*, no. 63, January.

— (1962), *Planning, The Rede Lecture*, Cambridge University Press.

— (1963), 'Changes in the industrial structure of Britain', *Lloyds Bank Review*, no. 67, January.

— (1966), *The Control of Economic Conditions*. The Jubilee Oration, 1960, University of Queensland Press.

— (1967), 'Problems of aggregation and dis-aggregation in macro-economic policy', Conference on Economic Policy, University of Queensland, August.

— (1968), 'Internal and external balance for an international currency', *Economic Papers*, no. 28, Economic Society of Australia and New Zealand, August.

— and Hitch, C.J. (1939), 'Price theory and business behaviour' *Oxford Economic Papers*, 2, May (see also Lord Roberthall).

Hancock, W. K. and Gowing, M. M. (1949), *British War Economy, History of the Second World War*, London, HMSO and Longmans Green and Co.

Harris, K. (1982), *Attlee*, Weidenfeld and Nicholson.

Henderson, H. B. (1938), 'The significance of the rate of interest', *Oxford Economic Papers*, 1, October.

Hennessy, P. (1989), *Whitehall*, Secker and Warburg.

— (1992), *Never Again: Britain 1945–61*, Jonathan Cape.

Howson and Moggeridge (eds) (1990), *Wartime Diaries of Lionel Robbins and James Meade*, Macmillan.

— (1990), *Collected Papers of James Meade. Vol. IV The Cabinet Office Diary 1944–46*, Unwin Hyman.

Hurstfield, J. (1953), *The Control of Raw Materials, History of the Second World War*, HMSO and Longmans, Green and Co.

Jay, D. P. T. (1980), *Change and Fortune*, Hutchinson.

Jones, K. (1988), 'Fifty years of economic research: a brief history of the National Institute of Economic and Social Research 1938–68', *National Institute Economic Review*, no. 124, May.

Knowles, K. G. J. C. and Winsten, G. B. (1959), 'Can the level of unemployment explain changes in wages?', *Oxford Bulletin of Economics and Statistics*, 21, 1.

Lee, F. S. (1981), 'Oxford Economists Research Group', *Oxford Economic Papers*, November.

Lindsay, J. (1962), *Fanfrolico and After*, Ringwood, Penguin.

Lipsey, R. G. (1960), 'The relation between unemployment and the rate of change of money wage rates in the United Kingdom 1862–1957. A further analysis', *Economica* NS, vol. 27, no. 105.

MacDougall, D. (1987), *Don and Mandarin*, John Murray.

Macmillan, H. (1969), *Tides of Fortune 1945–55*, Macmillan.

— (1971), *Riding the Storm 1956–59*, Macmillan.

Munro, C. (1984), *Wild Man of Letters, London 1980*, Melbourne University Press.

Philips, A. W. (1958), 'The relation between unemployment and the rate of change of money wage rates in the United Kingdom 1961–1957, *Economica*, NS vol. 25, no. 100.

Pimlott, B. (1992), *Harold Wilson*, HarperCollins.

Plowden, E. (1989), *An Industrialist in the Treasury. The Post War Years*, André Deutsch.

Plowden, Lord and Hall, Sir Robert (1968), 'The supremacy of politics', *The Political Quarterly*, vol. 39, no. 4.

Pressnell, L. S. (1987), *External Economic Policy since the War. Vol. 1 The Postwar Financial Settlement*, London, HMSO.

Robbins, Lord (1971), *Autobiography of an Economist*, Macmillan.

Roberthall, Lord (1969), 'Introduction to 50th issue', *National Institute Economic Review*, no. 50, November.

—   (1973), 'Economics and business', *The Business Economist*, vol. 5, no. 3, Autumn, Basil Blackwell.

—   (1974), 'Expatriate publishing', *Meanjin*, vol. 33.

—   (1980), Interview by Anthony Seldon, British Oral Archive of Political and Administrative History.

—   (1982), 'The end of full employment' in Kindleberger, C. P. and Tella, G. D. I., *Economics in the Long View: Applications and Cases*, Macmillan (see also R. L. Hall).

Roll, E. (1985), *Crowded Hours*, Faber and Faber.

Scammell, W. M. (1980), *The International Economy since 1945*, Macmillan.

Stewart, M. (1986), *Keynes and After*, Penguin Books.

University of Oxford (1966), *Report of Commission of Inquiry*, Clarendon Press, Oxford.

Williams, P. M. (1982), *Hugh Gaitskell*, Oxford University Press.

Wilson, T. and Andrews, P. W. S. (eds)(1951), *Oxford Studies in the Price Mechanism*, Oxford, Clarendon Press.

Index

Addison, Lord, 98
Allen, Maurice, 33, 133
Amery, Leo, 63
Andrews, Philip, 33
Archer, George, 53
Armstrong, Sir William, 95
Atkinson, Sir Fred, 99, 110
Attlee, C. R. (later Lord), lack of interest in economic affairs, 109; support for the setting up of NATO, 160; attitude towards European integration, 162

Baillieu, Sir Clive, 53
Bank of England, attitude towards release of the wartime sterling balances, 87; 'Robot' plan for limited convertibility and floating of sterling, 116–19; attitude towards restricting bank credit, 129–33, 136; recommendations of the Radcliffe Committee on the role of the Bank, 139
Batt, William, 53
Beaverbrook, Lord, 51, 63
Bevin, Ernest, unhappy with idea of fixed exchange rate after the war, 63; support for Marshall Plan, 74; as Foreign Secretary, participation in negotiations on devaluation, 94; setting up of NATO, 160
Bolton, Sir George, 94, 121
Bretherton, Russell, 33, 104, 110, 165
Bridges, Sir Edward (later Lord), as Permanent Secretary of the Treasury, presses Robert Hall to become Director of the Economic Section, 70;

warns Hall that Hugh Dalton not likely to seek his advice, 77; management of the Treasury, 81–3, 97, 124; retirement, 133
Brittain, Sir Herbert, 76, 131
Burton, Herbert, 20, 23
Butler, R. A. (later Lord), appointed Chancellor of the Exchequer, 114; indecisiveness, 115; supports increase in Robert Hall's salary and transfer of the Economic Section to the Treasury, 124; dealings with the Bank of England, 131
Butt, David Bensusan, 80, 104, 110, 118

Cairncross, Sir Alec, 138
Cannan, Edwin, 26, 35, 37
Catto, Lord, 89, 131
Cherwell, Lord, 117
Churchill, Sir Winston, figurehead of the European movement, 163
Clarke, Sir R. W. B. (Otto), 82, 83, 85, 90, 120, 125
Cole, Lord, 171
Council on Prices, Productivity and Incomes, 149
Cobbold, Lord, 89, 131, 140
Cripps, Sir Stafford, becomes Chancellor of the Exchequer, 80; first budget, 85; agreement to devalue sterling in 1949, 94; resignation, 101; appreciation of, 109
Cromer, Lord, 99, 142

Dalton, Hugh, regarding himself as his

241